BOOK 3 – FINANCIAL REPORTING AND ANALYSIS

D1319441

SCHWESERNOTES™ 2013 CFA LEVEL I BOOK 3: FINANCIAL REPORTING AND ANALYSIS

©2012 Kaplan, Inc. All rights reserved.

Published in 2012 by Kaplan Schweser

Printed in the United States of America.

ISBN: 978-1-4277-4267-4 / 1-4277-4267-7

PPN: 3200-2846

If this book does not have the hologram with the Kaplan Schweser logo on the back cover, it was distributed without permission of Kaplan Schweser, a Division of Kaplan, Inc., and is in direct violation of global copyright laws. Your assistance in pursuing potential violators of this law is greatly appreciated.

Required CFA Institute disclaimer: "CFA® and Chartered Financial Analyst® are trademarks owned by CFA Institute. CFA Institute (formerly the Association for Investment Management and Research) does not endorse, promote, review, or warrant the accuracy of the products or services offered by Kaplan Schweser."

Certain materials contained within this text are the copyrighted property of CFA Institute. The following is the copyright disclosure for these materials: "Copyright, 2012, CFA Institute. Reproduced and republished from 2013 Learning Outcome Statements, Level I, II, and III questions from CFA® Program Materials, CFA Institute Standards of Professional Conduct, and CFA Institute's Global Investment Performance Standards with permission from CFA Institute. All Rights Reserved."

These materials may not be copied without written permission from the author. The unauthorized duplication of these notes is a violation of global copyright laws and the CFA Institute Code of Ethics. Your assistance in pursuing potential violators of this law is greatly appreciated.

Disclaimer: The SchweserNotes should be used in conjunction with the original readings as set forth by CFA Institute in their 2013 CFA Level I Study Guide. The information contained in these Notes covers topics contained in the readings referenced by CFA Institute and is believed to be accurate. However, their accuracy cannot be guaranteed nor is any warranty conveyed as to your ultimate exam success. The authors of the referenced readings have not endorsed or sponsored these Notes.

©2012 Kaplan, Inc.

READING ASSIGNMENTS AND LEARNING OUTCOME STATEMENTS

The following material is a review of the Financial Reporting and Analysis principles designed to address the learning outcome statements set forth by CFA Institute.

STUDY SESSION 7

Reading Assignments
Financial Reporting and Analysis, CFA Program 2013 Curriculum, Volume 3
(CFA Institute, 2012)

STUDY SESSION 8

Reading Assignments
Financial Reporting and Analysis, CFA Program 2013 Curriculum, Volume 3
(CFA Institute, 2012)

STUDY SESSION 9

Reading Assignments
Financial Reporting and Analysis, CFA Program 2013 Curriculum, Volume 3
(CFA Institute, 2012)

STUDY SESSION 10

Reading Assignments
Financial Reporting and Analysis, CFA Program 2013 Curriculum, Volume 3
(CFA Institute, 2012)

LEARNING OUTCOME STATEMENTS (LOS)

The following material is a review of the Financial Reporting and Analysis principles designed to address the learning outcome statements set forth by CFA Institute.

STUDY SESSION 7

The topical coverage corresponds with the following CFA Institute assigned reading:

22. Financial Statement Analysis: An Introduction

The candidate should be able to:

a. describe the roles of financial reporting and financial statement analysis. (page 10)

b. describe the roles of the key financial statements (statement of financial position, statement of comprehensive income, statement of changes in equity, and statement of cash flows) in evaluating a company's performance and financial position. (page 11)

c. describe the importance of financial statement notes and supplementary information—including disclosures of accounting policies, methods, and estimates—and management's commentary. (page 12)

d. describe the objective of audits of financial statements, the types of audit reports, and the importance of effective internal controls. (page 12)

e. identify and explain information sources that analysts use in financial statement analysis besides annual financial statements and supplementary information. (page 13)

f. describe the steps in the financial statement analysis framework. (page 14)

The topical coverage corresponds with the following CFA Institute assigned reading:

23. Financial Reporting Mechanics

The candidate should be able to:

a. explain the relationship of financial statement elements and accounts, and classify accounts into the financial statement elements. (page 19)

b. explain the accounting equation in its basic and expanded forms. (page 20)

c. explain the process of recording business transactions using an accounting system based on the accounting equation. (page 21)

d. explain the need for accruals and other adjustments in preparing financial statements. (page 22)

e. explain the relationships among the income statement, balance sheet, statement of cash flows, and statement of owners' equity. (page 23)

f. describe the flow of information in an accounting system. (page 25)

g. explain the use of the results of the accounting process in security analysis. (page 25)

The topical coverage corresponds with the following CFA Institute assigned reading:

24. Financial Reporting Standards

The candidate should be able to:

a. describe the objective of financial statements and the importance of financial reporting standards in security analysis and valuation. (page 33)

b. describe the roles and desirable attributes of financial reporting standard-setting bodies and regulatory authorities in establishing and enforcing reporting standards, and describe the role of the International Organization of Securities Commissions. (page 34)

©2012 Kaplan, Inc.

c. describe the status of global convergence of accounting standards and ongoing barriers to developing one universally accepted set of financial reporting standards. (page 35)

d. describe the International Accounting Standards Board's conceptual framework, including the objective and qualitative characteristics of financial statements, required reporting elements, and constraints and assumptions in preparing financial statements. (page 36)

e. describe general requirements for financial statements under IFRS. (page 38)

f. compare key concepts of financial reporting standards under IFRS and U.S. GAAP reporting systems. (page 39)

g. identify the characteristics of a coherent financial reporting framework and the barriers to creating such a framework. (page 39)

h. explain the implications for financial analysis of differing financial reporting systems and the importance of monitoring developments in financial reporting standards. (page 40)

i. analyze company disclosures of significant accounting policies. (page 40)

STUDY SESSION 8

The topical coverage corresponds with the following CFA Institute assigned reading:

25. **Understanding Income Statements**
The candidate should be able to:

a. describe the components of the income statement and alternative presentation formats of that statement. (page 47)

b. describe the general principles of revenue recognition and accrual accounting, specific revenue recognition applications (including accounting for long-term contracts, installment sales, barter transactions, gross and net reporting of revenue), and the implications of revenue recognition principles for financial analysis. (page 49)

c. calculate revenue given information that might influence the choice of revenue recognition method. (page 49)

d. describe the general principles of expense recognition, specific expense recognition applications, and the implications of expense recognition choices for financial analysis. (page 55)

e. describe the financial reporting treatment and analysis of non-recurring items (including discontinued operations, extraordinary items, unusual or infrequent items) and changes in accounting standards. (page 61)

f. distinguish between the operating and non-operating components of the income statement. (page 63)

g. describe how earnings per share is calculated and calculate and interpret a company's earnings per share (both basic and diluted earnings per share) for both simple and complex capital structures. (page 64)

h. distinguish between dilutive and antidilutive securities, and describe the implications of each for the earnings per share calculation. (page 64)

i. convert income statements to common-size income statements. (page 73)

j. evaluate a company's financial performance using common-size income statements and financial ratios based on the income statement. (page 74)

k. describe, calculate, and interpret comprehensive income. (page 75)

l. describe other comprehensive income, and identify the major types of items included in it. (page 75)

The topical coverage corresponds with the following CFA Institute assigned reading:

26. **Understanding Balance Sheets**

The candidate should be able to:

a. describe the elements of the balance sheet: assets, liabilities, and equity. (page 86)

b. describe the uses and limitations of the balance sheet in financial analysis. (page 87)

c. describe alternative formats of balance sheet presentation. (page 87)

d. distinguish between current and non-current assets, and current and non-current liabilities. (page 87)

e. describe different types of assets and liabilities and the measurement bases of each. (page 88)

f. describe the components of shareholders' equity. (page 96)

g. analyze balance sheets and statements of changes in equity. (page 97)

h. convert balance sheets to common-size balance sheets and interpret the common-size balance sheets. (page 98)

i. calculate and interpret liquidity and solvency ratios. (page 100)

The topical coverage corresponds with the following CFA Institute assigned reading:

27. **Understanding Cash Flow Statements**

The candidate should be able to:

a. compare cash flows from operating, investing, and financing activities and classify cash flow items as relating to one of those three categories given a description of the items. (page 109)

b. describe how non-cash investing and financing activities are reported. (page 111)

c. contrast cash flow statements prepared under International Financial Reporting Standards (IFRS) and U.S. generally accepted accounting principles (U.S. GAAP). (page 111)

d. distinguish between the direct and indirect methods of presenting cash from operating activities and describe the arguments in favor of each method. (page 112)

e. describe how the cash flow statement is linked to the income statement and the balance sheet. (page 114)

f. describe the steps in the preparation of direct and indirect cash flow statements, including how cash flows can be computed using income statement and balance sheet data. (page 115)

g. convert cash flows from the indirect to direct method. (page 121)

h. analyze and interpret both reported and common-size cash flow statements. (page 124)

i. calculate and interpret free cash flow to the firm, free cash flow to equity, and performance and coverage cash flow ratios. (page 126)

The topical coverage corresponds with the following CFA Institute assigned reading:

28. **Financial Analysis Techniques**

The candidate should be able to:

a. describe tools and techniques used in financial analysis, including their uses and limitations. (page 142)

b. classify, calculate, and interpret activity, liquidity, solvency, profitability, and valuation ratios. (page 148)

c. describe the relationships among ratios and evaluate a company using ratio analysis. (page 157)

    d.   demonstrate the application of DuPont analysis of return on equity, and calculate and interpret the effects of changes in its components. (page 163)

    e.   calculate and interpret ratios used in equity analysis, credit analysis, and segment analysis. (page 167)

    f.   describe how ratio analysis and other techniques can be used to model and forecast earnings. (page 172)

STUDY SESSION 9

The topical coverage corresponds with the following CFA Institute assigned reading:

29. Inventories

The candidate should be able to:

    a.   distinguish between costs included in inventories and costs recognized as expenses in the period in which they are incurred. (page 182)

    b.   describe different inventory valuation methods (cost formulas). (page 184)

    c.   calculate cost of sales and ending inventory using different inventory valuation methods and explain the impact of the inventory valuation method choice on gross profit. (page 185)

    d.   calculate and compare cost of sales, gross profit, and ending inventory using perpetual and periodic inventory systems. (page 188)

    e.   compare and contrast cost of sales, ending inventory, and gross profit using different inventory valuation methods. (page 190)

    f.   describe the measurement of inventory at the lower of cost and net realisable value. (page 191)

    g.   describe the financial statement presentation of and disclosures relating to inventories. (page 194)

    h.   calculate and interpret ratios used to evaluate inventory management. (page 194)

The topical coverage corresponds with the following CFA Institute assigned reading:

30. Long-Lived Assets

The candidate should be able to:

    a.   distinguish between costs that are capitalized and costs that are expensed in the period in which they are incurred. (page 204)

    b.   compare the financial reporting of the following classifications of intangible assets: purchased, internally developed, acquired in a business combination. (page 208)

    c.   describe the different depreciation methods for property, plant, and equipment, the effect of the choice of depreciation method on the financial statements, and the effects of assumptions concerning useful life and residual value on depreciation expense. (page 211)

    d.   calculate depreciation expense. (page 211)

    e.   describe the different amortization methods for intangible assets with finite lives, the effect of the choice of amortization method on the financial statements, and the effects of assumptions concerning useful life and residual value on amortization expense. (page 216)

    f.   calculate amortization expense. (page 217)

    g.   describe the revaluation model. (page 218)

    h.   explain the impairment of property, plant, and equipment, and intangible assets. (page 218)

    i.   explain the derecognition of property, plant, and equipment, and intangible assets. (page 221)

    j.   describe the financial statement presentation of and disclosures relating to property, plant, and equipment, and intangible assets. (page 221)

    k.   compare the financial reporting of investment property with that of property, plant, and equipment. (page 222)

The topical coverage corresponds with the following CFA Institute assigned reading:

31. Income Taxes

The candidate should be able to:

    a.   describe the differences between accounting profit and taxable income, and define key terms, including deferred tax assets, deferred tax liabilities, valuation allowance, taxes payable, and income tax expense. (page 230)

    b.   explain how deferred tax liabilities and assets are created and the factors that determine how a company's deferred tax liabilities and assets should be treated for the purposes of financial analysis. (page 231)

    c.   determine the tax base of a company's assets and liabilities. (page 232)

    d.   calculate income tax expense, income taxes payable, deferred tax assets, and deferred tax liabilities, and calculate and interpret the adjustment to the financial statements related to a change in the income tax rate. (page 234)

    e.   evaluate the impact of tax rate changes on a company's financial statements and ratios. (page 238)

    f.   distinguish between temporary and permanent differences in pre-tax accounting income and taxable income. (page 239)

    g.   describe the valuation allowance for deferred tax assets—when it is required and what impact it has on financial statements. (page 241)

    h.   compare a company's deferred tax items. (page 242)

    i.   analyze disclosures relating to deferred tax items and the effective tax rate reconciliation, and explain how information included in these disclosures affects a company's financial statements and financial ratios. (page 244)

    j.   identify the key provisions of and differences between income tax accounting under IFRS and U.S. GAAP. (page 246)

The topical coverage corresponds with the following CFA Institute assigned reading:

32. Non-Current (Long-Term) Liabilities

The candidate should be able to:

    a.   determine the initial recognition, initial measurement and subsequent measurement of bonds. (page 257)

    b.   discuss the effective interest method and calculate interest expense, amortisation of bond discounts/premiums, and interest payments. (page 258)

    c.   discuss the derecognition of debt. (page 263)

    d.   explain the role of debt covenants in protecting creditors. (page 264)

    e.   discuss the financial statement presentation of and disclosures relating to debt. (page 264)

    f.   discuss the motivations for leasing assets instead of purchasing them. (page 265)

    g.   distinguish between a finance lease and an operating lease from the perspectives of the lessor and the lessee. (page 266)

    h.   determine the initial recognition, initial measurement, and subsequent measurement of finance leases. (page 267)

    i.   compare the disclosures relating to finance and operating leases. (page 275)

    j.   describe defined contribution and defined benefit pension plans. (page 275)

    k.   compare the presentation and disclosure of defined contribution and defined benefit pension plans. (page 276)

    l.   calculate and interpret leverage and coverage ratios. (page 278)

©2012 Kaplan, Inc.

STUDY SESSION 10

The topical coverage corresponds with the following CFA Institute assigned reading:

33. **Financial Reporting Quality: Red Flags and Accounting Warning Signs**
    The candidate should be able to:
    a. describe incentives that might induce a company's management to overreport or underreport earnings. (page 291)
    b. describe activities that will result in a low quality of earnings. (page 292)
    c. describe the three conditions that are generally present when fraud occurs, including the risk factors related to these conditions. (page 292)
    d. describe common accounting warning signs and methods for detecting each. (page 295)

The topical coverage corresponds with the following CFA Institute assigned reading:

34. **Accounting Shenanigans on the Cash Flow Statement**
    The candidate should be able to:
    a. analyze and describe the following ways to manipulate the cash flow statement: stretching out payables; financing of payables; securitization of receivables; and using stock buybacks to offset dilution of earnings. (page 302)

The topical coverage corresponds with the following CFA Institute assigned reading:

35. **Financial Statement Analysis: Applications**
    The candidate should be able to:
    a. evaluate a company's past financial performance and explain how a company's strategy is reflected in past financial performance. (page 308)
    b. prepare a basic projection of a company's future net income and cash flow. (page 309)
    c. describe the role of financial statement analysis in assessing the credit quality of a potential debt investment. (page 310)
    d. describe the use of financial statement analysis in screening for potential equity investments. (page 311)
    e. determine and justify appropriate analyst adjustments to a company's financial statements to facilitate comparison with another company. (page 311)

The following is a review of the Financial Reporting and Analysis principles designed to address the learning outcome statements set forth by CFA Institute. This topic is also covered in:

FINANCIAL STATEMENT ANALYSIS: AN INTRODUCTION

Study Session 7

EXAM FOCUS

This introduction may be useful to those who have no previous experience with financial statements. While the income statement, balance sheet, and statement of cash flows are covered in detail in subsequent readings, candidates should pay special attention here to the other sources of information for financial analysis. The nature of the audit report is important, as is the information that is contained in the footnotes to financial statements, proxy statements, Management's Discussion and Analysis, and the supplementary schedules. A useful framework enumerating the steps in financial statement analysis is presented.

LOS 22.a: Describe the roles of financial reporting and financial statement analysis.

CFA® Program Curriculum, Volume 3, page 6

Financial reporting refers to the way companies show their financial performance to investors, creditors, and other interested parties by preparing and presenting financial statements. According to the *IASB Conceptual Framework for Financial Reporting 2010*:

> "The objective of general purpose financial reporting is to provide financial information about the reporting entity that is useful to existing and potential investors, lenders, and other creditors in making decisions about providing resources to the entity. Those decisions involve buying, selling or holding equity and debt instruments, and providing or settling loans and other forms of credit."

The role of **financial statement analysis** is to use the information in a company's financial statements, along with other relevant information, to make economic decisions. Examples of such decisions include whether to invest in the company's securities or recommend them to investors and whether to extend trade or bank credit to the company. Analysts use financial statement data to evaluate a company's past performance and current financial position in order to form opinions about the company's ability to earn profits and generate cash flow in the future.

 Professor's Note: This topic review deals with financial analysis for external users. Management also performs financial analysis in making everyday decisions. However, management may rely on internal financial information that is likely maintained in a different format and unavailable to external users.

©2012 Kaplan, Inc.

LOS 22.b: Describe the roles of the key financial statements (statement of financial position, statement of comprehensive income, statement of changes in equity, and statement of cash flows) in evaluating a company's performance and financial position.

CFA® Program Curriculum, Volume 3, page 11

The **balance sheet** (also known as the *statement of financial position* or *statement of financial condition*) reports the firm's financial position at a point in time. The balance sheet consists of three elements:

1. *Assets* are the resources controlled by the firm.

2. *Liabilities* are amounts owed to lenders and other creditors.

3. *Owners' equity* is the residual interest in the net assets of an entity that remains after deducting its liabilities.

Transactions are measured so that the fundamental **accounting equation** holds:

assets = liabilities + owners' equity

The **statement of comprehensive income** reports all changes in equity expect for shareholder transactions (e.g., issuing stock, repurchasing stock, and paying dividends). The **income statement** (also known as the *statement of operations* or the *profit and loss statement*) reports on the financial performance of the firm over a period of time. The elements of the income statement include revenues, expenses, and gains and losses.

*   *Revenues* are inflows from delivering or producing goods, rendering services, or other activities that constitute the entity's ongoing major or central operations.
*   *Expenses* are outflows from delivering or producing goods or services that constitute the entity's ongoing major or central operations.
*   *Other income* includes gains that may or may not arise in the ordinary course of business.

Under IFRS, the income statement can be combined with "other comprehensive income" and presented as a single statement of comprehensive income. Alternatively, the income statement and the statement of comprehensive income can be presented separately. Presentation is similar under U.S. GAAP except that firms can choose to report comprehensive income in the statement of shareholders' equity.

The **statement of changes in equity** reports the amounts and sources of changes in equity investors' investment in the firm over a period of time.

The **statement of cash flows** reports the company's cash receipts and payments. These cash flows are classified as follows:

*   *Operating cash flows* include the cash effects of transactions that involve the normal business of the firm.
*   *Investing cash flows* are those resulting from the acquisition or sale of property, plant, and equipment; of a subsidiary or segment; of securities; and of investments in other firms.

- *Financing cash flows* are those resulting from issuance or retirement of the firm's debt and equity securities and include dividends paid to stockholders.

LOS 22.c: Describe the importance of financial statement notes and supplementary information—including disclosures of accounting policies, methods, and estimates—and management's commentary.

CFA® Program Curriculum, Volume 3, page 23

Financial statement notes (footnotes) include disclosures that provide further details about the information summarized in the financial statements. Footnotes allow users to improve their assessments of the amount, timing, and uncertainty of the estimates reported in the financial statements. Footnotes:

- Discuss the basis of presentation such as the fiscal period covered by the statements and the inclusion of consolidated entities.
- Provide information about accounting methods, assumptions, and estimates used by management.
- Provide additional information on items such as business acquisitions or disposals, legal actions, employee benefit plans, contingencies and commitments, significant customers, sales to related parties, and segments of the firm.

Management's commentary [also known as management's report, operating and financial review, and **management's discussion and analysis** (MD&A)] is one of the most useful sections of the annual report. In this section, management discusses a variety of issues, including the nature of the business, past performance, and future outlook. Analysts must be aware that some parts of management's commentary may be unaudited.

For publicly held firms in the United States, the SEC requires that MD&A discuss trends and identify significant events and uncertainties that affect the firm's liquidity, capital resources, and results of operations. MD&A must also discuss:

- Effects of inflation and changing prices if material.
- Impact of off-balance-sheet obligations and contractual obligations such as purchase commitments.
- Accounting policies that require significant judgment by management.
- Forward-looking expenditures and divestitures.

LOS 22.d: Describe the objective of audits of financial statements, the types of audit reports, and the importance of effective internal controls.

CFA® Program Curriculum, Volume 3, page 26

An **audit** is an independent review of an entity's financial statements. Public accountants conduct audits and examine the financial reports and supporting records. The objective of an audit is to enable the auditor to provide an opinion on the fairness and reliability of the financial statements.

The independent certified public accounting firm employed by the Board of Directors is responsible for seeing that the financial statements conform to the applicable accounting

©2012 Kaplan, Inc.

standards. The auditor examines the company's accounting and internal control systems, confirms assets and liabilities, and generally tries to determine that there are no material errors in the financial statements. The auditor's report is an important source of information.

The **standard auditor's opinion** contains three parts and states that:

1. Whereas the financial statements are prepared by management and are its responsibility, the auditor has performed an independent review.

2. Generally accepted auditing standards were followed, thus providing *reasonable assurance* that the financial statements contain no material errors.

3. The auditor is satisfied that the statements were prepared in accordance with accepted accounting principles and that the principles chosen and estimates made are reasonable. The auditor's report must also contain additional explanation when accounting methods have not been used consistently between periods.

An *unqualified opinion* (also known as a clean opinion) indicates that the auditor believes the statements are free from material omissions and errors. If the statements make any exceptions to the accounting principles, the auditor may issue a *qualified opinion* and explain these exceptions in the audit report. The auditor can issue an *adverse opinion* if the statements are not presented fairly or are materially nonconforming with accounting standards. If the auditor is unable to express an opinion (e.g., in the case of a scope limitation), a *disclaimer of opinion* is issued.

The auditor's opinion will also contain an explanatory paragraph when a material loss is probable but the amount cannot be reasonably estimated. These "uncertainties" may relate to the *going concern assumption* (the assumption that the firm will continue to operate for the foreseeable future), the valuation or realization of asset values, or to litigation. This type of disclosure may be a signal of serious problems and may call for close examination by the analyst.

Internal controls are the processes by which the company ensures that it presents accurate financial statements. Internal controls are the responsibility of management. Under U.S. Generally Accepted Accounting Principles (GAAP), the auditor must express an opinion on the firm's internal controls. The auditor can provide this opinion separately or as the fourth element of the standard opinion.

LOS 22.e: Identify and explain information sources that analysts use in financial statement analysis besides annual financial statements and supplementary information.

CFA® Program Curriculum, Volume 3, page 29

Besides the annual financial statements, an analyst should examine a company's *quarterly or semiannual reports.* These interim reports typically update the major financial statements and footnotes but are not necessarily audited.

Securities and Exchange Commission (SEC) filings are available from EDGAR (Electronic Data Gathering, Analysis, and Retrieval System, *www.sec.gov*). These include Form 8-K, which a company must file to report events such as acquisitions and disposals of major assets or changes in its management or corporate governance. Companies' annual and quarterly financial statements are also filed with the SEC (Form 10-K and Form 10-Q, respectively).

Proxy statements are issued to shareholders when there are matters that require a shareholder vote. These statements, which are also filed with the SEC and available from EDGAR, are a good source of information about the election of (and qualifications of) board members, compensation, management qualifications, and the issuance of stock options.

Corporate reports and *press releases* are written by management and are often viewed as public relations or sales materials. Not all of the material is independently reviewed by outside auditors. Such information can often be found on the company's Web site. Firms often provide **earnings guidance** before the financial statements are released. Once an earnings announcement is made, a conference call may be held whereby senior management is available to answer questions.

An analyst should also review pertinent information on economic conditions and the company's industry and compare the company to its competitors. The necessary information can be acquired from trade journals, statistical reporting services, and government agencies.

LOS 22.f: Describe the steps in the financial statement analysis framework.

CFA® Program Curriculum, Volume 3, page 30

The **financial statement analysis framework**[1] consists of six steps:

Step 1: *State the objective and context.* Determine what questions the analysis seeks to answer, the form in which this information needs to be presented, and what resources and how much time are available to perform the analysis.

Step 2: *Gather data.* Acquire the company's financial statements and other relevant data on its industry and the economy. Ask questions of the company's management, suppliers, and customers, and visit company sites.

Step 3: *Process the data.* Make any appropriate adjustments to the financial statements. Calculate ratios. Prepare exhibits such as graphs and common-size balance sheets.

Step 4: *Analyze and interpret the data.* Use the data to answer the questions stated in the first step. Decide what conclusions or recommendations the information supports.

Step 5: *Report the conclusions or recommendations.* Prepare a report and communicate it to its intended audience. Be sure the report and its dissemination comply with the Code and Standards that relate to investment analysis and recommendations.

Step 6: *Update the analysis.* Repeat these steps periodically and change the conclusions or recommendations when necessary.

---

1. Hennie van Greuning and Sonja Brajovic Bratanovic, *Analyzing and Managing Banking Risk: Framework for Assessing Corporate Governance and Financial Risk*, International Bank for Reconstruction and Development, April 2003, p. 300.

©2012 Kaplan, Inc.

KEY CONCEPTS

LOS 22.a

The role of financial reporting is to provide a variety of users with useful information about a company's performance and financial position.

The role of financial statement analysis is to use the data from financial statements to support economic decisions.

LOS 22.b

The statement of financial position (balance sheet) shows assets, liabilities, and owners' equity at a point in time.

The statement of comprehensive income shows the results of a firm's business activities over the period. Revenues, the cost of generating those revenues, and the resulting profit or loss are presented on the income statement.

The statement of changes in equity reports the amount and sources of changes in the equity owners' investment in the firm.

The statement of cash flows shows the sources and uses of cash over the period.

LOS 22.c

Important information about accounting methods, estimates, and assumptions is disclosed in the footnotes to the financial statements and supplementary schedules. These disclosures also contain information about segment results, commitments and contingencies, legal proceedings, acquisitions or divestitures, issuance of stock options, and details of employee benefit plans.

Management's commentary (management's discussion and analysis) contains an overview of the company and important information about business trends, future capital needs, liquidity, significant events, and significant choices of accounting methods requiring management judgment.

LOS 22.d

The objective of audits of financial statements is to provide an opinion on the statements' fairness and reliability.

The auditor's opinion gives evidence of an independent review of the financial statements that verifies that appropriate accounting principles were used, that standard auditing procedures were used to establish reasonable assurance that the statements contain no material errors, and that management's report on the company's internal controls has been reviewed.

An auditor can issue an unqualified (clean) opinion if the statements are free from material omissions and errors, a qualified opinion that notes any exceptions to accounting principles, an adverse opinion if the statements are not presented fairly in the auditor's opinion, or a disclaimer of opinion if the auditor is unable to express an opinion.

A company's management is responsible for maintaining an effective internal control system to ensure the accuracy of its financial statements.

LOS 22.e

Along with the annual financial statements, important information sources for an analyst include a company's quarterly and semiannual reports, proxy statements, press releases, and earnings guidance, as well as information on the industry and peer companies from external sources.

LOS 22.f

The framework for financial analysis has six steps:
1. State the objective of the analysis.
2. Gather data.
3. Process the data.
4. Analyze and interpret the data.
5. Report the conclusions or recommendations.
6. Update the analysis.

©2012 Kaplan, Inc.

CONCEPT CHECKERS

1. Which of the following statements *least accurately* describes a role of financial statement analysis?
    A. Use the information in financial statements to make economic decisions.
    B. Provide reasonable assurance that the financial statements are free of material errors.
    C. Evaluate an entity's financial position and past performance to form opinions about its future ability to earn profits and generate cash flow.

2. A firm's financial position at a specific point in time is reported in the:
    A. balance sheet.
    B. income statement.
    C. cash flow statement.

3. Information about accounting estimates, assumptions, and methods chosen for reporting is *most likely* found in:
    A. the auditor's opinion.
    B. financial statement notes.
    C. Management's Discussion and Analysis.

4. If an auditor finds that a company's financial statements have made a specific exception to applicable accounting principles, she is *most likely* to issue a:
    A. dissenting opinion.
    B. cautionary note.
    C. qualified opinion.

5. Information about elections of members to a company's Board of Directors is *most likely* found in:
    A. a 10-Q filing.
    B. a proxy statement.
    C. footnotes to the financial statements.

6. Which of these steps is *least likely* to be a part of the financial statement analysis framework?
    A. State the purpose and context of the analysis.
    B. Determine whether the company's securities are suitable for the client.
    C. Adjust the financial statement data and compare the company to its industry peers.

ANSWERS – CONCEPT CHECKERS

1. **B** This statement describes the role of an auditor, rather than the role of an analyst. The other responses describe the role of financial statement analysis.

2. **A** The balance sheet reports a company's financial position as of a specific date. The income statement, cash flow statement, and statement of changes in owners' equity show the company's performance during a specific period.

3. **B** Information about accounting methods and estimates is contained in the footnotes to the financial statements.

4. **C** An auditor will issue a qualified opinion if the financial statements make any exceptions to applicable accounting standards and will explain the effect of these exceptions in the auditor's report.

5. **B** Proxy statements contain information related to matters that come before shareholders for a vote, such as elections of board members.

6. **B** Determining the suitability of an investment for a client is not one of the six steps in the financial statement analysis framework. The analyst would only perform this function if he also had an advisory relationship with the client. Stating the objective and processing the data are two of the six steps in the framework. The others are gathering the data, analyzing the data, updating the analysis, and reporting the conclusions.

©2012 Kaplan, Inc.

The following is a review of the Financial Reporting and Analysis principles designed to address the learning outcome statements set forth by CFA Institute. This topic is also covered in:

FINANCIAL REPORTING MECHANICS

EXAM FOCUS

The analysis of financial statements requires an understanding of how a company's transactions are recorded in the various accounts. Candidates should focus on the financial statement elements (assets, liabilities, equity, revenues, and expenses) and be able to classify any account into its appropriate element. Candidates should also learn the basic and expanded accounting equations and why every transaction must be recorded in at least two accounts. The types of accruals, when each of them is used, how changes in accounts affect the financial statements, and the relationships among the financial statements, are all important topics.

LOS 23.a: Explain the relationship of financial statement elements and accounts, and classify accounts into the financial statement elements.

CFA® Program Curriculum, Volume 3, page 41

Financial statement elements are the major classifications of assets, liabilities, owners' equity, revenues, and expenses. **Accounts** are the specific records within each element where various transactions are entered. On the financial statements, accounts are typically presented in groups such as "inventory" or "accounts payable." A company's **chart of accounts** is a detailed list of the accounts that make up the five financial statement elements and the line items presented in the financial statements.

Contra accounts are used for entries that offset some part of the value of another account. For example, equipment is typically valued on the balance sheet at acquisition (historical) cost, and the estimated decrease in its value over time is recorded in a contra account titled "accumulated depreciation."

Classifying Accounts Into the Financial Statement Elements

Assets are the firm's economic resources. Examples of assets include:

- *Cash and cash equivalents.* Liquid securities with maturities of 90 days or less are considered cash equivalents.
- *Accounts receivable.* Accounts receivable often have an "allowance for bad debt expense" or "allowance for doubtful accounts" as a contra account.
- *Inventory.*
- *Financial assets* such as marketable securities.
- *Prepaid expenses.* Items that will be expenses on future income statements.
- *Property, plant, and equipment.* Includes a contra-asset account for accumulated depreciation.
- *Investment in affiliates* accounted for using the equity method.

- *Deferred tax assets.*
- *Intangible assets.* Economic resources of the firm that do not have a physical form, such as patents, trademarks, licenses, and goodwill. Except for goodwill, these values may be reduced by "accumulated amortization."

Liabilities are creditor claims on the company's resources. Examples of liabilities include:

- *Accounts payable* and *trade payables.*
- *Financial liabilities* such as short-term notes payable.
- *Unearned revenue.* Items that will show up on future income statements as revenues.
- *Income taxes payable.* The taxes accrued during the past year but not yet paid.
- *Long-term debt* such as bonds payable.
- *Deferred tax liabilities.*

Owners' equity is the owners' residual claim on a firm's resources, which is the amount by which assets exceed liabilities. Owners' equity includes:

- *Capital.* Par value of common stock.
- *Additional paid-in capital.* Proceeds from common stock sales in excess of par value. (Share repurchases that the company has made are represented in the contra account *treasury stock.*)
- *Retained earnings.* Cumulative net income that has not been distributed as dividends.
- *Other comprehensive income.* Changes resulting from foreign currency translation, minimum pension liability adjustments, or unrealized gains and losses on investments.

Revenue represents inflows of economic resources and includes:

- *Sales.* Revenue from the firm's day-to-day activities.
- *Gains.* Increases in assets from transactions incidental to the firm's day-to-day activities.
- *Investment income* such as interest and dividend income.

Expenses are outflows of economic resources and include:

- *Cost of goods sold.*
- *Selling, general, and administrative expenses.* These include such expenses as advertising, management salaries, rent, and utilities.
- *Depreciation and amortization.* To reflect the "using up" of tangible and intangible assets.
- *Tax expense.*
- *Interest expense.*
- *Losses.* Decreases in assets from transactions incidental to the firm's day-to-day activities.

LOS 23.b: Explain the accounting equation in its basic and expanded forms.

CFA® Program Curriculum, Volume 3, page 44

The **basic accounting equation** is the relationship among the three balance sheet elements:

assets = liabilities + owners' equity

©2012 Kaplan, Inc.

Owners' equity consists of capital contributed by the firm's owners and the cumulative earnings the firm has retained. With that in mind, we can state the **expanded accounting equation:**

assets = liabilities + contributed capital + ending retained earnings

Ending retained earnings for an accounting period are the result of adding that period's retained earnings (revenues minus expenses minus dividends) to beginning retained earnings. So the expanded accounting equation can also be stated as:

assets = liabilities
+ contributed capital
+ beginning retained earnings
+ revenue
− expenses
− dividends

LOS 23.c: Explain the process of recording business transactions using an accounting system based on the accounting equation.

CFA® Program Curriculum, Volume 3, page 49

Keeping the accounting equation in balance requires **double-entry accounting,** in which a transaction has to be recorded in at least two accounts. An increase in an asset account, for example, must be balanced by a decrease in another asset account or by an increase in a liability or owners' equity account.

Some typical examples of double entry accounting include:

- *Purchase equipment for $10,000 cash.* Property, plant, and equipment (an asset) increases by $10,000. Cash (an asset) decreases by $10,000.
- *Borrow $10,000 to purchase equipment.* PP&E increases by $10,000. Notes payable (a liability) increases by $10,000.
- *Buy office supplies for $100 cash.* Cash decreases by $100. Supply expense increases by $100. An expense reduces retained earnings, so owners' equity decreases by $100.
- *Buy inventory for $8,000 cash and sell it for $10,000 cash.* The purchase decreases cash by $8,000 and increases inventory (an asset) by $8,000. The sale increases cash by $10,000 and decreases inventory by $8,000, so assets increase by $2,000. At the same time, sales (a revenue account) increase by $10,000 and "cost of goods sold" (an expense) increases by the $8,000 cost of inventory. The $2,000 difference is an increase in net income and, therefore, in retained earnings and owners' equity (ignoring taxes).

LOS 23.d: Explain the need for accruals and other adjustments in preparing financial statements.

CFA® Program Curriculum, Volume 3, page 65

Revenues and expenses are not always recorded at the same time that cash receipts and payments are made. The principle of **accrual accounting** requires that revenue is recorded when the firm earns it and expenses are recorded as the firm incurs them, regardless of whether cash has actually been paid. Accruals fall into four categories:

1. *Unearned revenue.* The firm receives cash before it provides a good or service to customers. Cash increases and unearned revenue, a liability, increases by the same amount. When the firm provides the good or service, revenue increases and the liability decreases. For example, a newspaper or magazine subscription is typically paid in advance. The publisher records the cash received and increases the unearned revenue liability account. The firm recognizes revenues and decreases the liability as it fulfills the subscription obligation.

2. *Accrued revenue.* The firm provides goods or services before it receives cash payment. Revenue increases and accounts receivable (an asset) increases. When the customer pays cash, accounts receivable decreases. A typical example would be a manufacturer that sells goods to retail stores "on account." The manufacturer records revenue when it delivers the goods but does not receive cash until after the retailers sell the goods to consumers.

3. *Prepaid expenses.* The firm pays cash ahead of time for an anticipated expense. Cash (an asset) decreases and prepaid expense (also an asset) increases. Prepaid expense decreases and expenses increase when the expense is actually incurred. For example, a retail store that rents space in a shopping mall will often pay its rent in advance.

4. *Accrued expenses.* The firm owes cash for expenses it has incurred. Expenses increase and a liability for accrued expenses increases as well. The liability decreases when the firm pays cash to satisfy it. Wages payable are a common example of an accrued expense, as companies typically pay their employees at a later date for work they performed in the prior week or month.

Accruals require an accounting entry when the earliest event occurs (paying or receiving cash, providing a good or service, or incurring an expense) and require one or more offsetting entries as the exchange is completed. With unearned revenue and prepaid expenses, cash changes hands first and the revenue or expense is recorded later. With accrued revenue and accrued expenses, the revenue or expense is recorded first and cash is exchanged later. In all these cases, the effect of accrual accounting is to recognize revenues or expenses in the appropriate period.

Other Adjustments

Most assets are recorded on the financial statements at their historical costs. However, accounting standards require balance sheet values of certain assets to reflect their current market values. Accounting entries that update these assets' values are called **valuation adjustments**. To keep the accounting equation in balance, changes in asset values also change owners' equity, through gains or losses recorded on the income statement or in "other comprehensive income."

LOS 23.e: Explain the relationships among the income statement, balance sheet, statement of cash flows, and statement of owners' equity.

CFA® Program Curriculum, Volume 3, page 63

Figures 1 through 4 contain the financial statements for a sample corporation. The balance sheet summarizes the company's financial position at the end of the current accounting period (and in this example, it also shows the company's position at the end of the previous fiscal period). The income statement, cash flow statement, and statement of owners' equity show changes that occurred during the most recent accounting period.

Note these key relationships among the financial statements:

- The income statement shows that net income was $37,500 in 20X8. The company declared $8,500 of that income as dividends to its shareholders. The remaining $29,000 is an increase in retained earnings. Retained earnings on the balance sheet increased by $29,000, from $30,000 in 20X7 to $59,000 in 20X8.
- The cash flow statement shows a $24,000 net increase in cash. On the balance sheet, cash increased by $24,000, from $9,000 in 20X7 to $33,000 in 20X8.
- One of the uses of cash shown on the cash flow statement is a repurchase of stock for $10,000. The balance sheet shows this $10,000 repurchase as a decrease in common stock, from $50,000 in 20X7 to $40,000 in 20X8.
- The statement of owners' equity reflects the changes in retained earnings and contributed capital (common stock). Owners' equity increased by $19,000, from $80,000 in 20X7 to $99,000 in 20X8. This equals the $29,000 increase in retained earnings less the $10,000 decrease in common stock.

Figure 1: Income Statement for 20X8

Sales	$100,000
Expenses	
Cost of goods sold	40,000
Wages	5,000
Depreciation	7,000
Interest	500
Total expenses	$52,500
Income from continuing operations	47,500
Gain from sale of land	10,000
Pretax income	$57,500
Provision for taxes	20,000
Net income	$37,500
Common dividends declared	8,500

Figure 2: Balance Sheet for 20X7 and 20X8

	20X8	20X7
Assets		
Current assets		
Cash	$33,000	$9,000
Accounts receivable	10,000	9,000
Inventory	5,000	7,000
Noncurrent assets		
Land	$35,000	$40,000
Gross plant and equipment	85,000	60,000
less: Accumulated depreciation	(16,000)	(9,000)
Net plant and equipment	$69,000	$51,000
Goodwill	10,000	10,000
Total assets	$162,000	$126,000
Liabilities and Equity		
Current liabilities		
Accounts payable	$9,000	$5,000
Wages payable	4,500	8,000
Interest payable	3,500	3,000
Taxes payable	5,000	4,000
Dividends payable	6,000	1,000
Noncurrent liabilities		
Bonds	$15,000	$10,000
Deferred taxes	20,000	15,000
Stockholders' equity		
Common stock	$40,000	$50,000
Retained earnings	59,000	30,000
Total liabilities & stockholders' equity	$162,000	$126,000

Figure 3: Cash Flow Statement for 20X8

Cash collections	$99,000
Cash inputs	(34,000)
Cash expenses	(8,500)
Cash interest	0
Cash taxes	(14,000)
Cash flow from operations	$42,500
Cash from sale of land	$15,000
Purchase of plant and equipment	(25,000)
Cash flow from investments	($10,000)
Sale of bonds	$5,000
Repurchase of stock	(10,000)
Cash dividends	(3,500)
Cash flow from financing	($8,500)
Total cash flow	$24,000

©2012 Kaplan, Inc.

Figure 4: Statement of Owners' Equity for 20X8

	Contributed Capital	Retained Earnings	Total
Balance, 12/31/20X7	$50,000	$30,000	$80,000
Repurchase of stock	($10,000)		($10,000)
Net income		$37,500	$37,500
Distributions		($8,500)	($8,500)
Balance, 12/31/20X8	$40,000	$59,000	$99,000

LOS 23.f: Describe the flow of information in an accounting system.

CFA® Program Curriculum, Volume 3, page 68

Information flows through an accounting system in four steps:

1. **Journal entries** record every transaction, showing which accounts are changed and by what amounts. A listing of all the journal entries in order of their dates is called the **general journal**.

2. The **general ledger** sorts the entries in the general journal by account.

3. At the end of the accounting period, an **initial trial balance** is prepared that shows the balances in each account. If any adjusting entries are needed, they will be recorded and reflected in an **adjusted trial balance**.

4. The account balances from the adjusted trial balance are presented in the financial statements.

LOS 23.g: Explain the use of the results of the accounting process in security analysis.

CFA® Program Curriculum, Volume 3, page 69

An analyst does not have access to the detailed information that flows through a company's accounting system but sees only the end product (the financial statements). An analyst needs to understand the various accruals, adjustments, and management assumptions that go into the financial statements. Much of this detail is contained in the footnotes to the statements and Management's Discussion and Analysis, so it is crucial for an analyst to review these parts of the financial statements. With this information, the analyst can better judge how well the financial statements reflect the company's true performance and what adjustments to the data are necessary for appropriate analysis.

Because adjustments and assumptions within the financial statements are, at least to some extent, at the discretion of management, the possibility exists that management may attempt to manipulate or misrepresent the company's financial performance. A good understanding of the accounting process can help an analyst identify financial statement entries that appear to be out of line.

KEY CONCEPTS

LOS 23.a

Transactions are recorded in accounts that form the financial statement elements:

- Assets—the firm's economic resources.
- Liabilities—creditors' claims on the firm's resources.
- Owners' equity—paid-in capital (common and preferred stock), retained earnings, and cumulative other comprehensive income.
- Revenues—sales, investment income, and gains.
- Expenses—cost of goods sold, selling and administrative expenses, depreciation, interest, taxes, and losses.

LOS 23.b

The basic accounting equation:

$$\text{assets} = \text{liabilities} + \text{owners' equity}$$

The expanded accounting equation:

$$\text{assets} = \text{liabilities} + \text{contributed capital} + \text{ending retained earnings}$$

The expanded accounting equation can also be stated as:

$$\text{assets} = \text{liabilities} + \text{contributed capital} + \text{beginning retained earnings} + \text{revenue} - \text{expenses} - \text{dividends}$$

LOS 23.c

Keeping the accounting equation ($A - L = E$) in balance requires double entry accounting, in which a transaction is recorded in at least two accounts. An increase in an asset account, for example, must be balanced by a decrease in another asset account or by an increase in a liability or owners' equity account.

LOS 23.d

A firm must recognize revenues when they are earned and expenses when they are incurred. Accruals are required when the timing of cash payments made and received does not match the timing of the revenue or expense recognition on the financial statements.

LOS 23.e

The balance sheet shows a company's financial position at a point in time.

Changes in balance sheet accounts during an accounting period are reflected in the income statement, the cash flow statement, and the statement of owners' equity.

©2012 Kaplan, Inc.

LOS 23.f

Information enters an accounting system as journal entries, which are sorted by account into a general ledger. Trial balances are formed at the end of an accounting period. Accounts are then adjusted and presented in financial statements.

LOS 23.g

Since financial reporting requires choices of method, judgment, and estimates, an analyst must understand the accounting process used to produce the financial statements in order to understand the business and the results for the period. Analysts should be alert to the use of accruals, changes in valuations, and other notable changes that may indicate management judgment is incorrect or, worse, that the financial statements have been deliberately manipulated.

CONCEPT CHECKERS

1. Accounts receivable and accounts payable are *most likely* classified as which financial statement elements?

	Accounts receivable	Accounts payable
A.	Assets	Liabilities
B.	Revenues	Liabilities
C.	Revenues	Expenses

2. Annual depreciation and accumulated depreciation are *most likely* classified as which financial statement elements?

	Depreciation	Accumulated depreciation
A.	Expenses	Contra liabilities
B.	Expenses	Contra assets
C.	Liabilities	Contra assets

3. The accounting equation is *least accurately* stated as:
   A. owners' equity = liabilities – assets.
   B. ending retained earnings = assets – contributed capital – liabilities.
   C. assets = liabilities + contributed capital + beginning retained earnings + revenue – expenses – dividends.

4. A decrease in assets would *least likely* be consistent with a(n):
   A. increase in expenses.
   B. decrease in revenues.
   C. increase in contributed capital.

5. An electrician repaired the light fixtures in a retail shop on October 24 and sent the bill to the shop on November 3. If both the electrician and the shop prepare financial statements under the accrual method on October 31, how will they each record this transaction?

	Electrician	Retail shop
A.	Accrued revenue	Accrued expense
B.	Accrued revenue	Prepaid expense
C.	Unearned revenue	Accrued expense

6. If a firm raises $10 million by issuing new common stock, which of its financial statements will reflect the transaction?
   A. Income statement and statement of owners' equity.
   B. Balance sheet, income statement, and cash flow statement.
   C. Balance sheet, cash flow statement, and statement of owners' equity.

7. An auditor needs to review all of a company's transactions that took place between August 15 and August 17 of the current year. To find this information, she would *most likely* consult the company's:
   A. general ledger.
   B. general journal.
   C. financial statements.

©2012 Kaplan, Inc.

8.   Paul Schmidt, a representative for Westby Investments, is explaining how
      security analysts use the results of the accounting process. He states, "Analysts
      do not have access to all the entries that went into creating a company's
      financial statements. If the analyst carefully reviews the auditor's report for any
      instances where the financial statements deviate from the appropriate accounting
      principles, he can then be confident that management is not manipulating
      earnings." Schmidt is:

      A.   correct.
      B.   incorrect, because the entries that went into creating a company's financial
           statements are publicly available.
      C.   incorrect, because management can manipulate earnings even within the
           confines of generally accepted accounting principles.

CHALLENGE PROBLEMS

For each account listed, indicate whether the account should be classified as Assets (A), Liabilities (L), Owners' Equity (O), Revenues (R), or Expenses (X).

Account	Financial statement element				
Accounts payable	A	L	O	R	X
Accounts receivable	A	L	O	R	X
Accumulated depreciation	A	L	O	R	X
Additional paid-in capital	A	L	O	R	X
Allowance for bad debts	A	L	O	R	X
Bonds payable	A	L	O	R	X
Cash equivalents	A	L	O	R	X
Common stock	A	L	O	R	X
Cost of goods sold	A	L	O	R	X
Current portion of long-term debt	A	L	O	R	X
Deferred tax items	A	L	O	R	X
Depreciation	A	L	O	R	X
Dividends payable	A	L	O	R	X
Dividends received	A	L	O	R	X
Gain on sale of assets	A	L	O	R	X
Goodwill	A	L	O	R	X
Inventory	A	L	O	R	X
Investment securities	A	L	O	R	X
Loss on sale of assets	A	L	O	R	X
Notes payable	A	L	O	R	X
Other comprehensive income	A	L	O	R	X
Prepaid expenses	A	L	O	R	X
Property, plant, and equipment	A	L	O	R	X
Retained earnings	A	L	O	R	X
Sales	A	L	O	R	X
Unearned revenue	A	L	O	R	X

©2012 Kaplan, Inc.

ANSWERS – CONCEPT CHECKERS

1. **A** Accounts receivable are an asset and accounts payable are a liability.

2. **B** Annual depreciation is an expense. Accumulated depreciation is a contra asset account that typically offsets the historical cost of property, plant, and equipment.

3. **A** Owners' equity is equal to assets minus liabilities.

4. **C** The expanded accounting equation shows that assets = liabilities + contributed capital + beginning retained earnings + revenue – expenses – dividends. A decrease in assets is consistent with an increase in expenses or a decrease in revenues but not with an increase in contributed capital.

5. **A** The service is performed before cash is paid. This transaction represents accrued revenue to the electrician and an accrued expense to the retail shop. Since the invoice has not been sent as of the statement date, it is not shown in accounts receivable or accounts payable.

6. **C** The $10 million raised appears on the cash flow statement as a cash inflow from financing and on the statement of owners' equity as an increase in contributed capital. Both assets (cash) and equity (common stock) increase on the balance sheet. The income statement is unaffected by stock issuance.

7. **B** The general journal lists all of the company's transactions by date. The general ledger lists them by account.

8. **C** Schmidt is correct in stating that analysts do not have access to the detailed accounting entries that went into a company's financial statements. However, he is incorrect in stating that an analyst can be sure management is not manipulating earnings if the audit report does not list deviations from accounting principles. Because accruals and many valuations require management's judgment, there is considerable room within the accounting standards for management to manipulate earnings.

ANSWERS – CHALLENGE PROBLEMS

Account	Financial statement element			
Accounts payable		L		
Accounts receivable	A			
Accumulated depreciation	A			
Contra to the asset being depreciated.				
Additional paid-in capital			O	
Allowance for bad debts	A			
Contra to accounts receivable.				
Bonds payable		L		
Cash equivalents	A			
Common stock			O	
Cost of goods sold				X
Current portion of long-term debt		L		
Deferred tax items	A	L		
Both deferred tax assets and deferred tax liabilities are recorded.				
Depreciation				X
Dividends payable		L		
Dividends received				R
Gain on sale of assets				R
Goodwill	A			
Intangible asset.				
Inventory	A			
Investment securities	A			
Loss on sale of assets				X
Notes payable		L		
Other comprehensive income			O	
Prepaid expenses	A			
Accrual account.				
Property, plant, and equipment	A			
Retained earnings			O	
Sales				R
Unearned revenue		L		
Accrual account.				

©2012 Kaplan, Inc.

FINANCIAL REPORTING STANDARDS

EXAM FOCUS

This topic review covers accounting standards: why they exist, who issues them, and who enforces them. Know the difference between the roles of private standard-setting bodies and government regulatory authorities and be able to name the most important organizations of both kinds. Become familiar with the framework for International Financial Reporting Standards (IFRS), including qualitative characteristics, constraints and assumptions, and features for preparing financial statements. Be able to identify barriers to convergence of national accounting standards (such as U.S. GAAP) with IFRS, key differences between the IFRS and U.S. GAAP frameworks, and elements of and barriers to creating a coherent financial reporting network.

LOS 24.a: Describe the objective of financial statements and the importance of financial reporting standards in security analysis and valuation.

CFA® Program Curriculum, Volume 3, page 94

According to the IASB *Conceptual Framework for Financial Reporting 2010*, the objective of financial reporting is to provide information about the firm to current and potential investors and creditors that is useful for making their decisions about investing in or lending to the firm.

The conceptual framework is used in the development of accounting standards. Given the variety and complexity of possible transactions and the estimates and assumptions a firm must make when presenting its performance, financial statements could potentially take any form if reporting standards did not exist. Thus, financial reporting standards are needed to provide consistency by narrowing the range of acceptable responses.

Reporting standards ensure that transactions are reported by firms similarly. However, standards must remain flexible and allow discretion to management to properly describe the economics of the firm.

Financial reporting is not designed solely for valuation purposes; however, it does provide important inputs for valuation purposes.

LOS 24.b: Describe the roles and desirable attributes of financial reporting standard-setting bodies and regulatory authorities in establishing and enforcing reporting standards, and describe the role of the International Organization of Securities Commissions.

CFA® Program Curriculum, Volume 3, page 97

Standard-setting bodies are professional organizations of accountants and auditors that establish financial reporting standards. **Regulatory authorities** are government agencies that have the legal authority to enforce compliance with financial reporting standards.

The two primary standard-setting bodies are the *Financial Accounting Standards Board* (FASB) and the *International Accounting Standards Board* (IASB). In the United States, the FASB sets forth Generally Accepted Accounting Principles (GAAP). Outside the United States, the IASB establishes International Financial Reporting Standards (IFRS). Other national standard-setting bodies exist as well. Many of them (including the FASB) are working toward convergence with IFRS. Some of the older IASB standards are referred to as International Accounting Standards (IAS).

Desirable attributes of standard-setters:

- Observe high professional standards.
- Have adequate authority, resources, and competencies to accomplish its mission.
- Have clear and consistent standard-setting processes.
- Guided by a well-articulated framework.
- Operate independently while still seeking input from stakeholders.
- Should not be compromised by special interests.
- Decisions are made in the public interest.

Regulatory authorities, such as the *Securities and Exchange Commission* (SEC) in the United States and the *Financial Services Authority* (FSA) in the United Kingdom, are established by national governments. Figure 1 summarizes the SEC's filing requirements for publicly traded companies in the United States. These filings, which are available from the SEC Web site (*www.sec.gov*), are arguably the most important source of information for the analysis of publicly traded firms.

Most national authorities belong to the **International Organization of Securities Commissions** (IOSCO). The three objectives of financial market regulation according to IOSCO[1] are to (1) protect investors; (2) ensure the fairness, efficiency, and transparency of markets; and (3) reduce systemic risk. Because of the increasing globalization of securities markets, IOSCO has a goal of uniform financial regulations across countries.

---

1. International Organization of Securities Commissions, "Objectives and Principles of Securities Regulation," June 2010.

©2012 Kaplan, Inc.

Figure 1: Securities and Exchange Commission Required Filings

Form S-1. Registration statement filed prior to the sale of new securities to the public. The registration statement includes audited financial statements, risk assessment, underwriter identification, and the estimated amount and use of the offering proceeds.

Form 10-K. Required annual filing that includes information about the business and its management, audited financial statements and disclosures, and disclosures about legal matters involving the firm. Information required in Form 10-K is similar to that which a firm typically provides in its annual report to shareholders. However, a firm's annual report is not a substitute for the required 10-K filing. Equivalent SEC forms for foreign issuers in the U.S. markets are Form 40-F for Canadian companies and Form 20-F for other foreign issuers.

Form 10-Q. U.S. firms are required to file this form quarterly, with updated financial statements (unlike Form 10-K, these statements do not have to be audited) and disclosures about certain events such as significant legal proceedings or changes in accounting policy. Non-U.S. companies are typically required to file the equivalent Form 6-K semiannually.

Form DEF-14A. When a company prepares a proxy statement for its shareholders prior to the annual meeting or other shareholder vote, it also files the statement with the SEC as Form DEF-14A.

Form 8-K. Companies must file this form to disclose material events including significant asset acquisitions and disposals, changes in management or corporate governance, or matters related to its accountants, its financial statements, or the markets in which its securities trade.

Form 144. A company can issue securities to certain qualified buyers without registering the securities with the SEC but must notify the SEC that it intends to do so.

Forms 3, 4, and 5 involve the beneficial ownership of securities by a company's officers and directors. Analysts can use these filings to learn about purchases and sales of company securities by corporate insiders.

LOS 24.c: Describe the status of global convergence of accounting standards and ongoing barriers to developing one universally accepted set of financial reporting standards.

CFA® Program Curriculum, Volume 3, page 105

The European Union requires IFRS financial reporting by publicly listed companies. In most major countries that have not fully adopted IFRS, accounting standard setters are attempting to converge their standards with IFRS. Many aspects of U.S. GAAP and IFRS, for example, have converged over the past decade, and the Securities and Exchange Commission no longer requires IFRS reporting firms to reconcile their financial statements to U.S. GAAP. IFRS convergence efforts are also ongoing in Japan, China, and many other countries.

One barrier to convergence (developing one universally accepted set of accounting standards) is simply that different standard-setting bodies and the regulatory authorities of different countries can and do disagree on the best treatment of a particular item or issue. Other barriers result from the political pressures that regulatory bodies face from business groups and others who will be affected by changes in reporting standards.

LOS 24.d: Describe the International Accounting Standards Board's conceptual framework, including the objective and qualitative characteristics of financial statements, required reporting elements, and constraints and assumptions in preparing financial statements.

CFA® Program Curriculum, Volume 3, page 109

The ideas on which the IASB bases its standards are expressed in the "Conceptual Framework for Financial Reporting" that the organization adopted in 2010. The IASB framework details the qualitative characteristics of financial statements and specifies the required reporting elements. The framework also notes certain constraints and assumptions that are involved in financial statement preparation.

At the center of the IASB Conceptual Framework is the objective to provide financial information that is useful in making decisions about providing resources to an entity. The resource providers include investors, lenders, and other creditors. Users of financial statements need information about the firm's performance, financial position, and cash flow.

Qualitative Characteristics

There are two fundamental characteristics that make financial information useful: relevance and faithful representation.[2]

- *Relevance.* Financial statements are relevant if the information in them can influence users' economic decisions or affect users' evaluations of past events or forecasts of future events. To be relevant, information should have predictive value, confirmatory value (confirm prior expectations), or both. Materiality is an aspect of relevance.[3]
- *Faithful representation.* Information that is faithfully representative is complete, neutral (absence of bias), and free from error.

There are four characteristics that enhance relevance and faithful representation: comparability, verifiability, timeliness, and understandability.

- *Comparability.* Financial statement presentation should be consistent among firms and across time periods.
- *Verifiability.* Independent observers, using the same methods, obtain similar results.
- *Timeliness.* Information is available to decision makers before the information is stale.

---

2. *Conceptual Framework for Financial Reporting (2010).* paragraphs QC5-18.
3. Ibid., paragraphs QC19-34.

©2012 Kaplan, Inc.

- *Understandability*. Users with a basic knowledge of business and accounting and who make a reasonable effort to study the financial statements should be able to readily understand the information the statements present. Useful information should not be omitted just because it is complicated.

Required Reporting Elements

The elements of financial statements are the by-now familiar groupings of assets, liabilities, and owners' equity (for measuring financial position) and income and expenses (for measuring performance). The Conceptual Framework describes each of these elements:[4]

- *Assets*. Resources controlled as a result of past transactions that are expected to provide future economic benefits.
- *Liabilities*. Obligations as a result of past events that are expected to require an outflow of economic resources.
- *Equity*. The owners' residual interest in the assets after deducting the liabilities.
- *Income*. An increase in economic benefits, either increasing assets or decreasing liabilities in a way that increases owners' equity (but not including contributions by owners). Income includes revenues and gains.
- *Expenses*. Decreases in economic benefits, either decreasing assets or increasing liabilities in a way that decreases owners' equity (but not including distributions to owners). Losses are included in expenses.

An item should be *recognized* in its financial statement element if a future economic benefit from the item (flowing to or from the firm) is probable and the item's value or cost can be measured reliably.

The amounts at which items are reported in the financial statement elements depend on their **measurement base**. Measurement bases include *historical cost* (the amount originally paid for the asset), *amortized cost* (historical cost adjusted for depreciation, amortization, depletion, and impairment), *current cost* (the amount the firm would have to pay today for the same asset), *realizable value* (the amount for which the firm could sell the asset), *present value* (the discounted value of the asset's expected future cash flows), and *fair value* (the amount at which two parties in an arm's-length transaction would exchange the asset).

 Professor's Note: In the next Study Sessions, we will discuss these measurement bases in more detail and the situations in which each is appropriate.

Constraints and Assumptions

According to the Conceptual Framework, there is cost-benefit tradeoff of the enhancing characteristics.[5] Accordingly, the benefit that users gain from the information should be greater than the cost of presenting it. Another constraint, not specifically mentioned in the Conceptual Framework, is the fact that non-quantifiable information about a company (its reputation, brand loyalty, capacity for innovation, etc.) cannot be captured directly in financial statements.

---

4. Ibid., paragraphs 4.4-4.23.
5. Ibid., paragraphs QC35-39.

Two important underlying assumptions of financial statements are *accrual accounting* and *going concern*.[6] Accrual accounting means that financial statements should reflect transactions at the time they actually occur, not necessarily when cash is paid. Going concern assumes the company will continue to exist for the foreseeable future. If this is not the case, then presenting the company's financial position fairly requires a number of adjustments (e.g., its inventory or other assets may only be worth their liquidation values).

LOS 24.e: Describe general requirements for financial statements under IFRS.

CFA® Program Curriculum, Volume 3, page 115

International Accounting Standard (IAS) No. 1 defines which financial statements are required and how they must be presented. The **required financial statements** are:

- Balance sheet.
- Statement of comprehensive income.
- Cash flow statement.
- Statement of changes in owners' equity.
- Explanatory notes, including a summary of accounting policies.

The general **features for preparing financial statements** are stated in IAS No. 1:

- *Fair presentation,* defined as faithfully representing the effects of the entity's transactions and events according to the standards for recognizing assets, liabilities, revenues, and expenses.
- *Going concern basis,* meaning the financial statements are based on the assumption that the firm will continue to exist unless its management intends to (or must) liquidate it.
- *Accrual basis* of accounting is used to prepare the financial statements other than the statement of cash flows.
- *Consistency* between periods in how items are presented and classified, with prior-period amounts disclosed for comparison.
- *Materiality,* meaning the financial statements should be free of misstatements or omissions that could influence the decisions of users of financial statements.
- *Aggregation* of similar items and separation of dissimilar items.
- *No offsetting* of assets against liabilities or income against expenses unless a specific standard permits or requires it.
- *Reporting frequency* must be at least annually.
- *Comparative information* for prior periods should be included unless a specific standard states otherwise.

Also stated in IAS No. 1 are the **structure and content of financial statements:**

- Most entities should present a *classified balance sheet* showing current and noncurrent assets and liabilities.
- *Minimum information* is required on the face of each financial statement and in the notes. For example, the face of the balance sheet must show specific items such as cash and cash equivalents, plant, property and equipment, and inventories. Items listed on the face of the comprehensive income statement must include revenue, profit or loss, tax expense, and finance costs, among others.

---

6. Ibid., paragraphs OB17 and 4.1.

©2012 Kaplan, Inc.

- *Comparative information* for prior periods should be included unless a specific standard states otherwise.

LOS 24.f: Compare key concepts of financial reporting standards under IFRS and U.S. GAAP reporting systems.

CFA® Program Curriculum, Volume 3, page 119

U.S. GAAP consists of standards issued by the FASB, along with numerous other pronouncements and interpretations. Like the IASB, the FASB has a framework for preparing and presenting financial statements. The two organizations are working toward a common framework, but at present the two frameworks differ in several respects.

- The IASB framework lists income and expenses as elements related to performance, while the FASB framework includes revenues, expenses, gains, losses, and comprehensive income.
- The FASB defines an asset as a future economic benefit, whereas the IASB defines it as a resource from which a future economic benefit is expected to flow. Also, the FASB uses the word *probable* in its definition of assets and liabilities.
- The FASB does not allow the upward valuation of most assets.

Until these frameworks converge, analysts will need to interpret financial statements that are prepared under different standards. In many cases, however, a company will present a **reconciliation statement** showing what its financial results would have been under an alternative reporting system. For example, firms that list their shares in the United States but do not use U.S. GAAP or IFRS are required to reconcile their financial statements with U.S. GAAP. For IFRS firms listing their shares in the United States, reconciliation is no longer required.

Even when a unified framework emerges, special reporting standards that apply to particular industries (e.g., insurance and banking) will continue to exist.

LOS 24.g: Identify the characteristics of a coherent financial reporting framework and the barriers to creating such a framework.

CFA® Program Curriculum, Volume 3, page 121

A coherent financial reporting framework is one that fits together logically. Such a framework should be transparent, comprehensive, and consistent.

- *Transparency*—Full disclosure and fair presentation reveal the underlying economics of the company to the financial statement user.
- *Comprehensiveness*—All types of transactions that have financial implications should be part of the framework, including new types of transactions that emerge.
- *Consistency*—Similar transactions should be accounted for in similar ways across companies, geographic areas, and time periods.

Barriers to creating a coherent financial reporting framework include issues related to valuation, standard setting, and measurement.

- *Valuation*—Measurement bases for valuation that require little judgment, such as historical cost, may be less relevant than a basis like fair value that requires more judgment.
- *Standard setting*—Three approaches to standard setting are a "principles-based" approach that relies on a broad framework, a "rules-based" approach that gives specific guidance about how to classify transactions, and an "objectives-oriented" approach that blends the other two approaches. IFRS is largely a principles-based approach. U.S. GAAP has traditionally been more rules-based, but the common conceptual framework is moving toward an objectives-oriented approach.
- *Measurement*—Another trade-off in financial reporting is between properly valuing the elements at one point in time (as on the balance sheet) and properly valuing the changes between points in time (as on the income statement). An "asset/liability" approach, which standard setters have largely used, focuses on balance sheet valuation. A "revenue/expense" approach would tend to place more significance on the income statement.

LOS 24.h: Explain the implications for financial analysis of differing financial reporting systems and the importance of monitoring developments in financial reporting standards.

CFA® Program Curriculum, Volume 3, page 123

As financial reporting standards continue to evolve, analysts need to monitor how these developments will affect the financial statements they use. An analyst should be aware of new products and innovations in the financial markets that generate new types of transactions. These might not fall neatly into the existing financial reporting standards. The analyst can use the financial reporting framework as a guide for evaluating what effect new products or transactions might have on financial statements.

To keep up to date on the evolving standards, an analyst can monitor professional journals and other sources, such as the IASB (*www.iasb.org*) and FASB (*www.fasb.org*) Web sites. CFA Institute produces position papers on financial reporting issues through the CFA Centre for Financial Market Integrity (*www.cfainstitute.org/cfacentre*).

Finally, analysts must monitor company disclosures for significant accounting standards and estimates.

LOS 24.i: Analyze company disclosures of significant accounting policies.

CFA® Program Curriculum, Volume 3, page 126

Companies that prepare financial statements under IFRS or U.S. GAAP must disclose their accounting policies and estimates in the footnotes. Significant policies and estimates that require management judgement are also addressed in Management's Discussion and Analysis. An analyst should use these disclosures to evaluate what policies are discussed, whether they cover all the relevant data in the financial statements, which policies required management to make estimates, and whether the disclosures and estimates have changed since the prior period.

Another disclosure that is required for public companies is the likely impact of implementing recently issued accounting standards. Management can discuss the impact of adopting a new standard, conclude that the standard does not apply or will not affect the financial statements materially, or state that they are still evaluating the effects of the new standards. Analysts should be aware of the uncertainty this last statement implies.

KEY CONCEPTS

LOS 24.a
The objective of financial statements is to provide economic decision makers with useful information about a firm's financial performance and changes in financial position.

Reporting standards are designed to ensure that different firms' statements are comparable to one another and to narrow the range of reasonable estimates on which financial statements are based. This aids users of the financial statements who rely on them for information about the company's activities, profitability, and creditworthiness.

LOS 24.b
Standard-setting bodies are private sector organizations that establish financial reporting standards. The two primary standard-setting bodies are the International Accounting Standards Board (IASB) and, in the United States, the Financial Accounting Standards Board (FASB).

Regulatory authorities are government agencies that enforce compliance with financial reporting standards. Regulatory authorities include the Securities and Exchange Commission (SEC) in the United States and the Financial Services Authority (FSA) in the United Kingdom. Many national regulatory authorities belong to the International Organization of Securities Commissions (IOSCO).

LOS 24.c
Efforts to achieve convergence of local accounting standards with IFRS are underway in most major countries that have not adopted IFRS.

Barriers to developing one universally accepted set of financial reporting standards include differences of opinion among standard-setting bodies and regulatory authorities from different countries and political pressure within countries from groups affected by changes in reporting standards.

LOS 24.d
The IFRS "Conceptual Framework for Financial Reporting" defines the fundamental and enhancing qualitative characteristics of financial statements, specifies the required reporting elements, and notes the constraints and assumptions involved in preparing financial statements.

The fundamental characteristics of financial statements are relevance and faithful representation. The enhancing characteristics include comparability, verifiability, timeliness, and understandability.

Elements of financial statements are assets, liabilities, and owners' equity (for measuring financial position) and income and expenses (for measuring performance).

Constraints on financial statement preparation include cost versus benefit and the difficulty of capturing non-quantifiable information in financial statements.

©2012 Kaplan, Inc.

The two primary assumptions that underlie the preparation of financial statements are the accrual basis and the going concern assumption.

LOS 24.e
Required financial statements are the balance sheet, comprehensive income statement, cash flow statement, statement of changes in owners' equity, and explanatory notes.

The general features of financial statements according to IAS No. 1 are:
- Fair presentation.
- Going concern.
- Accrual accounting.
- Consistency.
- Materiality.
- Aggregation.
- No offsetting.
- Reporting frequency.
- Comparative information.

Other presentation requirements include a classified balance sheet and specific minimum information that must be reported in the notes and on the face of the financial statements.

LOS 24.f
The IASB and FASB frameworks are similar but are moving towards convergence. Some of the remaining differences are:
- The IASB lists income and expenses as performance elements, while the FASB lists revenues, expenses, gains, losses, and comprehensive income.
- There are minor differences in the definition of assets. Also, the FASB uses the word *probable* when defining assets and liabilities.
- The FASB does not allow the upward revaluation of most assets.

Firms that list their shares in the United States but do not use U.S. GAAP or IFRS are required to reconcile their financial statements with U.S. GAAP. For IFRS firms listing their shares in the United States, reconciliation is no longer required.

LOS 24.g
A coherent financial reporting framework should exhibit transparency, comprehensiveness, and consistency.

Barriers to creating a coherent framework include issues of valuation, standard setting, and measurement.

LOS 24.h
An analyst should be aware of evolving financial reporting standards and new products and innovations that generate new types of transactions.

LOS 24.i
Under IFRS and U.S. GAAP, companies must disclose their accounting policies and estimates in the footnotes and MD&A. Public companies are also required to disclose the likely impact of recently issued accounting standards on their financial statements.

CONCEPT CHECKERS

1. Standard-setting bodies are responsible for:
   A. establishing financial reporting standards only.
   B. establishing and enforcing standards for financial reporting.
   C. enforcing compliance with financial reporting standards only.

2. Which of the following organizations is *least likely* involved with enforcing compliance with financial reporting standards?
   A. Financial Services Authority (FSA).
   B. Securities and Exchange Commission (SEC).
   C. International Accounting Standards Board (IASB).

3. Dawn Czerniak is writing an article about international financial reporting standards. In her article she states, "Despite strong support from business groups for a universally accepted set of financial reporting standards, disagreements among the standard-setting bodies and regulatory authorities of various countries remain a barrier to developing one." Czerniak's statement is:
   A. correct.
   B. incorrect, because business groups have not supported a uniform set of financial reporting standards.
   C. incorrect, because disagreements among national standard-setting bodies and regulatory agencies have not been a barrier to developing a universal set of standards.

4. According to the IASB Conceptual Framework, the fundamental qualitative characteristics that make financial statements useful are:
   A. verifiability and timeliness.
   B. relevance and faithful representation.
   C. understandability and relevance.

5. Which of the following *most accurately* lists a required reporting element that is used to measure a company's financial position and one that is used to measure a company's performance?

	Position	Performance
A.	Assets	Liabilities
B.	Income	Expenses
C.	Liabilities	Income

6. International Accounting Standard (IAS) No. 1 *least likely* requires which of the following?
   A. Neither assets and liabilities, nor income and expenses, may be offset unless required or permitted by a financial reporting standard.
   B. Audited financial statements and disclosures, along with updated information about the firm and its management, must be filed at least quarterly.
   C. Fair presentation of financial statements means faithfully representing the firm's events and transactions according to the financial reporting standards.

©2012 Kaplan, Inc.

7.   Which of the following statements about the FASB conceptual framework, as compared to the IASB conceptional framework, is *most accurate*?
     A.   The FASB framework allows for upward revaluations of tangible, long-lived assets.
     B.   The FASB framework and IASB framework are now fully converged.
     C.   The FASB framework lists revenue, expenses, gains, losses, and comprehensive income related to financial performance.

8.   Which is *least likely* one of the conclusions about the impact of a change in financial reporting standards that might appear in management's discussion and analysis?
     A.   Management has chosen not to implement the new standard.
     B.   Management is currently evaluating the impact of the new standard.
     C.   The new standard will not have a material impact on the company's financial statements.

ANSWERS – CONCEPT CHECKERS

1. **A** Standard-setting bodies are private-sector organizations that establish financial reporting standards. Enforcement is the responsibility of regulatory authorities.

2. **C** The IASB is a standard-setting body. The SEC (in the United States) and the FSA (in the United Kingdom) are regulatory authorities.

3. **B** Political pressure from business groups and other interest groups who are affected by financial reporting standards has been a barrier to developing a universally accepted set of financial reporting standards. Disagreements among national standard-setting bodies and regulatory agencies have also been a barrier.

4. **B** The fundamental qualitative characteristics are relevance and faithful representation. Verifiability, timeliness, and understandability are enhancing qualitative characteristics.

5. **C** Balance sheet reporting elements (assets, liabilities, and owners' equity) measure a company's financial position. Income statement reporting elements (income, expenses) measure its financial performance.

6. **B** According to IAS No. 1, financial statements must be presented at least *annually*. Fair presentation is one of the IAS No. 1 principles for preparing financial statements. The ban against offsetting is one of the IAS No. 1 principles for presenting financial statements.

7. **C** The FASB framework lists revenues, expenses, gains, losses, and comprehensive income. The IASB framework only lists income and expenses.

8. **A** Management can discuss the impact of adopting the new standard, conclude that it does not apply or will have no material impact, or state that they are still evaluating the potential impact.

©2012 Kaplan, Inc.

The following is a review of the Financial Reporting and Analysis principles designed to address the learning outcome statements set forth by CFA Institute. This topic is also covered in:

UNDERSTANDING INCOME STATEMENTS

Study Session 8

EXAM FOCUS

Now we're getting to the heart of the matter. Since forecasts of future earnings, and therefore estimates of firm value, depend crucially on understanding a firm's income statement, everything in this topic review is important. Some of the items requiring calculation include depreciation, COGS, and inventory under different cost flow assumptions, as well as basic and diluted EPS. The separation of items into operating and non-operating categories is important when estimating recurring income as a first step in forecasting future firm earnings. Note that questions regarding the effect on financial ratios of the choice of accounting method and of accounting estimates are one common way to test your understanding of the material on those topics presented here.

INCOME STATEMENT COMPONENTS AND FORMAT

The income statement reports the revenues and expenses of the firm over a period of time. The income statement is sometimes referred to as the "statement of operations," the "statement of earnings," or the "profit and loss statement." The income statement equation is:

revenues − expenses = net income

Under IFRS, the income statement can be combined with "other comprehensive income" and presented as a single statement of comprehensive income. Alternatively, the income statement and the statement of comprehensive income can be presented separately. Presentation is similar under U.S. GAAP except that firms can choose to report comprehensive income in the statement of shareholders' equity.

Investors examine a firm's income statement for valuation purposes while lenders examine the income statement for information about the firm's ability to make the promised interest and principal payments on its debt.

LOS 25.a: Describe the components of the income statement and alternative presentation formats of that statement.

CFA® Program Curriculum, Volume 3, page 140

Revenues are the amounts reported from the sale of goods and services in the normal course of business. Revenue less adjustments for estimated returns and allowances is known as **net revenue**.

Professor's Note: The terms "revenue" and "sales" are sometimes used synonymously. However, sales is just one component of revenue in many firms. In some countries, revenues are referred to as "turnover."

Expenses are the amounts incurred to generate revenue and include cost of goods sold, operating expenses, interest, and taxes. Expenses are grouped together by their nature or function. Presenting all depreciation expense from manufacturing and administration together in one line of the income statement is an example of grouping by nature of the expense. Combining all costs associated with manufacturing (e.g., raw materials, depreciation, labor, etc.) as cost of goods sold is an example of grouping by function. Grouping expenses by function is sometimes referred to as the cost of sales method.

Professor's Note: Firms can present columnar data in chronological order from left-to-right or vice versa. Also, some firms present expenses as negative numbers while other firms use parentheses to signify expenses. Still other firms present expenses as positive numbers with the assumption that users know that expenses are subtracted in the income statement. Watch for these different treatments on the exam.

The income statement also includes **gains and losses,** which result in an increase (gains) or decrease (losses) of economic benefits. Gains and losses may or may not result from ordinary business activities. For example, a firm might sell surplus equipment used in its manufacturing operation that is no longer needed. The difference between the sales price and book value is reported as a gain or loss on the income statement. Summarizing, net income is equal to income (revenues + gains) minus expenses (including losses). Thus, the components can be rearranged as follows:

net income = revenues − ordinary expenses + other income − other expense + gains − losses

If a firm has a controlling interest in a subsidiary, the pro rata share of the subsidiary's income not owned by the parent is reported in parent's income statement as the **noncontrolling interest** (also known as **minority interest** or **minority owners' interest**). The noncontrolling interest is subtracted in arriving at net income because the parent is reporting all of the subsidiary's revenue and expense.

Presentation Formats

A firm can present its income statement using a single-step or multi-step format. In a single-step statement, all revenues are grouped together and all expenses are grouped together. A multi-step format includes *gross profit*, revenues minus cost of goods sold.

Figure 1 is an example of a multi-step income statement format for the BHG Company.

©2012 Kaplan, Inc.

Figure 1: Multi-Step Income Statement

BHG Company Income Statement
For the year ended December 31, 20X7

Revenue	$579,312
Cost of goods sold	(362,520)
Gross profit	216,792
Selling, general, and administrative expense	(109,560)
Depreciation expense	(69,008)
Operating profit	38,224
Interest expense	(2,462)
Income before tax	35,762
Provision for income taxes	(14,305)
Income from continuing operations	21,457
Earnings (losses) from discontinued operations, net of tax	1,106
Net income	$22,563

Gross profit is the amount that remains after the direct costs of producing a product or service are subtracted from revenue. Subtracting operating expenses, such as selling, general, and administrative expenses, from gross profit results in another subtotal known as **operating profit** or operating income. For nonfinancial firms, operating profit is profit before financing costs, income taxes, and non-operating items are considered. Subtracting interest expense and income taxes from operating profit results in the firm's net income, sometimes referred to as "earnings" or the "bottom line."

 Professor's Note: Interest expense is usually considered an operating expense for financial firms.

LOS 25.b: Describe the general principles of revenue recognition and accrual accounting, specific revenue recognition applications (including accounting for long-term contracts, installment sales, barter transactions, gross and net reporting of revenue), and the implications of revenue recognition principles for financial analysis.

LOS 25.c: Calculate revenue given information that might influence the choice of revenue recognition method.

CFA® Program Curriculum, Volume 3, page 145

Under the accrual method of accounting, revenue is recognized when earned and expenses are recognized when incurred. The important point to remember is that accrual accounting does not necessarily coincide with the receipt or payment of cash.

Consequently, firms can manipulate net income by recognizing revenue earlier or later or by delaying or accelerating the recognition of expenses.

According to the International Accounting Standards Board (IASB), revenue is recognized from the sale of goods when:[1]

1. The risk and reward of ownership is transferred.

2. There is no continuing control or management over the goods sold.

3. Revenue can be reliably measured.

4. There is a probable flow of economic benefits.

5. The cost can be reliably measured.

For services rendered, revenue is recognized when:[2]

1. The amount of revenue can be reliably measured.

2. There is a probable flow of economic benefits.

3. The stage of completion can be measured.

4. The cost incurred and cost of completion can be reliably measured.

According to the Financial Accounting Standards Board (FASB), revenue is recognized in the income statement when (a) realized or realizable and (b) earned.[3] The Securities and Exchange Commission (SEC) provides additional guidance by listing four criteria to determine whether revenue should be recognized:[4]

1. There is evidence of an arrangement between the buyer and seller.

2. The product has been delivered or the service has been rendered.

3. The price is determined or determinable.

4. The seller is reasonably sure of collecting money.

---

1. IAS No. 18, *Revenue*, paragraph 14.
2. IAS No. 18, *Revenue*, paragraph 20.
3. FASB Accounting Standards Codification, section 605-10-25.
4. SEC Staff Accounting Bulletin 101.

©2012 Kaplan, Inc.

If a firm receives cash before revenue recognition is complete, the firm reports it as *unearned revenue*. Unearned revenue is reported on the balance sheet as a liability. The liability is reduced in the future as the revenue is earned. For example, a magazine publisher typically receives subscription payments in advance of delivery. When payments are received, both assets (cash) and liabilities (unearned revenue) increase. As the magazines are delivered, the publisher recognizes revenue on the income statement and the liability is reduced.

Specific Revenue Recognition Applications

Revenue is usually recognized at delivery using the revenue recognition criteria previously discussed. However, in some cases, revenue may be recognized before delivery occurs or even after delivery takes place.

Long-Term Contracts

The percentage-of-completion method and the completed-contract method are used for contracts that extend beyond one accounting period, often contracts related to construction projects.

In certain cases involving service contracts or licensing agreements, the firm may simply recognize revenue equally over the term of the contract or agreement.

When the outcome of a long-term contract can be reliably estimated, the **percentage-of-completion method** is used under both IFRS and U.S. GAAP. Accordingly, revenue, expense, and therefore profit, are recognized as the work is performed. The percentage of completion is measured by the total cost incurred to date divided by the total expected cost of the project.

Under International Financial Reporting Standards (IFRS), if the firm cannot reliably measure the outcome of the project, revenue is recognized to the extent of contract costs, costs are expensed when incurred, and profit is recognized only at completion. Under U.S. GAAP, the **completed-contract method** is used when the outcome of the project cannot be reliably estimated. Accordingly, revenue, expense, and profit are recognized only when the contract is complete.

If a loss is expected, the loss must be recognized immediately under IFRS and U.S. GAAP.

The effect of using these different revenue recognition methods for long-term contracts on the income statement is illustrated in the following examples.

Example: Revenue recognition for long-term contracts

Assume that AAA Construction Corp. has a contract to build a ship for $1,000 and a reliable estimate of the contract's total cost is $800. Project costs incurred by AAA are as follows:

AAA Project Costs

Year	20X5	20X6	20X7	Total
Cost incurred	$400	$300	$100	$800

Determine AAA's net income from this project for each year using the percentage-of-completion and completed contract methods in accordance with U.S. GAAP.

Answer:

Since one-half of the total contract cost [$400 / $800] was incurred during 20X5, the project was 50% complete at year-end. Under the *percentage-of-completion method,* 20X5 revenue is $500 [$1,000 × 50%]. Expenses (cost incurred) were $400; thus, net income for 20X5 was $100 [$500 revenue – $400 expense].

At the end of 20X6, the project is 87.5% complete [($400 + $300) / $800]. Revenue to date should total $875 [$1,000 × 87.5%]. Since AAA already recognized $500 of revenue in 20X5, 20X6 revenue is $375 [$875 – $500]. 20X6 expenses were $300 so 20X6 net income was $75 [$375 revenue – $300 expense].

At the end of 20X7, the project is 100% complete [($400 + $300 +$100) / $800]. Revenue to date should total $1,000 [$1,000 × 100%]. Since AAA already recognized $875 of revenue in 20X5 and 20X6, 20X7 revenue is $125 [$1,000 – $875]. 20X7 expenses were $100 so 20X7 net income was $25 [$125 revenue – $100 expense].

The table below summarizes the AAA's revenue, expense, and net income over the term of project under the percentage-of-completion method.

AAA Income Statements

	20X5	20X6	20X7	Total
Revenue	$500	$375	$125	$1,000
Expense	400	300	100	800
Net income	$100	$75	$25	$200

Under the *completed contract method,* revenue, expenses, and profit are not recognized until the contract is complete. Therefore, at the end of 20X7, AAA reports revenue of $1,000, expense of $800, and net income of $200.

©2012 Kaplan, Inc.

Example: Long-term contracts under IFRS

Using the data from the previous example, determine AAA's net income from this project each year in accordance with IFRS.

Answer:

If the outcome of the project can be reliably estimated, the results under the percentage-of-completion method would be identical to U.S. GAAP. If the outcome cannot be reliably estimated, revenues would be recognized only to the extent of costs incurred in 20X5 and 20X6. The remainder of the revenue, and all of the profit, is recognized in 20X7 as follows:

AAA Income Statements

	20X5	20X6	20X7	Total
Revenue	$400	$300	$300	$1,000
Expense	400	300	100	800
Net income	$0	$0	$200	$200

As compared to the completed contract method, the percentage-of-completion method is more aggressive since revenue is reported sooner. Also, the percentage-of-completion method is more subjective because it involves cost estimates. However, the percentage-of-completion method provides smoother earnings and results in better matching of revenues and expenses over time. Cash flows are the same under both methods.

Installment Sales

An **installment sale** occurs when a firm finances a sale and payments are expected to be received over an extended period. If collectibility is certain, revenue is recognized at the time of sale using the normal revenue recognition criteria. If collectibility cannot be reasonably estimated, the installment method is used. If collectibility is highly uncertain, the cost recovery method is used.

Under the **installment method**, profit is recognized as cash is collected. Profit is equal to the cash collected during the period multiplied by the total expected profit as a percentage of sales. The installment method is used in limited circumstances, usually involving the sale of real estate or other firm assets.

Under the **cost recovery method**, profit is recognized only when cash collected exceeds costs incurred.

The effects of using the installment and the cost recovery methods are illustrated in the following example.

Example: Revenue recognition for installment sales

Assume that BBB Property Corp. sells a piece of land for $1,000. The original cost of the land was $800. Collections received by BBB for the sale are as follows:

BBB Installment Collections

Year	20X5	20X6	20X7	Total
Collections	$400	$400	$200	$1,000

Determine BBB's profit under the installment and cost recovery methods.

Answer:

Total expected profit as a percentage of sales is 20% [($1,000 – $800) / $1,000]. Under the installment method, BBB will report profit in 20X5 and 20X6 of $80 [$400 × 20%] each year. In 20X7, BBB will report profit of $40 [$200 × 20%].

Under the cost recovery method, the collections received during 20X5 and 20X6 are applied to the recovery of costs. In 20X7, BBB will report $200 of profit.

Under IFRS, the discounted present value of the installment payments is recognized at the time of sale. The difference between the installment payments and the discounted present value is recognized as interest over time. If the outcome of the project cannot be reliably estimated, revenue recognition under IFRS is similar to the cost recovery method.

Barter Transactions

In a **barter transaction**, two parties exchange goods or services without cash payment. A **round-trip transaction** involves the sale of goods to one party with the simultaneous purchase of almost identical goods from the same party. The underlying issue with these transactions is whether revenue should be recognized. In the late 1990s, several internet companies increased their revenue significantly by "buying" equal values of advertising space on each others' websites.

According to U.S. GAAP, revenue from a barter transaction can be recognized at fair value only if the firm has historically received cash payments for such goods and services and can use this historical experience to determine fair value. Otherwise, the revenue is recorded at the carrying value of the asset surrendered.[5]

Under IFRS, revenue from barter transactions must be based on the fair value of revenue from similar nonbarter transactions with unrelated parties.[6]

---

5. FASB ASC paragraph 605-20-25-14 (Revenue Recognition-Services-Recognition-Advertising Barter Services).
6. IASB, SIC Interpretation 31, Revenue – Barter Transactions Involving Advertising Services, paragraph 5.

©2012 Kaplan, Inc.

Gross and Net Reporting of Revenue

Under **gross revenue reporting**, the selling firm reports sales revenue and cost of goods sold separately. Under **net revenue reporting**, only the difference in sales and cost is reported. While profit is the same, sales are higher using gross revenue reporting.

For example, consider a travel agent who arranges a first-class ticket for a customer flying to Singapore. The ticket price is $10,000, and the travel agent receives a $1,000 commission. Using gross reporting, the travel agent would report $10,000 of revenue, $9,000 of expense, and $1,000 of profit. Using net reporting, the travel agent would simply report $1,000 of revenue and no expense.

The following criteria must be met in order to use gross revenue reporting under U.S. GAAP.[7] The firm must:

- Be the primary obligor under the contract.
- Bear the inventory risk and credit risk.
- Be able to choose its supplier.
- Have reasonable latitude to establish the price.

Implications for Financial Analysis

As noted previously, firms can recognize revenue before delivery, at the time of delivery, or after delivery takes place, as appropriate. Different revenue recognition methods can be used within the firm. Firms disclose their revenue recognition policies in the financial statement footnotes.

Users of financial information must consider two points when analyzing a firm's revenue: (1) how conservative are the firm's revenue recognition policies (recognizing revenue sooner rather than later is more aggressive), and (2) the extent to which the firm's policies rely on judgment and estimates.

LOS 25.d: Describe the general principles of expense recognition, specific expense recognition applications, and the implications of expense recognition choices for financial analysis.

CFA® Program Curriculum, Volume 3, page 157

Expenses are subtracted from revenue to calculate net income. According to the IASB, expenses are decreases in economic benefits during the accounting period in the form of outflows or depletions of assets or incurrence of liabilities that result in decreases in equity other than those relating to distributions to equity participants.[8]

If the financial statements were prepared on a cash basis, neither revenue recognition nor expense recognition would be an issue. The firm would simply recognize cash received as revenue and cash payments as expense.

---

7. FASB ASC Section 605-45-45 [Revenue Recognition-Principal Agent Considerations-Other Presentation Matters].

8. IASB *Framework for the Preparation and Presentation of Financial Statements,* paragraph 70.

Under the accrual method of accounting, expense recognition is based on the **matching principle** whereby expenses to generate revenue are recognized in the same period as the revenue. Inventory provides a good example. Assume inventory is purchased during the fourth quarter of one year and sold during the first quarter of the following year. Using the matching principle, both the revenue and the expense (cost of goods sold) are recognized in the first quarter, when the inventory is sold, not the period in which the inventory was purchased.

Not all expenses can be directly tied to revenue generation. These costs are known as **period costs**. Period costs, such as administrative costs, are expensed in the period incurred.

Inventory Expense Recognition

If a firm can identify exactly which items were sold and which items remain in inventory, it can use the **specific identification** method. For example, an auto dealer records each vehicle sold or in inventory by its identification number.

Under the **first-in, first-out** (FIFO) method, the first item purchased is assumed to be the first item sold. The cost of inventory acquired first (beginning inventory and early purchases) is used to calculate the cost of goods sold for the period. The cost of the most recent purchases is used to calculate ending inventory. FIFO is appropriate for inventory that has a limited shelf life. For example, a food products company will sell its oldest inventory first to keep the inventory on hand fresh.

Under the **last-in, first-out** (LIFO) method, the last item purchased is assumed to be the first item sold. The cost of inventory most recently purchased is assigned to the cost of goods sold for the period. The costs of beginning inventory and earlier purchases are assigned to ending inventory. LIFO is appropriate for inventory that does not deteriorate with age. For example, a coal distributor will sell coal off the top of the pile.

In the United States, LIFO is popular because of its income tax benefits. In an inflationary environment, LIFO results in higher cost of goods sold. Higher cost of goods sold results in lower taxable income and, therefore, lower income taxes.

The **weighted average cost** method makes no assumption about the physical flow of the inventory. It is popular because of its ease of use. The cost per unit is calculated by dividing cost of available goods by total units available, and this average cost is used to determine both cost of goods sold and ending inventory. Average cost results in cost of goods sold and ending inventory values between those of LIFO and FIFO.

FIFO and average cost are permitted under both U.S. GAAP and IFRS. LIFO is allowed under U.S. GAAP but is prohibited under IFRS.

Figure 2 summarizes the effects of the inventory methods.

Figure 2: Inventory Method Comparison

Method	Assumption	Cost of Goods Sold Consists of…	Ending Inventory Consists of…
FIFO (U.S. and IFRS)	The items first purchased are the first to be sold.	first purchased	most recent purchases
LIFO (U.S. only)	The items last purchased are the first to be sold.	last purchased	earliest purchases
Weighted average cost (U.S. and IFRS)	Items sold are a mix of purchases.	average cost of all items	average cost of all items

Example: Inventory costing

Use the inventory data in the table below to calculate the cost of goods sold and ending inventory under each of the three methods.

Inventory Data

January 1 (beginning inventory)	2 units @ $2 per unit =	$4
January 7 purchase	3 units @ $3 per unit =	$9
January 19 purchase	5 units @ $5 per unit =	$25
Cost of goods available	10 units	$38
Units sold during January	7 units	

Answer:

FIFO cost of goods sold: Value the seven units sold using the unit cost of first units purchased. Start with the beginning inventory and the earliest units purchased and work down, as illustrated in the following table.

FIFO COGS Calculation		
From beginning inventory	2 units @ $2 per unit	$4
From first purchase	3 units @ $3 per unit	$9
From second purchase	2 units @ $5 per unit	$10
FIFO cost of goods sold	7 units	$23
Ending inventory	3 units @ $5 per unit	$15

LIFO cost of goods sold: Value the seven units sold at unit cost of last units purchased. Start with the most recently purchased units and work up, as illustrated in the following table.

LIFO COGS Calculation

From second purchase	5 units @ $5 per unit	$25
From first purchase	2 units @ $3 per unit	$6
LIFO cost of goods sold	7 units	$31
Ending inventory	2 units @ $2 + 1 unit @ $3	$7

Average cost of goods sold:
Value the seven units sold at the average unit cost of goods available.

Weighted Average COGS Calculation

Average unit cost	$38 / 10 units	$3.80 per unit
Weighted average cost of goods sold	7 units @ $3.80 per unit	$26.60
Ending inventory	3 units @ $3.80 per unit	$11.40

The following table summarizes the calculations of COGS and ending inventory for each method.

Summary:

Inventory system	COGS	Ending Inventory
FIFO	$23.00	$15.00
LIFO	$31.00	$7.00
Average Cost	$26.60	$11.40

Depreciation Expense Recognition

The cost of long-lived assets must also be matched with revenues. Long-lived assets are expected to provide economic benefits beyond one accounting period. The allocation of cost over an asset's life is known as depreciation (tangible assets), depletion (natural resources), or amortization (intangible assets). Most firms use the **straight-line depreciation** method for financial reporting purposes. The straight-line method recognizes an equal amount of depreciation expense each period. However, most assets generate more benefits in the early years of their economic life and fewer benefits in the later years. In this case, an *accelerated depreciation method* is more appropriate for matching the expenses to revenues.

©2012 Kaplan, Inc.

In the early years of an asset's life, the straight-line method will result in lower depreciation expense as compared to an accelerated method. Lower expense results in higher net income. In the later years of the asset's life, the effect is reversed, and straight-line depreciation results in higher expense and lower net income compared to accelerated methods.

Straight-line depreciation (SL) allocates an equal amount of depreciation each year over the asset's useful life as follows:

$$\text{SL depreciation expense} = \frac{\text{cost} - \text{residual value}}{\text{useful life}}$$

> **Example: Calculating straight-line depreciation expense**
>
> Littlefield Company recently purchased a machine at a cost of $12,000. The machine is expected to have a residual value of $2,000 at the end of its useful life in five years. Calculate depreciation expense using the straight-line method.
>
> **Answer:**
>
> The annual depreciation expense each year will be:
>
> $$\frac{\text{cost} - \text{residual value}}{\text{useful life}} = \frac{(\$12,000 - \$2,000)}{5} = \$2,000$$

Accelerated depreciation speeds up the recognition of depreciation expense in a systematic way to recognize more depreciation expense in the early years of the asset's life and less depreciation expense in the later years of its life. Total depreciation expense over the life of the asset will be the same as it would be if straight-line depreciation were used.

The **declining balance method** (DB) applies a constant rate of depreciation to an asset's (declining) book value each year.

 Professor's Note: The declining balance method is also known as the diminishing balance method.

The most common declining balance method is *double-declining balance* (DDB), which applies two times the straight-line rate to the declining balance. If an asset's life is ten years, the straight-line rate is 1/10 or 10%, and the DDB rate would be 2/10 or 20%.

$$\text{DDB depreciation} = \left(\frac{2}{\text{useful life}}\right)(\text{cost} - \text{accumulated depreciation})$$

DB does not explicitly use the asset's residual value in the calculations, but depreciation ends once the estimated residual value has been reached. If the asset is expected to have no residual value, the DB method will never fully depreciate it, so the DB method is typically changed to straight-line at some point in the asset's life.

Example: Calculating double-declining balance depreciation expense

Littlefield Company recently purchased a machine at a cost of $12,000. The machine is expected to have a residual value of $2,000 at the end of its useful life in five years. Calculate depreciation expense for all five years using the double-declining balance method.

Answer:

The depreciation expense using the double declining balance method is:

- Year 1: (2 / 5)($12,000) = $4,800
- Year 2: (2 / 5)($12,000 – $4,800) = $2,880
- Year 3: (2 / 5)($12,000 – $7,680) = $1,728

In years 1 through 3, the company has recognized cumulative depreciation expense of $9,408. Since the total depreciation expense is limited to $10,000 ($12,000 – $2,000 salvage value), the depreciation in year 4 is limited to $592, rather than the (2 / 5)($12,000 – $9,408) = $1,036.80 using the DDB formula.

Year 5: Depreciation expense is $0, since the asset is fully depreciated.

Note that the rate of depreciation is doubled (2 / 5) from straight-line, and the only thing that changes from year to year is the base amount (book value) used to calculate annual depreciation.

 Professor's Note: We've been discussing the "double" declining balance method, which uses a factor of two times the straight-line rate. You can compute declining balance depreciation based on any factor (e.g., 1.5, double, triple).

Amortization Expense Recognition

Amortization is the allocation of the cost of an intangible asset (such as a franchise agreement) over its useful life. Amortization expense should match the proportion of the asset's economic benefits used during the period. Most firms use the straight-line method to calculate annual amortization expense for financial reporting. Straight-line amortization is calculated exactly like straight-line depreciation.

Intangible assets with indefinite lives (e.g., goodwill) are not amortized. However, they must be tested for impairment at least annually. If the asset value is impaired, an expense equal to the impairment amount is recognized on the income statement.

Bad Debt Expense and Warranty Expense Recognition

If a firm sells goods or services on credit or provides a warranty to the customer, the matching principle requires the firm to estimate bad debt expense and/or warranty expense. By doing so, the firm is recognizing the expense in the period of the sale, rather than a later period.

©2012 Kaplan, Inc.

Implications for Financial Analysis

Like revenue recognition, expense recognition requires a number of estimates. Since estimates are involved, it is possible for firms to delay or accelerate the recognition of expenses. Delayed expense recognition increases current net income and is therefore more aggressive.

Analysts must consider the underlying reasons for a change in an expense estimate. If a firm's bad debt expense has recently decreased, did the firm lower its expense estimate because its collection experience improved, or was the expense decreased to manipulate net income?

Analysts should also compare a firm's estimates to those of other firms within the firm's industry. If a firm's warranty expense is significantly less than that of a peer firm, is the lower warranty expense a result of higher quality products, or is the firm's expense recognition more aggressive than that of the peer firm?

Firms disclose their accounting policies and significant estimates in the financial statement footnotes and in the management discussion and analysis (MD&A) section of the annual report.

LOS 25.e: Describe the financial reporting treatment and analysis of non-recurring items (including discontinued operations, extraordinary items, unusual or infrequent items) and changes in accounting standards.

CFA® Program Curriculum, Volume 3, page 167

Non-Recurring Items

Discontinued operations. A *discontinued operation* is one that management has decided to dispose of, but either has not yet done so, or has disposed of in the current year after the operation had generated income or losses. To be accounted for as a discontinued operation, the business—in terms of assets, operations, and investing and financing activities—must be physically and operationally distinct from the rest of the firm.

The date when the company develops a formal plan for disposing of an operation is referred to as the *measurement date*, and the time between the measurement period and the actual disposal date is referred to as the *phaseout period*. Any income or loss from discontinued operations is reported separately in the income statement, net of tax, after income from continuing operations. Any past income statements presented must be restated, separating the income or loss from the discontinued operations. On the measurement date, the company will accrue any estimated loss during the phaseout period and any estimated loss on the sale of the business. Any expected gain on the disposal cannot be reported until after the sale is completed.

Analytical implications: The analysis is straightforward. Discontinued operations do not affect net income from continuing operations. Discontinued operations should be excluded by the analyst when forecasting future earnings. The actual event of discontinuing a business segment or selling assets may provide information about the future cash flows of the firm, however.

Unusual or infrequent items. The definition of these items is obvious—these events are either unusual in nature *or* infrequent in occurrence, but *not* both. Examples of unusual or infrequent items include:

- Gains or losses from the sale of assets or part of a business.
- Impairments, write-offs, write-downs, and restructuring costs.

Unusual or infrequent items are included in income from continuing operations and are reported before tax.

Analytical implications: Even though unusual or infrequent items affect net income from continuing operations, an analyst may want to review them to determine whether they truly should be included when forecasting future firm earnings.

Extraordinary items. Under U.S. GAAP, an *extraordinary item* is a material transaction or event that is *both* unusual *and* infrequent in occurrence. Examples of these include:

- Losses from an expropriation of assets.
- Gains or losses from early retirement of debt (when it is judged to be both unusual and infrequent).
- Uninsured losses from natural disasters that are both unusual and infrequent.

Extraordinary items are reported separately in the income statement, net of tax, after income from continuing operations.

IFRS does not allow extraordinary items to be separated from operating results in the income statement.

Analytical implications: Judgment is required in determining whether a transaction or event is extraordinary. Although extraordinary items do not affect income from continuing operations, an analyst may want to review them to determine whether some portion should be included when forecasting future income. Some companies appear to be accident-prone and have "extraordinary" losses every year or every few years.

Changes in Accounting Standards

Accounting changes include changes in accounting principles, changes in accounting estimates, and prior-period adjustments.

A **change in accounting principle** refers to a change from one GAAP or IFRS method to another (e.g., a change in inventory accounting from LIFO to FIFO). A change in accounting principle requires **retrospective application**. Accordingly, all of the prior-period financial statements currently presented are restated to reflect the change. Retrospective application enhances the comparability of the financial statements over time.

©2012 Kaplan, Inc.

Professor's Note: Under U.S. GAAP, a firm that changes to LIFO from another inventory cost method does not apply the change retrospectively, but instead uses the carrying value of inventory as the first LIFO layer. This exception to retrospective application is described in the topic review of Inventories.

Generally, a **change in accounting estimate** is the result of a change in management's judgment, usually due to new information. For example, management may change the estimated useful life of an asset because new information indicates the asset has a longer or shorter life than originally expected. A change in estimate is applied prospectively and does not require the restatement of prior financial statements.

Analytical implications: Accounting estimate changes typically do not affect cash flow. An analyst should review changes in accounting estimates to determine the impact on future operating results.

A change from an incorrect accounting method to one that is acceptable under GAAP or IFRS or the correction of an accounting error made in previous financial statements is reported as a **prior-period adjustment.** Prior-period adjustments are made by restating results for all prior periods presented in the current financial statements. Disclosure of the nature of the adjustment and its effect on net income is also required.

Analytical implications: Prior-period adjustments usually involve errors or new accounting standards and do not typically affect cash flow. Analysts should review adjustments carefully because errors may indicate weaknesses in the firm's internal controls.

LOS 25.f: Distinguish between the operating and non-operating components of the income statement.

CFA® Program Curriculum, Volume 3, page 172

Operating and nonoperating transactions are usually reported separately in the income statement. For a nonfinancial firm, nonoperating transactions may result from investment income and financing expenses. For example, a nonfinancial firm may receive dividends and interest from investments in other firms. The investment income and any gains and losses from the sale of these securities are not a part of the firm's normal business operations. Interest expense is based on the firm's capital structure, which is also independent of the firm's operations. Conversely, for a financial firm, investment income and financing expenses are usually considered operating activities.

LOS 25.g: Describe how earnings per share is calculated and calculate and interpret a company's earnings per share (both basic and diluted earnings per share) for both simple and complex capital structures.

LOS 25.h: Distinguish between dilutive and antidilutive securities, and describe the implications of each for the earnings per share calculation.

CFA® Program Curriculum, Volume 3, page 173

Earnings per share (EPS) is one of the most commonly used corporate profitability performance measures for publicly-traded firms (nonpublic companies are not required to report EPS data). EPS is reported only for shares of common stock (also known as ordinary stock).

A company may have either a simple or complex capital structure:

- A **simple capital structure** is one that contains *no* potentially dilutive securities. A simple capital structure contains only common stock, nonconvertible debt, and nonconvertible preferred stock.
- A **complex capital structure** contains *potentially dilutive securities* such as options, warrants, or convertible securities.

All firms with complex capital structures must report both *basic* and *diluted* EPS. Firms with simple capital structures report only basic EPS.

BASIC EPS

The basic EPS calculation does not consider the effects of any dilutive securities in the computation of EPS.

$$\text{basic EPS} = \frac{\text{net income} - \text{preferred dividends}}{\text{weighted average number of common shares outstanding}}$$

The current year's preferred dividends are subtracted from net income because EPS refers to the per-share earnings *available to common shareholders*. Net income minus preferred dividends is the income available to common stockholders. Common stock dividends are *not* subtracted from net income because they are a part of the net income available to common shareholders.

The **weighted average number of common shares** is the number of shares outstanding during the year, weighted by the portion of the year they were outstanding.

©2012 Kaplan, Inc.

Example: Weighted average shares and basic EPS

Johnson Company has net income of $10,000 and paid $1,000 cash dividends to its preferred shareholders and $1,750 cash dividends to its common shareholders. At the beginning of the year, there were 10,000 shares of common stock outstanding. 2,000 new shares were issued on July 1. Assuming a simple capital structure, what is Johnson's basic EPS?

Answer:

Calculate Johnson's weighted average number of shares.

Shares outstanding all year = 10,000(12) = 120,000

Shares outstanding 1/2 year = 2,000(6) = 12,000

Weighted average shares = 132,000 / 12 = 11,000 shares

$$\text{Basic EPS} = \frac{\text{net income} - \text{pref. div.}}{\text{wt. avg. shares of common}} = \frac{\$10,000 - \$1,000}{11,000} = \$0.82$$

 Professor's Note: Remember, the payment of a cash dividend on common shares is not considered in the calculation of EPS.

Effect of Stock Dividends and Stock Splits

A **stock dividend** is the distribution of additional shares to each shareholder in an amount proportional to their current number of shares. If a 10% stock dividend is paid, the holder of 100 shares of stock would receive 10 additional shares.

A **stock split** refers to the division of each "old" share into a specific number of "new" (post-split) shares. The holder of 100 shares will have 200 shares after a 2-for-1 split or 150 shares after a 3-for-2 split.

The important thing to remember is that each shareholder's proportional ownership in the company is unchanged by either of these events. Each shareholder has more shares but the same percentage of the total shares outstanding.

 Professor's Note: For our purposes here, a stock dividend and a stock split are two ways of doing the same thing. For example, a 50% stock dividend and a 3-for-2 stock split both result in three "new" shares for every two "old" shares. Stock dividends and stock splits are explained further in the Study Session on corporate finance.

The effect of a stock dividend or a stock split on the weighted average number of common shares is illustrated in the following example.

Example: Effect of stock dividends

During the past year, R & J, Inc. had net income of $100,000, paid dividends of $50,000 to its preferred stockholders, and paid $30,000 in dividends to its common shareholders. R & J's common stock account showed the following:

January 1	Shares issued and outstanding at the beginning of the year	10,000
April 1	Shares issued	4,000
July 1	10% stock dividend	
September 1	Shares repurchased for the treasury	3,000

Compute the weighted average number of common shares outstanding during the year, and compute EPS.

Answer:

Step 1: Adjust the number of pre-stock-dividend shares to post-stock-dividend units (to reflect the 10% stock dividend) by multiplying all share numbers prior to the stock dividend by 1.1. Shares issued or retired after the stock dividend are not affected.

January 1	Initial shares adjusted for the 10% dividend	11,000
April 1	Shares issued adjusted for the 10% dividend	4,400
September 1	Shares of treasury stock repurchased (no adjustment)	−3,000

Step 2: Compute the weighted average number of post-stock dividend shares:

Initial shares	11,000 × 12 months outstanding	132,000
Issued shares	4,400 × 9 months outstanding	39,600
Retired treasury shares	−3,000 × 4 months retired	−12,000
Total share-month		159,600
Average shares	159,600 / 12	13,300

Step 3: Compute basic EPS:

$$\text{basic EPS} = \frac{\text{net income} - \text{pref. div.}}{\text{wt. avg. shares of common}} = \frac{\$100,000 - \$50,000}{13,300} = \$3.76$$

©2012 Kaplan, Inc.

Study Session 8

Things to know about the weighted average shares outstanding calculation:

- The weighting system is days outstanding divided by the number of days in a year, but on the exam, the monthly approximation method will probably be used.
- Shares issued enter into the computation from the date of issuance.
- Reacquired shares are excluded from the computation from the date of reacquisition.
- Shares sold or issued in a purchase of assets are included from the date of issuance.
- A stock split or stock dividend is applied to all shares outstanding prior to the split or dividend and to the beginning-of-period weighted average shares. A stock split or stock dividend adjustment is not applied to any shares issued or repurchased after the split or dividend date.

DILUTED EPS

Before calculating diluted EPS, it is necessary to understand the following terms:

- **Dilutive securities** are stock options, warrants, convertible debt, or convertible preferred stock that would *decrease EPS* if exercised or converted to common stock.
- **Antidilutive securities** are stock options, warrants, convertible debt, or convertible preferred stock that would *increase EPS* if exercised or converted to common stock.

The numerator of the basic EPS equation contains income available to common shareholders (net income less preferred dividends). In the case of diluted EPS, if there are dilutive securities, then the numerator must be adjusted as follows:

- If convertible preferred stock is dilutive (meaning EPS will fall if it is converted to common stock), the convertible preferred dividends must be added to earnings available to common shareholders.
- If convertible bonds are dilutive, then the bonds' after-tax interest expense is not considered an interest expense for diluted EPS. Hence, interest expense multiplied by (1 – the tax rate) must be added back to the numerator.

 Professor's Note: Interest paid on bonds is typically tax deductible for the firm. If convertible bonds are converted to stock, the firm saves the interest cost but loses the tax deduction. Thus, only the after-tax interest savings are added back to income available to common shareholders.

The basic EPS denominator is the weighted average number of shares. When the firm has dilutive securities outstanding, the denominator is the basic EPS denominator adjusted for the equivalent number of common shares that would be created by the conversion of all dilutive securities outstanding (convertible bonds, convertible preferred shares, warrants, and options), with each one considered separately to determine if it is dilutive.

If a dilutive security was issued during the year, the increase in the weighted average number of shares for diluted EPS is based on only the portion of the year the dilutive security was outstanding.

Dilutive stock options or warrants increase the number of common shares outstanding in the denominator for diluted EPS. There is no adjustment to the numerator.

Stock options and warrants are dilutive only when their exercise prices are less than the average market price of the stock over the year. If the options or warrants are dilutive, use the **treasury stock method** to calculate the number of shares used in the denominator.

- The treasury stock method assumes that the funds received by the company from the exercise of the options would be used to hypothetically purchase shares of the company's common stock in the market at the average market price.
- The net increase in the number of shares outstanding (the adjustment to the denominator) is the number of shares created by exercising the options less the number of shares hypothetically repurchased with the proceeds of exercise.

Example: Treasury stock method

Baxter Company has 5,000 shares outstanding all year. Baxter had 2,000 outstanding warrants all year, convertible into one share each at $20 per share. The year-end price of Baxter stock was $40, and the average stock price was $30. What effect will these warrants have on the weighted average number of shares?

Answer:

If the warrants are exercised, the company will receive 2,000 × $20 = $40,000 and issue 2,000 new shares. The treasury stock method assumes the company uses these funds to repurchase shares at the average market price of $30. The company would repurchase $40,000 / $30 = 1,333 shares. Net shares issued would be 2,000 − 1,333 = 667 shares.

The **diluted EPS equation** is:

$$\text{diluted EPS} = \frac{\text{adjusted income available for common shares}}{\text{weighted-average common and potential common shares outstanding}}$$

where *adjusted income available for common shares* is:

> net income − preferred dividends
> + dividends on convertible preferred stock
> + after-tax interest on convertible debt

Therefore, diluted EPS is:

$$\text{diluted EPS} = \frac{\left[\begin{array}{c}\text{net income} - \text{preferred} \\ \text{dividends}\end{array}\right] + \left[\begin{array}{c}\text{convertible} \\ \text{preferred} \\ \text{dividends}\end{array}\right] + \left[\begin{array}{c}\text{convertible} \\ \text{debt} \\ \text{interest}\end{array}\right](1-t)}{\left(\begin{array}{c}\text{weighted} \\ \text{average} \\ \text{shares}\end{array}\right) + \left(\begin{array}{c}\text{shares from} \\ \text{conversion of} \\ \text{conv. pfd. shares}\end{array}\right) + \left(\begin{array}{c}\text{shares from} \\ \text{conversion of} \\ \text{conv. debt}\end{array}\right) + \left(\begin{array}{c}\text{shares} \\ \text{issuable from} \\ \text{stock options}\end{array}\right)}$$

©2012 Kaplan, Inc.

Remember, each potentially dilutive security must be examined separately to determine if it is actually dilutive (i.e., would reduce EPS if converted to common stock). The effect of conversion to common is included in the calculation of diluted EPS for a given security only if it is, in fact, dilutive.

Example 1: EPS with convertible debt

During 20X6, ZZZ Corp. reported net income of $115,600 and had 200,000 shares of common stock outstanding for the entire year. ZZZ also had 1,000 shares of 10%, $100 par, preferred stock outstanding during 20X6. During 20X5, ZZZ issued 600, $1,000 par, 7% bonds for $600,000 (issued at par). Each of these bonds is convertible to 100 shares of common stock. The tax rate is 40%. Compute the 20X6 basic and diluted EPS.

Answer:

Step 1: Compute 20X6 basic EPS:

$$\text{basic EPS} = \frac{\$115,600 - \$10,000}{200,000} = \$0.53$$

Step 2: Calculate diluted EPS:

- Compute the increase in common stock outstanding if the convertible debt is converted to common stock at the beginning of 20X6:

    shares issuable for debt conversion = (600)(100) = 60,000 shares

- If the convertible debt is considered converted to common stock at the beginning of 20X6, then there would be no interest expense related to the convertible debt. Therefore, it is necessary to increase ZZZ's after-tax net income for the after-tax effect of the decrease in interest expense:

    increase in income = [(600)($1,000)(0.07)] (1 − 0.40) = $25,200

- Compute diluted EPS as if the convertible debt were common stock:

    $$\text{diluted EPS} = \frac{\text{net. inc.} - \text{pref. div.} + \text{convert. int. } (1-t)}{\text{wt. avg. shares} + \text{convertible debt shares}}$$

    $$\text{diluted EPS} = \frac{\$115,600 - \$10,000 + \$25,200}{200,000 + 60,000} = \$0.50$$

- Check to make sure that *diluted EPS is less than basic EPS* [$0.50 < $0.53]. If diluted EPS is more than the basic EPS, the convertible bonds are *antidilutive* and should not be treated as common stock in computing diluted EPS.

A quick way to determine whether the convertible debt is dilutive is to calculate its per share impact by:

$$\frac{\text{convertible debt interest } (1-t)}{\text{convertible debt shares}}$$

If this per share amount is greater than basic EPS, the convertible debt is antidilutive, and the effects of conversion should not be included when calculating diluted EPS.

If this per share amount is less than basic EPS, the convertible debt is dilutive, and the effects of conversion should be included in the calculation of diluted EPS.

For ZZZ:

$$\frac{\$25,200}{60,000} = \$0.42$$

The company's basic EPS is $0.53, so the convertible debt is dilutive, and the effects of conversion should be included in the calculation of diluted EPS.

Example 2: EPS with convertible preferred stock

During 20X6, ZZZ reported net income of $115,600 and had 200,000 shares of common stock and 1,000 shares of preferred stock outstanding for the entire year. ZZZ's 10%, $100 par value preferred shares are each convertible into 40 shares of common stock. The tax rate is 40%. Compute basic and diluted EPS.

Answer:

Step 1: Calculate 20X6 basic EPS:

$$\text{basic EPS} = \frac{\$115,600 - \$10,000}{200,000} = \$0.53$$

Step 2: Calculate diluted EPS:

- Compute the increase in common stock outstanding if the preferred stock is converted to common stock at the beginning of 20X6: (1,000)(40) = 40,000 shares.
- If the convertible preferred shares were converted to common stock, there would be no preferred dividends paid. Therefore, you should add back the convertible preferred dividends that had previously been subtracted from net income in the numerator.

©2012 Kaplan, Inc.

- Compute diluted EPS as if the convertible preferred stock were converted into common stock:

$$\text{diluted EPS} = \frac{\text{net. inc.} - \text{pref. div.} + \text{convert. pref. dividends}}{\text{wt. avg. shares} + \text{convert. pref. common shares}}$$

$$\text{diluted EPS} = \frac{\$115{,}600 - \$10{,}000 + \$10{,}000}{200{,}000 + 40{,}000} = \$0.48$$

- Check to see if diluted EPS is less than basic EPS ($0.48 < $0.53). If the answer is yes, the preferred stock is dilutive and must be included in diluted EPS as computed above. If the answer is no, the preferred stock is antidilutive and conversion effects are not included in diluted EPS.

A quick way to check whether convertible preferred stock is dilutive is to divide the preferred dividend by the number of shares that will be created if the preferred stock is converted. For ZZZ: $\dfrac{\$100 \times 0.10}{40} = \$0.25$. Since this is less than basic EPS, the convertible preferred is dilutive.

Example 3: EPS with stock options

During 20X6, ZZZ reported net income of $115,600 and had 200,000 shares of common stock outstanding for the entire year. ZZZ also had 1,000 shares of 10%, $100 par, preferred stock outstanding during 20X6. ZZZ has 10,000 stock options (or warrants) outstanding the entire year. Each option allows its holder to purchase one share of common stock at $15 per share. The average market price of ZZZ's common stock during 20X6 is $20 per share. Compute the diluted EPS.

Answer:

Number of common shares created if the options are exercised:	10,000 shares
Cash inflow if the options are exercised ($15/share)(10,000):	$150,000
Number of shares that can be purchased with these funds is: $150,000 / $20	7,500 shares
Net increase in common shares outstanding from the exercise of the stock options (10,000 – 7,500)	2,500 shares

$$\text{diluted EPS} = \frac{\$115,600 - \$10,000}{200,000 + 2,500} = \$0.52$$

A quick way to calculate the net increase in common shares from the potential exercise of stock options or warrants when the exercise price is less than the average market price is:

$$\left[\frac{AMP - EP}{AMP}\right] \times N$$

where:
AMP = average market price over the year
EP   = exercise price of the options or warrants
N   = number of common shares that the options and warrants can be converted into

For ZZZ: $\dfrac{\$20 - \$15}{\$20} \times 10,000 \text{ shares} = 2,500 \text{ shares}$

Example 4: EPS with convertible bonds, convertible preferred, and options

During 20X6, ZZZ reported net income of $115,600 and had 200,000 shares of common stock outstanding for the entire year. ZZZ had 1,000 shares of 10%, $100 par convertible preferred stock, convertible into 40 shares each, outstanding for the entire year. ZZZ also had 600, 7%, $1,000 par value convertible bonds, convertible into 100 shares each, outstanding for the entire year. Finally, ZZZ had 10,000 stock options outstanding during the year. Each option is convertible into one share of stock at $15 per share. The average market price of the stock for the year was $20. What are ZZZ's basic and diluted EPS? (Assume a 40% tax rate.)

©2012 Kaplan, Inc.

Answer:

Step 1: From Examples 1, 2, and 3, we know that the convertible preferred stock, convertible bonds, and stock options are all dilutive. Recall that basic EPS was calculated as:

$$\text{basic EPS} = \frac{\$115{,}600 - \$10{,}000}{200{,}000} = \$0.53$$

Step 2: Review the number of shares created by converting the convertible securities and options (the denominator):

Converting the convertible preferred shares	40,000 shares
Converting the convertible bonds	60,000 shares
Exercising the options	2,500 shares

Step 3: Review the adjustments to net income (the numerator):

Converting the convertible preferred shares	$10,000
Converting the convertible bonds	$25,200
Exercising the options	$0

Step 4: Compute ZZZ's diluted EPS:

$$\text{diluted EPS} = \frac{115{,}600 - 10{,}000 + 10{,}000 + 25{,}200}{200{,}000 + 40{,}000 + 60{,}000 + 2{,}500} = \$0.47$$

LOS 25.i: Convert income statements to common-size income statements.

CFA® Program Curriculum, Volume 3, page 182

A vertical **common-size income statement** expresses each category of the income statement as a percentage of revenue. The common-size format standardizes the income statement by eliminating the effects of size. This allows for comparison of income statement items over time (time-series analysis) and across firms (cross-sectional analysis). For example, the following are year-end income statements of industry competitors North Company and South Company:

	North Co.	South Co.
Revenue	$75,000,000	$3,500,000
Cost of goods sold	52,500,000	700,000
Gross profit	$22,500,000	$2,800,000
Administrative expense	11,250,000	525,000
Research expense	3,750,000	700,000
Operating profit	$7,500,000	$1,575,000

Notice that North is significantly larger and more profitable than South when measured in absolute dollars. North's gross profit is $22,500,000, as compared to South's gross profit of $2,800,000. Similarly, North's operating profit of $7,500,000 is significantly greater than South's operating profit of $1,575,000.

Once we convert the income statements to common-size format, we can see that South is the more profitable firm on a relative basis. South's gross profit of 80% and operating profit of 45% are significantly greater than North's gross profit of 30% and operating profit of 10%.

	North Co.	South Co.
Revenue	100%	100%
Cost of goods sold	70%	20%
Gross profit	30%	80%
Administrative expense	15%	15%
Research expense	5%	20%
Operating profit	10%	45%

Common-size analysis can also be used to examine a firm's strategy. South's higher gross profit margin may be the result of technologically superior products. Notice that South spends more on research than North on a relative basis. This may allow South to charge a higher price for its products.

In most cases, expressing expenses as a percentage of revenue is appropriate. One exception is income tax expense. Tax expense is more meaningful when expressed as a percentage of pretax income. The result is known as the **effective tax rate**.

LOS 25.j: Evaluate a company's financial performance using common-size income statements and financial ratios based on the income statement.

CFA® Program Curriculum, Volume 3, page 184

Margin ratios can be used to measure a firm's profitability quickly. **Gross profit margin** is the ratio of gross profit (revenue minus cost of goods sold) to revenue (sales).

$$\text{gross profit margin} = \frac{\text{gross profit}}{\text{revenue}}$$

Gross profit margin can be increased by raising prices or reducing production costs. A firm might be able to increase prices if its products can be differentiated from other firms' products as a result of factors such as brand names, quality, technology, or patent protection. This was illustrated in the previous example whereby South's gross profit margin was higher than North's.

©2012 Kaplan, Inc.

Another popular margin ratio is **net profit margin**. Net profit margin is the ratio of net income to revenue.

$$\text{net profit margin} = \frac{\text{net income}}{\text{revenue}}$$

Net profit margin measures the profit generated after considering all expenses. Like gross profit margin, net profit margin should be compared over time and with the firm's industry peers.

Any subtotal found in the income statement can be expressed as a percentage of revenue. For example, operating profit divided by revenue is known as **operating profit margin**. Pretax accounting profit divided by revenue is known as **pretax margin**.

LOS 25.k: Describe, calculate, and interpret comprehensive income.

LOS 25.l: Describe other comprehensive income, and identify the major types of items included in it.

CFA® Program Curriculum, Volume 3, page 186

At the end of each accounting period, the net income of the firm is added to stockholders' equity through an account known as **retained earnings**. Therefore, any transaction that affects the income statement (net income) will also affect stockholders' equity.

Recall that net income is equal to revenue minus expenses. **Comprehensive income** is a more inclusive measure that includes all changes in equity except for owner contributions and distributions. That is, comprehensive income is the sum of net income and **other comprehensive income**. Other comprehensive income includes transactions that are *not* included in net income, such as:

1. Foreign currency translation gains and losses.

2. Adjustments for minimum pension liability.

3. Unrealized gains and losses from cash flow hedging derivatives.

4. Unrealized gains and losses from available-for-sale securities.

Available-for-sale securities are investment securities that are not expected to be held to maturity or sold in the near term. Available-for-sale securities are reported on the balance sheet at fair value. The unrealized gains and losses (the changes in fair value before the securities are sold) are not reported in the income statement but are reported directly in stockholders' equity as a component of other comprehensive income.

Under IFRS, firms can choose to report certain long-lived assets at fair value rather than historical cost. In this case, the changes in fair value are also included in other comprehensive income.

Example: Calculating comprehensive income

Calculate comprehensive income for Triple C Corporation using the selected financial statement data found in the following table.

Triple C Corporation – Selected Financial Statement Data

Net income	$1,000
Dividends received from available-for-sale securities	60
Unrealized loss from foreign currency translation	(15)
Dividends paid	(110)
Reacquire common stock	(400)
Unrealized gain from cash flow hedge	30
Unrealized loss from available-for-sale securities	(10)
Realized gain on sale of land	65

Answer:

Net income	$1,000
Unrealized loss from foreign currency translation	(15)
Unrealized gain from cash flow hedge	30
Unrealized loss from available-for-sale securities	(10)
Comprehensive income	$1,005

The dividends received for available-for-sale securities and the realized gain on the sale of land are already included in net income. Dividends paid and the reacquisition of common stock are transactions with shareholders, so they are not included in comprehensive income.

Because firms have some flexibility of including or excluding transactions from net income, analysts must examine comprehensive income when comparing financial performance with other firms.

©2012 Kaplan, Inc.

KEY CONCEPTS

LOS 25.a

The income statement shows an entity's revenues, expenses, gains and losses during a reporting period.

A multi-step income statement provides a subtotal for gross profit and a single step income statement does not. Expenses on the income statement can be grouped by the nature of the expense items or by their function, such as with expenses grouped into cost of goods sold.

LOS 25.b

Revenue is recognized when earned and expenses are recognized when incurred.

Methods for accounting for long-term contracts include:
- Percentage-of-completion—recognizes revenue in proportion to costs incurred.
- Completed-contract—recognizes revenue only when the contract is complete.

Revenue recognition methods for installment sales are:
- Normal revenue recognition at time of sale if collectability is reasonably assured.
- Installment sales method if collectability cannot be reasonably estimated.
- Cost recovery method if collectability is highly uncertain.

Revenue from barter transactions can only be recognized if its fair value can be estimated from historical data on similar non-barter transactions.

Gross revenue reporting shows sales and cost of goods sold, while net revenue reporting shows only the difference between sales and cost of goods sold and should be used when the firm is acting essentially as a selling agent and does not stock inventory, take credit risk, or have control over supplier and price.

LOS 25.c

A firm using a revenue recognition method that is aggressive will inflate current period earnings at a minimum and perhaps inflate overall earnings. Because of the estimates involved, the percentage-of-completion method is more aggressive than the completed-contract method. Also, the installment method is more aggressive than the cost recovery method.

LOS 25.d

The matching principle requires that firms match revenues recognized in a period with the expenses required to generate them. One application of the matching principle is seen in accounting for inventory, with cost of goods sold as the cost of units sold from inventory that are included in current-period revenue. Other costs, such as straight-line depreciation of fixed assets or administrative overhead, are period costs and are taken without regard to revenues generated during the period.

Depreciation methods:

- Straight-line: Equal amount of depreciation expense in each year of the asset's useful life.
- Declining balance: Apply a constant rate of depreciation to the declining book value until book value equals residual value.

Inventory valuation methods:

- FIFO: Inventory reflects cost of most recent purchases, COGS reflects cost of oldest purchases.
- LIFO: COGS reflects cost of most recent purchases, inventory reflects cost of oldest purchases.
- Average cost: Unit cost equals cost of goods available for sale divided by total units available and is used for both COGS and inventory.
- Specific identification: Each item in inventory is identified and its historical cost is used for calculating COGS when the item is sold.

Intangible assets with limited lives should be amortized using a method that reflects the flow over time of their economic benefits. Intangible assets with indefinite lives (e.g., goodwill) are not amortized.

Users of financial data should analyze the reasons for any changes in estimates of expenses and compare these estimates with those of peer companies.

LOS 25.e

Results of discontinued operations are reported below income from continuing operations, net of tax, from the date the decision to dispose of the operations is made. These results are segregated because they likely are non-recurring and do not affect future net income.

Unusual or infrequent items are reported before tax and above income from continuing operations. An analyst should determine how "unusual" or "infrequent" these items really are for the company when estimating future earnings or firm value.

Extraordinary items (both unusual and infrequent) are reported below income from continuing operations, net of tax under U.S. GAAP, but this treatment is not allowed under IFRS. Extraordinary items are not expected to continue in future periods.

Changes in accounting standards, changes in accounting methods applied, and corrections of accounting errors require retrospective restatement of all prior-period financial statements included in the current statement. A change in an accounting estimate, however, is applied prospectively (to subsequent periods) with no restatement of prior-period results.

LOS 25.f

Operating income is generated from the firm's normal business operations. For a nonfinancial firm, income that results from investing or financing transactions is classified as non-operating income, while it is operating income for a financial firm since its business operations include investing in and financing securities.

©2012 Kaplan, Inc.

LOS 25.g

$$\text{basic EPS} = \frac{\text{net income} - \text{preferred dividends}}{\text{weighted average number of common shares outstanding}}$$

When a company has potentially dilutive securities, it must report diluted EPS.

For any convertible preferred stock, convertible debt, warrants, or stock options that are dilutive, the calculation of diluted EPS is:

$$\text{diluted EPS} = \frac{\left[\begin{array}{c}\text{net income} - \text{preferred} \\ \text{dividends}\end{array}\right] + \left[\begin{array}{c}\text{convertible} \\ \text{preferred} \\ \text{dividends}\end{array}\right] + \left[\begin{array}{c}\text{convertible} \\ \text{debt} \\ \text{interest}\end{array}\right](1-t)}{\left(\begin{array}{c}\text{weighted} \\ \text{average} \\ \text{shares}\end{array}\right) + \left(\begin{array}{c}\text{shares from} \\ \text{conversion of} \\ \text{conv. pfd. shares}\end{array}\right) + \left(\begin{array}{c}\text{shares from} \\ \text{conversion of} \\ \text{conv. debt}\end{array}\right) + \left(\begin{array}{c}\text{shares} \\ \text{issuable from} \\ \text{stock options}\end{array}\right)}$$

LOS 25.h

A dilutive security is one that, if converted to its common stock equivalent, would decrease EPS. An antidilutive security is one that would not reduce EPS if converted to its common stock equivalent.

LOS 25.i

A vertical common-size income statement expresses each item as a percentage of revenue. The common-size format standardizes the income statement by eliminating the effects of size. Common-size income statements are useful for trend analysis and for comparisons with peer firms.

LOS 25.j

Common-size income statements are useful in examining a firm's business strategies.

Two popular profitability ratios are gross profit margin (gross profit / revenue) and net profit margin (net income / revenue). A firm can often achieve higher profit margins by differentiating its products from the competition.

LOS 25.k

Comprehensive income is the sum of net income and other comprehensive income. It measures all changes to equity other than those from transactions with shareholders.

LOS 25.l

Transactions with shareholders, such as dividends paid and shares issued or repurchased, are not reported on the income statement.

Other comprehensive income includes other transactions that affect equity but do not affect net income, including:
- Gains and losses from foreign currency translation.
- Pension obligation adjustments.
- Unrealized gains and losses from cash flow hedging derivatives.
- Unrealized gains and losses on available-for-sale securities.

CONCEPT CHECKERS

1. For a nonfinancial firm, are depreciation expense and interest expense included or excluded from operating expenses in the income statement?

	Depreciation expense	Interest expense
A.	Included	Included
B.	Included	Excluded
C.	Excluded	Included

2. Are income taxes and cost of goods sold examples of expenses classified by nature or classified by function in the income statement?

	Income taxes	Cost of goods sold
A.	Nature	Function
B.	Function	Nature
C.	Function	Function

3. Which of the following is *least likely* a condition necessary for revenue recognition?
   A. Cash has been collected.
   B. The goods have been delivered.
   C. The price has been determined.

4. AAA has a contract to build a building for $100,000 with an estimated time to completion of three years. A reliable cost estimate for the project is $60,000. In the first year of the project, AAA incurred costs totaling $24,000. How much profit should AAA report at the end of the first year under the percentage-of-completion method and the completed-contract method?

	Percentage-of-completion	Completed-contract
A.	$16,000	$0
B.	$16,000	$40,000
C.	$40,000	$0

5. Which principle requires that cost of goods sold be recognized in the same period in which the sale of the related inventory is recorded?
   A. Going concern.
   B. Certainty.
   C. Matching.

6. Which of the following would *least likely* increase pretax income?
   A. Decreasing the bad debt expense estimate.
   B. Increasing the useful life of an intangible asset.
   C. Decreasing the residual value of a depreciable tangible asset.

7. When accounting for inventory, are the first-in, first-out (FIFO) and last-in, first-out (LIFO) cost flow assumptions permitted under U.S. GAAP?

	FIFO	LIFO
A.	Yes	Yes
B.	Yes	No
C.	No	Yes

©2012 Kaplan, Inc.

8. Which of the following *best* describes the impact of depreciating equipment with a useful life of 6 years using the declining balance method as compared to the straight-line method?
   A. Total depreciation expense will be higher over the life of the equipment.
   B. Depreciation expense will be higher in the first year.
   C. Scrapping the equipment after five years will result in a larger loss.

9. CC Corporation reported the following inventory transactions (in chronological order) for the year:

Purchase	Sales
40 units at $30	13 units at $35
20 units at $40	35 units at $45
90 units at $50	60 units at $60

   Assuming inventory at the beginning of the year was zero, calculate the year-end inventory using FIFO and LIFO.

	FIFO	LIFO
A.	$5,220	$1,040
B.	$2,100	$1,280
C.	$2,100	$1,040

10. At the beginning of the year, Triple W Corporation purchased a new piece of equipment to be used in its manufacturing operation. The cost of the equipment was $25,000. The equipment is expected to be used for 4 years and then sold for $4,000. Depreciation expense to be reported for the second year using the double-declining-balance method is *closest* to:
    A. $5,250.
    B. $6,250.
    C. $7,000.

11. Which of the following is *least likely* considered a nonoperating transaction from the perspective of a manufacturing firm?
    A. Dividends received from available-for-sale securities.
    B. Interest expense on subordinated debentures.
    C. Accruing bad debt expense for goods sold on credit.

12. Changing an accounting estimate:
    A. is reported prospectively.
    B. requires restatement of all prior-period statements presented in the current financial statements.
    C. is reported by adjusting the beginning balance of retained earnings for the cumulative effect of the change.

13. Which of the following transactions would *most likely* be reported below income from continuing operations, net of tax?
    A. Gain or loss from the sale of equipment used in a firm's manufacturing operation.
    B. A change from the accelerated method of depreciation to the straight-line method.
    C. The operating income of a physically and operationally distinct division that is currently for sale, but not yet sold.

14. Which of the following statements about nonrecurring items is *least accurate*?
    A. Gains from extraordinary items are reported net of taxes at the bottom of the income statement before net income.
    B. Unusual or infrequent items are reported before taxes above net income from continuing operations.
    C. A change in accounting principle is reported in the income statement net of taxes after extraordinary items and before net income.

15. The Hall Corporation had 100,000 shares of common stock outstanding at the beginning of the year. Hall issued 30,000 shares of common stock on May 1. On July 1, the company issued a 10% stock dividend. On September 1, Hall issued 1,000, 10% bonds, each convertible into 21 shares of common stock. What is the weighted average number of shares to be used in computing basic and diluted EPS, assuming the convertible bonds are dilutive?

	Average shares, basic	Average shares, dilutive
A.	132,000	139,000
B.	132,000	146,000
C.	139,000	146,000

16. Given the following information, how many shares should be used in computing diluted EPS?
    - 300,000 shares outstanding.
    - 100,000 warrants exercisable at $50 per share.
    - Average share price is $55.
    - Year-end share price is $60.
    A. 9,091.
    B. 90,909.
    C. 309,091.

17. An analyst gathered the following information about a company:
    - 100,000 common shares outstanding from the beginning of the year.
    - Earnings of $125,000.
    - 1,000, 7%, $1,000 par bonds convertible into 25 shares each, outstanding as of the beginning of the year.
    - The tax rate is 40%.

    The company's diluted EPS is *closest* to:
    A. $1.22.
    B. $1.25.
    C. $1.34.

©2012 Kaplan, Inc.

18. An analyst has gathered the following information about a company:
    - 50,000 common shares outstanding from the beginning of the year.
    - Warrants outstanding all year on 50,000 shares, exercisable at $20 per share.
    - Stock is selling at year end for $25.
    - The average price of the company's stock for the year was $15.

    How many shares should be used in calculating the company's diluted EPS?
    A. 16,667.
    B. 50,000.
    C. 66,667.

19. Which of the following transactions affects owners' equity but does not affect net income?
    A. Foreign currency translation gain.
    B. Repaying the face amount on a bond issued at par.
    C. Dividends received from available-for-sale securities.

20. Which of the following is *least likely* to be included when calculating comprehensive income?
    A. Unrealized loss from cash flow hedging derivatives.
    B. Unrealized gain from available-for-sale securities.
    C. Dividends paid to common shareholders.

21. A vertical common-size income statement expresses each category of the income statement as a percentage of:
    A. assets.
    B. gross profit.
    C. revenue.

22. Which of the following would *most likely* result in higher gross profit margin, assuming no fixed costs?
    A. A 10% increase in the number of units sold.
    B. A 5% decrease in production cost per unit.
    C. A 7% decrease in administrative expenses.

ANSWERS – CONCEPT CHECKERS

1. **B** Depreciation is included in the computation of operating expenses. Interest expense is a financing cost. Thus, it is excluded from operating expenses.

2. **A** Income taxes are expenses grouped together by their nature. Cost of goods sold includes a number of expenses related to the same function, the production of inventory.

3. **A** In order to recognize revenue, the seller must know the sales price and be reasonably sure of collection, and must have delivered the goods or rendered the service. Actual collection of cash is not required.

4. **A** $24,000 / $60,000 = 40% of the project completed. 40% of $100,000 = $40,000 revenue. $40,000 revenue – $24,000 cost = $16,000 profit for the period. No profit would be reported in the first year using the completed contract method.

5. **C** The matching principle requires that the expenses incurred to generate the revenue be recognized in the same accounting period as the revenue.

6. **C** Decreasing the residual (salvage) value of a depreciable long-lived asset will result in higher depreciation expense and, thus, lower pretax income.

7. **A** LIFO and FIFO are both permitted under U.S. GAAP. LIFO is prohibited under IFRS.

8. **B** Accelerated depreciation will result in higher depreciation in the early years and lower depreciation in the later years compared to the straight-line method. Total depreciation expense will be the same under both methods. The book value would be higher in the later years using straight-line depreciation, so the loss from scrapping the equipment under an accelerated method is less compared to the straight-line method.

9. **B** 108 units were sold (13 + 35 + 60) and 150 units were available for sale (beginning inventory of 0 plus purchases of 40 + 20 + 90), so there are 150 − 108 = 42 units in ending inventory. Under FIFO, units from the last batch purchased would remain in inventory: 42 × $50 = $2,100. Under LIFO, the first 42 units purchased would be in inventory: (40 × $30) + (2 × $40) = $1,280.

10. **B** Year 1: (2 / 4) × 25,000 = $12,500. Year 2: (2 / 4) × (25,000 − 12,500) = $6,250.

11. **C** Bad debt expense is an operating expense. The other choices are nonoperating items from the perspective of a manufacturing firm.

12. **A** A change in an accounting estimate is reported prospectively. No restatement of prior period statements is necessary.

13. **C** A physically and operationally distinct division that is currently for sale is treated as a discontinued operation. The income from the division is reported net of tax below income from continuing operations. Changing a depreciation method is a change of accounting principle, which is applied retrospectively and will change operating income.

14. **C** A change in accounting principle requires retrospective application; that is, all prior period financial statements currently presented are restated to reflect the change.

©2012 Kaplan, Inc.

15. **A**   The new stock is weighted by 8 / 12. The bonds are weighted by 4 / 12 and are not affected by the stock dividend.

Basic shares = {[100,000 × (12 / 12)] + [30,000 × (8 / 12)]} × 1.10 = 132,000

Diluted shares = 132,000 + [21,000 × (4 / 12)] = 139,000

16. **C**   Since the exercise price of the warrants is less than the average share price, the warrants are dilutive. Using the treasury stock method to determine the denominator impact:

$$\frac{\$55 - \$50}{\$55} \times 100,000 \text{ shares} = 9,091 \text{ shares}$$

Thus, the denominator will increase by 9,091 shares to 309,091 shares. The question asks for the total, not just the impact of the warrants.

17. **B**   First, calculate basic EPS = $\dfrac{\$125,000}{100,000} = \$1.25$

Next, check if the convertible bonds are dilutive:

numerator impact = (1,000 × 1,000 × 0.07) × (1 – 0.4) = $42,000

denominator impact = (1,000 × 25) = 25,000 shares

$$\text{per share impact} = \frac{\$42,000}{25,000 \text{ shares}} = \$1.68$$

Since $1.68 is greater than the basic EPS of $1.25, the bonds are antidilutive. Thus, diluted EPS = basic EPS = $1.25.

18. **B**   The warrants in this case are antidilutive. The average price per share of $15 is less than the exercise price of $20. The year-end price per share is not relevant. The denominator consists of only the common stock for basic EPS.

19. **A**   A foreign currency translation gain is not included in net income but the gain increases owners' equity. Dividends received are reported in the income statement. The repayment of principal does not affect owners' equity.

20. **C**   Comprehensive income includes all changes in equity except transactions with shareholders. Therefore, dividends paid to common shareholders are not included in comprehensive income.

21. **C**   Each category of the income statement is expressed as a percentage of revenue (sales).

22. **B**   A 5% decrease in per unit production cost will increase gross profit by lowering cost of goods sold. Assuming no fixed costs, gross profit margin will remain the same if sale quantities increase. Administrative expenses are not included in gross profit margin.

The following is a review of the Financial Reporting and Analysis principles designed to address the learning outcome statements set forth by CFA Institute. This topic is also covered in:

UNDERSTANDING BALANCE SHEETS

EXAM FOCUS

While the income statement presents a picture of a firm's economic activities over a period of time, its balance sheet is a snapshot of its financial and physical assets and its liabilities at a point in time. Just as with the income statement, understanding balance sheet accounts, how they are valued, and what they represent, is also crucial to the financial analysis of a firm. Again, different choices of accounting methods and different accounting estimates will affect a firm's financial ratios, and an analyst must be careful to make the necessary adjustments in order to compare two or more firms. Special attention should be paid to the method by which each balance sheet item is calculated and how changes in balance sheet values relate to the income statement and to shareholders' equity. The next Study Session includes more detailed information on several balance sheet accounts, including inventories, long-lived assets, deferred taxes, and long-term liabilities.

LOS 26.a: Describe the elements of the balance sheet: assets, liabilities, and equity.

CFA® Program Curriculum, Volume 3, page 200

The **balance sheet** (also known as the statement of financial position or statement of financial condition) reports the firm's financial position at a point in time. The balance sheet consists of assets, liabilities, and equity.[1]

Assets: Resources controlled as a result of past transactions that are expected to provide future economic benefits.

Liabilities: Obligations as a result of past events that are expected to require an outflow of economic resources.

Equity: The owners' residual interest in the assets after deducting the liabilities. Equity is also referred to as stockholders' equity, shareholders' equity, or owners' equity. Analysts sometimes refer to equity as "net assets."

A financial statement item should be recognized if a future economic benefit from the item (flowing to or from the firm) is *probable* and the item's value or cost can be measured reliably.

---

1. Conceptual Framework for Financial Reporting (2010), paragraphs 4.4-4.23.

 ©2012 Kaplan, Inc.

LOS 26.b: Describe the uses and limitations of the balance sheet in financial analysis.

CFA® Program Curriculum, Volume 3, page 200

The balance sheet can be used to assess a firm's liquidity, solvency, and ability to make distributions to shareholders. From the firm's perspective, **liquidity** is the ability to meet short-term obligations and **solvency** is the ability to meet long-term obligations.

The balance sheet elements (assets, liabilities, and equity) should not be interpreted as market value or intrinsic value. For most firms, the balance sheet consists of a mixture of values. For example, some assets are reported at historical cost, some are reported at amortized cost, and others may be reported at fair value. There are numerous valuation bases. Even if the balance sheet was reported at fair value, the value may have changed since the balance sheet date. Also, there are a number of assets and liabilities that do not appear on the balance sheet but certainly have value. For example, the value of a firm's employees and reputation is not reported on the balance sheet.

LOS 26.c: Describe alternative formats of balance sheet presentation.

CFA® Program Curriculum, Volume 3, page 201

Both IFRS and U.S. GAAP require firms to separately report their current assets and noncurrent assets and current and noncurrent liabilities. The current/noncurrent format is known as a **classified balance sheet** and is useful in evaluating liquidity.

Under IFRS, firms can choose to use a **liquidity-based format** if the presentation is more relevant and reliable. Liquidity-based presentations, which are often used in the banking industry, present assets and liabilities in the order of liquidity.

LOS 26.d: Distinguish between current and non-current assets, and current and non-current liabilities.

CFA® Program Curriculum, Volume 3, page 204

Current assets include cash and other assets that will likely be converted into cash or used up within one year or one operating cycle, whichever is greater. The **operating cycle** is the time it takes to produce or purchase inventory, sell the product, and collect the cash. Current assets are usually presented in the order of their liquidity, with cash being the most liquid. Current assets reveal information about the operating activities of the firm.

Current liabilities are obligations that will be satisfied within one year or one operating cycle, whichever is greater. More specifically, a liability that meets any of the following criteria is considered current:

- Settlement is expected during the normal operating cycle.
- Settlement is expected within one year.
- Held primarily for trading purposes.
- There is not an unconditional right to defer settlement for more than one year.

Current assets minus current liabilities equals **working capital**. Not enough working capital may indicate liquidity problems. Too much working capital may be an indication of inefficient use of assets.

Noncurrent assets do not meet the definition of current assets because they will not be converted into cash or used up within one year or operating cycle. Noncurrent assets provide information about the firm's investing activities, which form the foundation upon which the firm operates.

Noncurrent liabilities do not meet the criteria of current liabilities. Noncurrent liabilities provide information about the firm's long-term financing activities.

LOS 26.e: Describe different types of assets and liabilities and the measurement bases of each.

CFA® Program Curriculum, Volume 3, page 204

Current Assets

Current assets include cash and other assets that will be converted into cash or used up within one year or operating cycle, whichever is greater.

Cash and cash equivalents. Cash equivalents are short-term, highly liquid investments that are readily convertible to cash and near enough to maturity that interest rate risk is insignificant. Examples of cash equivalents include Treasury bills, commercial paper, and money market funds. Cash and equivalents are considered financial assets. Generally, financial assets are reported on the balance sheet at amortized cost or fair value. For cash equivalents, either measurement base should result in about the same value.

Marketable securities. Marketable securities are financial assets that are traded in a public market and whose value can be readily determined. Examples include Treasury bills, notes, bonds, and equity securities. Details of the investment are disclosed in the financial footnotes. Measurement bases for marketable securities will be discussed later in this topic review.

Accounts receivable. Accounts receivable (also known as trade receivables) are financial assets that represent amounts owed to the firm by customers for goods or services sold on credit. Accounts receivable are reported at **net realizable value**, which is based on estimated **bad debt expense**. Bad debt expense increases the **allowance for doubtful accounts**, a contra-asset account. A **contra account** is used to reduce the value of its controlling account. Thus, gross receivables less the allowance for doubtful accounts is equal to accounts receivable at net realizable value, the amount the firm expects to collect. When receivables are "written off" (removed from the balance sheet because they are uncollectable), both gross receivables and the allowance account are reduced.

Firms are required to disclose significant concentrations of credit risk, including customer, geographic, and industry concentrations.

Analyzing receivables relative to sales can reveal collection problems. The allowance for doubtful accounts should also be considered relative to the level and growth rate of sales. Firms can underestimate bad debt expense, thereby increasing reported earnings.

©2012 Kaplan, Inc.

Inventories. Inventories are goods held for sale to customers or used in manufacture of goods to be sold. Manufacturing firms separately report inventories of raw materials, work-in-process, and finished goods.

The costs included in inventory include purchase cost, conversion costs, and other costs necessary to bring the inventory to its present location and condition. Costs that are excluded from inventory include abnormal waste of material, labor, and overhead, storage costs (unless they are necessary as a part of the production process), administrative overhead, and selling costs.

Standard costing and the retail method are used by some firms to measure inventory costs. **Standard costing**, often used by manufacturing firms, involves assigning predetermined amounts of materials, labor, and overhead to goods produced. Firms that use the **retail method** measure inventory at retail prices and then subtract gross profit in order to determine cost.

Using different cost flow assumptions (also known as cost flow methods), firms assign inventory costs to the income statement (cost of goods sold). As discussed in the topic review of Understanding Income Statements, FIFO and average cost are permitted under both IFRS and U.S. GAAP. LIFO is permitted under U.S. GAAP but is prohibited under IFRS.

Under IFRS, inventories are reported at the lower of cost or net realizable value. Net realizable value is equal to the selling price less any completion costs and disposal (selling) costs. Under U.S. GAAP, inventories are reported at the lower of cost or market. Market is usually equal to replacement cost; however, market cannot be greater than net realizable value or less than net realizable value less a normal profit margin. If net realizable value (IFRS) or market (U.S. GAAP) is less than the inventory's carrying value, the inventory is written down and a loss is recognized in the income statement. If there is a subsequent recovery in value, the inventory can be written back up under IFRS. No write-up is allowed under U.S. GAAP; the firm simply reports higher profit when the inventory is sold.

 Professor's Note: Inventories are described in more detail in the next Study Session.

Other current assets. Other current assets are amounts that may not be material if shown separately; thus, the items are combined into a single amount. Examples include prepaid expenses and deferred tax assets. **Prepaid expenses** are operating costs that have been paid in advance. As the costs are actually incurred, an expense is recognized in the income statement and prepaid expenses (an asset) decrease. For example, if a firm makes an annual rent payment of $400,000 at the beginning of the year, an asset (cash) decreases and another asset (prepaid rent) increases by the amount of the payment. At the end of three months, one-quarter of the prepaid rent has been used. At this point, the firm will recognize $100,000 of rent expense in its income statement and reduce assets (prepaid rent) by $100,000.

As we will discuss in our topic review of Income Taxes, deferred taxes are the result of temporary differences between financial reporting income and tax reporting income. **Deferred tax assets** are created when the amount of taxes payable exceeds the amount of income tax expense recognized in the income statement. This can occur when expenses or losses are recognized in the income statement before they are tax deductible, or when revenues or gains are taxable before they are recognized in the income statement. Eventually, the deferred tax asset will reverse when the expense is deducted for tax purposes or the revenue is recognized in the income statement. Deferred tax assets can also be created from unused tax losses.

Current Liabilities

Current liabilities are obligations that will be satisfied within one year or operating cycle, whichever is greater.

Accounts payable. Accounts payable (also known as trade payables) are amounts the firm owes to suppliers for goods or services purchased on credit. Analyzing payables relative to purchases can signal credit problems with suppliers.

Notes payable and current portion of long-term debt. Notes payable are obligations in the form of promissory notes owed to creditors and lenders. Notes payable can also be reported as noncurrent liabilities if their maturities are greater than one year. The current portion of long-term debt is the principal portion of debt due within one year or operating cycle, whichever is greater.

Accrued liabilities. Accrued liabilities (accrued expenses) are expenses that have been recognized in the income statement but are not yet contractually due. Accrued liabilities result from the accrual method of accounting, under which expenses are recognized as incurred. For example, consider a firm that is required to make annual year-end interest payments of $100,000 on an outstanding bank loan. At the end of March, the firm would recognize one-quarter ($25,000) of the total interest expense in its income statement and an accrued liability would be increased by the same amount, even though the liability is not actually due until the end of the year.

Some firms include income tax payable as an accrued liability. **Taxes payable** are current taxes that have been recognized in the income statement but have not yet been paid. Other examples of accrued liabilities include interest payable, wages payable, and accrued warranty expense.

Unearned revenue. Unearned revenue (also known as unearned income, deferred revenue, or deferred income) is cash collected in advance of providing goods and services. For example, a magazine publisher receives subscription payments in advance of delivery. When payment is received, assets (cash) and liabilities (unearned revenue) increase by the same amount. As the magazines are delivered, the publisher recognizes revenue in the income statement and reduces the liability.

When analyzing liquidity, keep in mind that unearned revenue does not require a future outflow of cash like accounts payable. Also, unearned revenue may be an indication of future growth as the revenue will ultimately be recognized in the income statement.

Non-Current Assets

Property, plant, and equipment. Property, plant, and equipment (PP&E) are tangible assets used in the production of goods and services. PP&E includes land and buildings, machinery and equipment, furniture, and natural resources. Under IFRS, PP&E can be reported using the **cost model** or the **revaluation model**. Under U.S. GAAP, only the cost model is allowed.

©2012 Kaplan, Inc.

Under the cost model, PP&E is reported at amortized cost (historical cost minus accumulated depreciation, amortization, depletion, and impairment losses). **Historical cost** includes the purchase price plus any cost necessary to get the asset ready for use, such as delivery and installation costs. As discussed in the topic review of Understanding Income Statements, there are several depreciation methods (e.g., straight-line and declining balance methods) used to allocate the cost to the income statement over time. Thus, the balance sheet and income statement are affected by the depreciation method and related estimates (i.e., salvage value and useful life of assets).

Also under the cost model, PP&E must be tested for **impairment**. An asset is impaired if its carrying value exceeds the **recoverable amount**. Under IFRS, the recoverable amount of an asset is the greater of fair value less any selling costs, or the asset's **value in use**. Value in use is the present value of the asset's future cash flow stream. If impaired, the asset is written down to its recoverable amount and a loss is recognized in the income statement. Loss recoveries are allowed under IFRS but not under U.S. GAAP.

Under the revaluation model, PP&E is reported at fair value less any accumulated depreciation. Changes in fair value are reflected in shareholders' equity and may be recognized in the income statement in certain circumstances.

 Professor's Note: The revaluation model will be discussed in more detail in the topic review of Long-Lived Assets.

Investment property. Under IFRS, investment property includes assets that generate rental income or capital appreciation. U.S. GAAP does not have a specific definition of investment property. Under IFRS, investment property can either be reported at amortized cost (just like PP&E) or fair value. Under the **fair value model**, any change in fair value is recognized in the income statement.

Intangible assets. Intangible assets are non-monetary assets that lack physical substance. Securities are not considered intangible assets. Intangible assets are either identifiable or unidentifiable. **Identifiable intangible assets** can be acquired separately or are the result of rights or privileges conveyed to their owner. Examples of identifiable intangibles are patents, trademarks, and copyrights. **Unidentifiable intangible assets** cannot be acquired separately and may have an unlimited life. The best example of an unidentifiable intangible asset is goodwill.

Under IFRS, identifiable intangibles that are *purchased* can be reported on the balance sheet using the cost model or the revaluation model, although the revaluation model can only be used if an active market for the intangible asset exists. Both models are basically the same as the measurement models used for PP&E. Under U.S. GAAP, only the cost model is allowed.

Except for certain legal costs, intangible assets that are *created internally*, such as research and development costs, are expensed as incurred under U.S. GAAP. Under IFRS, a firm must identify the research stage (discovery of new scientific or technical knowledge) and the development stage (using research results to plan or design products). Under IFRS, the firm must expense costs incurred during the research stage but can capitalize costs incurred during the development stage.

Finite-lived intangible assets are amortized over their useful lives and tested for impairment in the same way as PP&E. The amortization method and useful life

Study Session 8

estimates are reviewed at least annually. Intangible assets with infinite lives are not amortized, but are tested for impairment at least annually.

Under IFRS and U.S. GAAP, all of the following should be expensed as incurred:
- Start-up and training costs.
- Administrative overhead.
- Advertising and promotion costs.
- Relocation and reorganization costs.
- Termination costs.

Some analysts choose to eliminate intangible assets for analytical purposes. However, analysts should consider the value to the firm of each intangible asset before making any adjustments.

Goodwill. Goodwill is the excess of purchase price over the fair value of the identifiable net assets (assets minus liabilities) acquired in a business acquisition. Let's look at an example of calculating goodwill.

Example: Goodwill

Wood Corporation paid $600 million for the outstanding stock of Pine Corporation. At the acquisition date, Pine reported the following condensed balance sheet.

Pine Corporation – Condensed Balance Sheet

	Book value (millions)
Current assets	$80
Plant and equipment, net	760
Goodwill	30
Liabilities	400
Stockholders' equity	470

The fair value of the plant and equipment was $120 million more than its recorded book value. The fair values of all other identifiable assets and liabilities were equal to their recorded book values. Calculate the amount of goodwill Wood should report on its consolidated balance sheet.

©2012 Kaplan, Inc.

Answer:

	Book value (millions)
Current assets	$80
Plant and equipment, net	880
Liabilities	(400)
Fair value of net assets	560
Purchase price	600
Less: Fair value of net assets	(560)
Acquisition goodwill	40

Goodwill is equal to the excess of purchase price over the fair value of identifiable assets and liabilities acquired. Plant and equipment was "written up" by $120 million to reflect fair value. The goodwill reported on Pine's balance sheet is an unidentifiable asset and is thus ignored in the calculation of Wood's goodwill.

Acquirers are often willing to pay more than the fair value of the target's identifiable net assets because the target may have assets that are not reported on its balance sheet. For example, the target's reputation and customer loyalty certainly have value; however, the value is not quantifiable. Also, the target may have research and development assets that remain off-balance-sheet because of current accounting standards. Finally, part of the acquisition price may reflect perceived synergies from the business combination. For example, the acquirer may be able to eliminate duplicate facilities and reduce payroll as a result of the acquisition.

 Professor's Note: Occasionally the purchase price of an acquisition is less than fair value of the identifiable net assets. In this case, the difference is immediately recognized as a gain in the acquirer's income statement.

Goodwill is only created in a purchase acquisition. Internally generated goodwill is expensed as incurred.

Goodwill is not amortized but must be tested for impairment at least annually. If impaired, goodwill is reduced and a loss is recognized in the income statement. The impairment loss does not affect cash flow. As long as goodwill is not impaired, it can remain on the balance sheet indefinitely.

Since goodwill is not amortized, firms can manipulate net income upward by allocating more of the acquisition price to goodwill and less to the identifiable assets. The result is less depreciation and amortization expense, resulting in higher net income.

Accounting goodwill should not be confused with economic goodwill. Economic goodwill derives from the expected future performance of the firm, while accounting goodwill is the result of past acquisitions.

When computing ratios, analysts should eliminate goodwill from the balance sheet and goodwill impairment charges from the income statement for comparability. Also, analysts should evaluate future acquisitions in terms of the price paid relative to the earning power of the acquired assets.

Financial assets. Financial instruments are contracts that give rise to both a financial asset of one entity and a financial liability or equity instrument of another entity.[2] Financial instruments can be found on the asset side and the liability side of the balance sheet. Financial assets include investment securities (stocks and bonds), derivatives, loans, and receivables.

Financial instruments are measured at historical cost, amortized cost, or fair value. Financial assets measured at cost include unquoted equity investments (whereby fair value cannot be reliably measured) and loans to and receivables from other entities.

Financial assets measured at amortized cost are known as held-to-maturity securities. **Held-to-maturity securities** are debt securities acquired with the intent to be held to maturity. Amortized cost is equal to the original issue price minus any principal payments, plus any amortized discount or minus any amortized premium, minus any impairment losses. Subsequent changes in market value are ignored.

Financial assets measured at fair value, also known as **mark-to-market** accounting, include trading securities, available-for-sale securities, and derivatives.

Trading securities (also known as held-for-trading securities) are debt and equity securities acquired with the intent to profit over the near term. Trading securities are reported on the balance sheet at fair value, and the unrealized gains and losses (changes in market value before the securities are sold) are recognized in the income statement. Unrealized gains and losses are also known as holding period gains and losses. **Derivative instruments** are treated the same as trading securities.

Available-for-sale securities are debt and equity securities that are not expected to be held to maturity or traded in the near term. Like trading securities, available-for-sale securities are reported on the balance sheet at fair value. However, any unrealized gains and losses are not recognized in the income statement, but are reported in other comprehensive income as a part of shareholders' equity.

For all three classifications of securities, dividend and interest income and realized gains and losses (actual gains or losses when the securities are sold) are recognized in the income statement.

Figure 1 summarizes the different classifications and measurement bases of financial assets.

---

2.   IAS 32, *Financial Instruments*: Presentation, paragraph 11.

                     ©2012 Kaplan, Inc.

Figure 1: Financial Asset Classifications and Measurement Bases

Historical Cost	*Amortized Cost*	*Fair Value*
Unlisted equity investments	Held-to-maturity securities	Trading securities
Loans and receivables		Available-for-sale securities
		Derivatives

 Professor's Note: Beginning in 2015, the available-for-sale classification will no longer exist in accordance with a newly issued standard, IFRS 9, Financial Instruments.

Example: Classification of investment securities

Triple D Corporation purchased a 6% bond, at par, for $1,000,000 at the beginning of the year. Interest rates have recently increased and the market value of the bond declined $20,000. Determine the bond's effect on Triple D's financial statements under each classification of securities.

Answer:

If the bond is classified as a *held-to-maturity* security, the bond is reported on the balance sheet at $1,000,000. Interest income of $60,000 [$1,000,000 × 6%] is reported in the income statement.

If the bond is classified as a *trading* security, the bond is reported on the balance sheet at $980,000. The $20,000 unrealized loss and $60,000 of interest income are both recognized in the income statement.

If the bond is classified as an *available-for-sale* security, the bond is reported on the balance sheet at $980,000. Interest income of $60,000 is recognized in the income statement. The $20,000 unrealized loss is not recognized in the income statement. Rather, it is reported as a change in stockholders' equity.

Non-Current Liabilities

Long-term financial liabilities. Financial liabilities include bank loans, notes payable, bonds payable, and derivatives. If the financial liabilities are not issued at face amount, the liabilities are usually reported on the balance sheet at amortized cost. Amortized cost is equal to the issue price minus any principal payments, plus any amortized discount or minus any amortized premium.

In some cases, financial liabilities are reported at fair value. Examples include held-for-trading liabilities (such as a short position in a stock), derivative liabilities, and non-derivative liabilities with exposures hedged by derivatives.

Deferred tax liabilities. Deferred tax liabilities are amounts of income taxes payable in future periods as a result of taxable temporary differences. Deferred tax liabilities are created when the amount of income tax expense recognized in the income statement is greater than taxes payable. This can occur when expenses or losses are tax deductible before they are recognized in the income statement. A good example is when a firm uses an accelerated depreciation method for tax purposes and the straight-line method for financial reporting. Deferred tax liabilities are also created when revenues or gains are recognized in the income statement before they are taxable. For example, a firm often recognizes the earnings of a subsidiary before any distributions (dividends) are made. Eventually, deferred tax liabilities will reverse when the taxes are paid.

LOS 26.f: Describe the components of shareholders' equity.

CFA® Program Curriculum, Volume 3, page 228

Owners' equity is the residual interest in assets that remains after subtracting an entity's liabilities. Owners' equity includes contributed capital, preferred stock, treasury stock, retained earnings, non-controlling interest, and accumulated other comprehensive income.

Contributed capital (also known as issued capital) is the amount contributed by the common shareholders.

The **par value** of common stock is a stated or legal value. Par value has no relationship to fair value. Some common shares are even issued without a par value. When par value exists, it is reported separately in stockholders' equity.

Also disclosed is the number of common shares that are authorized, issued, and outstanding. **Authorized shares** are the number of shares that may be sold under the firm's articles of incorporation. **Issued shares** are the number of shares that have actually been sold to shareholders. The number of **outstanding shares** is equal to the issued shares less shares that have been reacquired by the firm (i.e., treasury stock).

Preferred stock has certain rights and privileges not conferred by common stock. For example, preferred shareholders are paid dividends at a specified rate, usually expressed as a percentage of par value, and have priority over the claims of the common shareholders in the event of liquidation.

Preferred stock can be classified as debt or equity, depending on the terms. For example, perpetual preferred stock that is non-redeemable is considered equity. However, preferred stock that calls for *mandatory redemption* in fixed amounts is considered a financial liability.

Noncontrolling interest (minority interest) is the minority shareholders' pro-rata share of the net assets (equity) of a subsidiary that is not wholly owned by the parent.

Retained earnings are the undistributed earnings (net income) of the firm since inception, the cumulative earnings that have not been paid out to shareholders as dividends.

©2012 Kaplan, Inc.

Treasury stock is stock that has been reacquired by the issuing firm but not yet retired. Treasury stock reduces stockholders' equity. It does not represent an investment in the firm. Treasury stock has no voting rights and does not receive dividends.

Accumulated other comprehensive income includes all changes in stockholders' equity except for transactions recognized in the income statement (net income) and transactions with shareholders, such as issuing stock, reacquiring stock, and paying dividends.

As discussed in the topic review of Understanding Income Statements, comprehensive income aggregates net income and certain special transactions that are not reported in the income statement but that affect stockholders' equity. These special transactions comprise what is known as "other comprehensive income." Comprehensive income is equal to net income plus other comprehensive income.

> *Professor's Note: It is easy to confuse the two terms "comprehensive income" and "accumulated other comprehensive income." Comprehensive income is an income measure over a period of time. It includes net income and other comprehensive income for the period. Accumulated other comprehensive income does not include net income but is a component of stockholders' equity at a point in time.*

LOS 26.g: Analyze balance sheets and statements of changes in equity.

CFA® Program Curriculum, Volume 3, page 231

The balance sheet reports the economic resources and obligations of the firm. Thus, the balance sheet can be used to analyze a firm's capital structure and ability to pay its short-term and long-term obligations.

The **statement of changes in stockholders' equity** summarizes all transactions that increase or decrease the equity accounts for the period. The statement includes transactions with shareholders and reconciles the beginning and ending balance of each equity account, including capital stock, additional paid-in-capital, retained earnings, and accumulated other comprehensive income. In addition, the components of accumulated other comprehensive income are disclosed (i.e., unrealized gains and losses from available-for-sale securities, cash flow hedging derivatives, foreign currency translation, and adjustments for minimum pension liability).

A statement of changes in stockholders' equity is illustrated in Figure 2.

Figure 2: Sample Statement of Changes in Stockholders' Equity

	Common Stock	Retained Earnings (in thousands)	Accumulated Other Comprehensive Income (loss)	Total
Beginning balance	$49,234	$26,664	($406)	$75,492
Net income		6,994		6,994
Net unrealized loss on available-for-sale securities			(40)	(40)
Net unrealized loss on cash flow hedges			(56)	(56)
Minimum pension liability			(26)	(26)
Cumulative translation adjustment			42	42
Comprehensive income				6,914
Issuance of common stock	1,282			1,282
Repurchases of common stock	(6,200)			(6,200)
Dividends		(2,360)		(2,360)
Ending balance	$44,316	$31,298	($486)	$75,128

LOS 26.h: Convert balance sheets to common-size balance sheets and interpret the common-size balance sheets.

CFA® Program Curriculum, Volume 3, page 232

A vertical **common-size balance sheet** expresses each item of the balance sheet as a percentage of total assets. The common-size format standardizes the balance sheet by eliminating the effects of size. This allows for comparison over time (time-series analysis) and across firms (cross-sectional analysis). For example, following are the balance sheets of industry competitors East Company and West Company.

©2012 Kaplan, Inc.

	East	West
Cash	$2,300	$1,500
Accounts receivable	3,700	1,100
Inventory	5,500	900
Current assets	11,500	3,500
Plant and equipment	32,500	11,750
Goodwill	1,750	0
Total assets	$45,750	$15,250
Current liabilities	$10,100	$1,000
Long-term debt	26,500	5,100
Total liabilities	36,600	6,100
Equity	9,150	9,150
Total liabilities & equity	$45,750	$15,250

East is obviously the larger company. By converting the balance sheets to common-size format, we can eliminate the size effect.

	East	West
Cash	5%	10%
Accounts receivable	8%	7%
Inventory	12%	6%
Current assets	25%	23%
Plant and equipment	71%	77%
Goodwill	4%	0%
Total assets	100%	100%
Current liabilities	22%	7%
Long-term debt	58%	33%
Total liabilities	80%	40%
Equity	20%	60%
Total liabilities & equity	100%	100%

East's investment in current assets of 25% of total assets is slightly higher than West's current assets of 23%. However, East's current liabilities of 22% of total assets are significantly higher than West's current liabilities of 7%. Thus, East is less liquid and may have more difficulty paying its current obligations when due. However, West's superior working capital position may not be an efficient use of resources. The investment returns on working capital are usually lower than the returns on long-term assets.

A closer look at current assets reveals that East reports less cash as a percentage of assets than West. In fact, East does not have enough cash to satisfy its current liabilities without selling more inventory and collecting receivables. East's inventories of 12% of total assets are higher than West's inventories of 6%. Carrying higher inventories may be an indication of inventory obsolescence. Further analysis of inventory is necessary.

Not only are East's current liabilities higher than West's, but East's long-term debt of 58% of total assets is much greater than West's long-term debt of 33%. Thus, East may have trouble satisfying its long-term obligations since its capital structure consists of more debt.

Common-size analysis can also be used to examine a firm's strategies. East appears to be growing through acquisitions since it is reporting goodwill. West is growing internally since no goodwill is reported. It could be that East is financing the acquisitions with debt.

LOS 26.i: Calculate and interpret liquidity and solvency ratios.

CFA® Program Curriculum, Volume 3, page 239

Balance sheet ratios compare balance sheet items only. Balance sheet ratios, along with common-size analysis, can be used to evaluate a firm's liquidity and solvency. The results should be compared over time (time-series analysis) and across firms (cross-sectional analysis).

 Professor's Note: Ratio analysis is covered in more detail in the topic review of Financial Analysis Techniques.

Liquidity ratios measure the firm's ability to satisfy its short-term obligations as they come due. Liquidity ratios include the current ratio, the quick ratio, and the cash ratio.

$$\text{current ratio} = \frac{\text{current assets}}{\text{current liabilities}}$$

$$\text{quick ratio} = \frac{\text{cash} + \text{marketable securities} + \text{receivables}}{\text{current liabilities}}$$

$$\text{cash ratio} = \frac{\text{cash} + \text{marketable securities}}{\text{current liabilities}}$$

Although all three ratios measure the firm's ability to pay current liabilities, they should be considered collectively. For example, assume Firm A has a higher current ratio but a lower quick ratio as compared to Firm B. This is the result of higher inventory as compared to Firm B. The quick ratio (also known as the acid-test ratio) is calculated by excluding inventory from current assets. Similar analysis can be performed by comparing the quick ratio and the cash ratio. The cash ratio is calculated by excluding inventory and receivables.

©2012 Kaplan, Inc.

Solvency ratios measure the firm's ability to satisfy its long-term obligations. Solvency ratios include the long-term debt-to-equity ratio, the total debt-to-equity ratio, the debt ratio, and the financial leverage ratio.

$$\text{long-term debt-to-equity} = \frac{\text{long-term debt}}{\text{total equity}}$$

$$\text{total debt-to-equity} = \frac{\text{total debt}}{\text{total equity}}$$

$$\text{debt ratio} = \frac{\text{total debt}}{\text{total assets}}$$

$$\text{financial leverage} = \frac{\text{total assets}}{\text{total equity}}$$

All four ratios measure solvency but they should be considered collectively. For example, Firm A might have a higher long-term debt-to-equity ratio but a lower total debt-to-equity ratio as compared to Firm B. This is an indication that Firm B is utilizing more short-term debt to finance itself.

When calculating solvency ratios, debt is considered to be any interest bearing obligation. On the other hand, the financial leverage ratio captures the impact of all obligations, both interest bearing and non-interest bearing.

Analysts must understand the limitations of balance sheet ratio analysis:

- Comparisons with peer firms are limited by differences in accounting standards and estimates.
- Lack of homogeneity as many firms operate in different industries.
- Interpretation of ratios requires significant judgment.
- Balance sheet data are only measured at a single point in time.

KEY CONCEPTS

LOS 26.a

Assets are resources controlled as result of past transactions that are expected to provide future economic benefits. Liabilities are obligations as a result of past events that are expected to require an outflow of economic resources. Equity is the owners' residual interest in the assets after deducting the liabilities.

A financial statement item should be recognized if a future economic benefit to or from the firm is probable and the item's value or cost can be measured reliably.

LOS 26.b

The balance sheet can be used to assess a firm's liquidity, solvency, and ability to pay dividends to shareholders.

Balance sheet assets, liabilities, and equity should not be interpreted as market value or intrinsic value. For most firms, the balance sheet consists of a mixture of values including historical cost, amortized cost, and fair value.

Some assets and liabilities are difficult to quantify and are not reported on the balance sheet.

LOS 26.c

A classified balance sheet separately reports current and noncurrent assets and current and noncurrent liabilities. Alternatively, liquidity-based presentations, often used in the banking industry, present assets and liabilities in order of liquidity.

LOS 26.d

Current (noncurrent) assets are those expected to be used up or converted to cash in less than (more than) one year or the firm's operating cycle, whichever is greater.

Current (noncurrent) liabilities are those the firm expects to satisfy in less than (more than) one year or the firm's operating cycle, whichever is greater.

LOS 26.e

Cash equivalents are short-term, highly liquid financial assets that are readily convertible to cash. Their balance sheet values are generally close to identical using either amortized cost or fair value.

Accounts receivable are reported at net realizable value by estimating bad debt expense.

Inventories are reported at the lower of cost or net realizable value (IFRS) or the lower of cost or market (U.S. GAAP). Cost can be measured using standard costing or the retail method. Different cost flow assumptions can affect inventory values.

Property, plant, and equipment (PP&E) can be reported using the cost model or the revaluation model under IFRS. Under U.S. GAAP, only the cost model is allowed. PP&E is impaired if its carrying value exceeds the recoverable amount. Recoveries of impairment losses are allowed under IFRS but not U.S. GAAP.

©2012 Kaplan, Inc.

Intangible assets created internally are expensed as incurred. Purchased intangibles are reported similar to PP&E. Under IFRS, research costs are expensed as incurred and development costs are capitalized. Both research and development costs are expensed under U.S. GAAP.

Goodwill is the excess of purchase price over the fair value of the identifiable net assets (assets minus liabilities) acquired in a business acquisition. Goodwill is not amortized but must be tested for impairment at least annually.

Held-to-maturity securities are reported at amortized cost. Trading securities, available-for-sale securities, and derivatives are reported at fair value. For trading securities and derivatives, unrealized gains and losses are recognized in the income statement. Unrealized gains and losses for available-for-sale securities are reported in equity (other comprehensive income).

Accounts payable are amounts owed to suppliers for goods or services purchased on credit. Accrued liabilities are expenses that have been recognized in the income statement but are not yet contractually due. Unearned revenue is cash collected in advance of providing goods and services.

Financial liabilities not issued at face value, like bonds payable, are reported at amortized cost. Held-for-trading liabilities and derivative liabilities are reported at fair value.

LOS 26.f
Owners' equity includes:
- Contributed capital—the amount paid in by common shareholders.
- Preferred stock—capital stock that has certain rights and privileges not possessed by the common shareholders. Classified as debt if mandatorily redeemable.
- Treasury stock—issued common stock that has been repurchased by the firm.
- Retained earnings—the cumulative undistributed earnings of the firm since inception.
- Noncontrolling (minority) interest—the portion of a subsidiary that is not owned by the parent.
- Accumulated other comprehensive income—includes all changes to equity from sources other than net income and transactions with shareholders.

LOS 26.g
The statement of changes in stockholders' equity summarizes the transactions during a period that increase or decrease equity, including transactions with shareholders.

LOS 26.h
A vertical common-size balance sheet expresses each item of the balance sheet as a percentage of total assets. The common-size format standardizes the balance sheet by eliminating the effects of size. This allows for comparison over time (time-series analysis) and across firms (cross-sectional analysis).

LOS 26.i

Balance sheet ratios, along with common-size analysis, can be used to evaluate a firm's liquidity and solvency. Liquidity ratios measure the firm's ability to satisfy its short-term obligations as they come due. Liquidity ratios include the current ratio, the quick ratio, and the cash ratio.

Solvency ratios measure the firm's ability to satisfy its long-term obligations. Solvency ratios include the long-term debt-to-equity ratio, the total debt-to-equity ratio, the debt ratio, and the financial leverage ratio.

©2012 Kaplan, Inc.

CONCEPT CHECKERS

1. Which of the following is *most likely* an essential characteristic of an asset?
    A. An asset is tangible.
    B. An asset is obtained at a cost.
    C. An asset provides future benefits.

2. Which of the following statements about analyzing the balance sheet is *most accurate*?
    A. The value of the firm's reputation is reported on the balance sheet at amortized cost.
    B. Shareholders' equity is equal to the intrinsic value of the firm.
    C. The balance sheet can be used to measure the firm's capital structure.

3. Century Company's balance sheet follows:

    Century Company
    Balance Sheet
    (in millions)

	20X7	20X6
Current assets	$340	$280
Noncurrent assets	660	630
Total assets	$1,000	$910
Current liabilities	$170	$110
Noncurrent liabilities	50	50
Total liabilities	$220	$160
Equity	$780	$750
Total liabilities and equity	$1,000	$910

    Century's balance sheet presentation is known as a(n)?
    A. classified balance sheet.
    B. liquidity-based balance sheet.
    C. account form balance sheet.

4. Which of the following would *most likely* result in a current liability?
    A. Possible warranty claims.
    B. Future operating lease payments.
    C. Estimated income taxes for the current year.

5. How should the proceeds received from the advance sale of tickets to a sporting event be treated by the seller, assuming the tickets are nonrefundable?
    A. Unearned revenue is recognized to the extent that costs have been incurred.
    B. Revenue is recognized to the extent that costs have been incurred.
    C. Revenue is deferred until the sporting event is held.

6. A vertical common-size balance sheet expresses each category of the balance sheet as a percentage of:
    A. assets.
    B. equity.
    C. revenue.

7. Which of the following inventory valuation methods is required by the accounting standard-setting bodies?
    A. Lower of cost or net realizable value.
    B. Weighted average cost.
    C. First-in, first-out.

8. SF Corporation has created employee goodwill by reorganizing its retirement benefit package. An independent management consultant estimated the value of the goodwill at $2 million. In addition, SF recently purchased a patent that was developed by a competitor. The patent has an estimated useful life of five years. Should SF report the goodwill and patent on its balance sheet?

	Goodwill	Patent
A.	Yes	No
B.	No	Yes
C.	No	No

9. At the beginning of the year, Parent Company purchased all 500,000 shares of Sub Incorporated for $15 per share. Just before the acquisition date, Sub's balance sheet reported net assets of $6 million. Parent determined the fair value of Sub's property and equipment was $1 million higher than reported by Sub. What amount of goodwill should Parent report as a result of its acquisition of Sub?
    A. $0.
    B. $500,000.
    C. $1,500,000.

Use the following information to answer Questions 10 and 11.

At the beginning of the year, Company P purchased 1,000 shares of Company S for $80 per share. During the year, Company S paid a dividend of $4 per share. At the end of the year, Company S's share price was $75.

10. What amount should Company P report on its balance sheet at year-end if the investment in Company S is considered a trading security, and what amount should be reported if the investment is considered an available-for-sale security?

	Trading	Available-for-sale
A.	$75,000	$75,000
B.	$75,000	$80,000
C.	$80,000	$80,000

©2012 Kaplan, Inc.

11.   What amount of investment income should Company P recognize in its income statement if the investment in Company S is considered trading, and what amount should be recognized if the investment is considered available-for-sale?

Trading	Available-for-sale
A. ($1,000)	($1,000)
B. ($1,000)	$4,000
C. ($5,000)	$4,000

12.   Miller Corporation has 160,000 shares of common stock authorized. There are 92,000 shares issued and 84,000 shares outstanding. How many shares of treasury stock does Miller own?
   A. 8,000.
   B. 68,000.
   C. 76,000.

13.   Selected data from Alpha Company's balance sheet at the end of the year follows:

Investment in Beta Company, at fair value	$150,000
Deferred taxes	$86,000
Common stock, $1 par value	$550,000
Preferred stock, $100 par value	$175,000
Retained earnings	$893,000
Accumulated other comprehensive income	$46,000

The investment in Beta Company had an original cost of $120,000. Assuming the investment in Beta is classified as available-for-sale, Alpha's total owners' equity at year-end is *closest* to:
   A. $1,618,000.
   B. $1,664,000.
   C. $1,714,000.

14.   Which of the following ratios are used to measure a firm's liquidity and solvency?

Liquidity	Solvency
A. Current ratio	Quick ratio
B. Debt-to-equity ratio	Financial leverage ratio
C. Cash ratio	Total debt ratio

ANSWERS – CONCEPT CHECKERS

1. **C** An asset is a future economic benefit obtained or controlled as a result of past transactions. Some assets are intangible (e.g., goodwill), and others may be donated.

2. **C** The balance sheet lists the firm's assets, liabilities, and equity. The capital structure is measured by the mix of debt and equity used to finance the business.

3. **A** A classified balance sheet groups together similar items (e.g., current and noncurrent assets and liabilities) to arrive at significant subtotals.

4. **C** Estimated income taxes for the current year are likely reported as a current liability. To recognize the warranty expense, it must be probable, not just possible. Future operating lease payments are not reported on the balance sheet.

5. **C** The ticket revenue should not be recognized until it is earned. Even though the tickets are nonrefundable, the seller is still obligated to hold the event.

6. **A** Each category of the balance sheet is expressed as a percentage of total assets.

7. **A** Inventories are required to be valued at the lower of cost or net realizable value (or "market" under U.S. GAAP). FIFO and average cost are two of the inventory cost flow assumptions among which a firm has a choice.

8. **B** Goodwill developed internally is expensed as incurred. The purchased patent is reported on the balance sheet.

9. **B** Purchase price of $7,500,000 [$15 per share × 500,000 shares] – fair value of net assets of $7,000,000 [$6,000,000 book value + $1,000,000 increase in property and equipment] = goodwill of $500,000.

10. **A** Both trading securities and available-for-sale securities are reported on the balance sheet at their fair values. At year-end, the fair value is $75,000 [$75 per share × 1,000 shares].

11. **B** A loss of $1,000 is recognized if the securities are considered trading securities ($4 dividend × $1,000 shares) – ($5 unrealized loss × 1,000 shares). Income is $4,000 if the investment in Company S is considered available-for-sale [$4 dividend × $1,000].

12. **A** The difference between the issued shares and the outstanding shares is the treasury shares.

13. **B** Total stockholders' equity consists of common stock of $550,000, preferred stock of $175,000, retained earnings of $893,000, and accumulated other comprehensive income of $46,000, for a total of $1,664,000. The $30,000 unrealized gain from the investment in Beta is already included in accumulated other comprehensive income.

14. **C** The current ratio, quick ratio, and cash ratio measure liquidity. Debt-to-equity, the total debt ratio, and the financial leverage ratio measure solvency.

©2012 Kaplan, Inc.

The following is a review of the Financial Reporting and Analysis principles designed to address the learning outcome statements set forth by CFA Institute. This topic is also covered in:

UNDERSTANDING CASH FLOW STATEMENTS

EXAM FOCUS

This topic review covers the third important required financial statement: the statement of cash flows. Since the income statement is based on the accrual method, net income may not represent cash generated from operations. A company may be generating positive and growing net income but may be headed for insolvency because insufficient cash is being generated from operating activities. Constructing a statement of cash flows, by either the direct or indirect method, is therefore very important in an analysis of a firm's activities and prospects. Make sure you understand the preparation of a statement of cash flows by either method, the classification of various cash flows as operating, financing, or investing cash flows, and the key differences in these classifications between U.S. GAAP and international accounting standards.

THE CASH FLOW STATEMENT

The **cash flow statement** provides information beyond that available from the income statement, which is based on accrual, rather than cash, accounting. The cash flow statement provides the following:

- Information about a company's cash receipts and cash payments during an accounting period.
- Information about a company's operating, investing, and financing activities.
- An understanding of the impact of accrual accounting events on cash flows.

The cash flow statement provides information to assess the firm's liquidity, solvency, and financial flexibility. An analyst can use the statement of cash flows to determine whether:

- Regular operations generate enough cash to sustain the business.
- Enough cash is generated to pay off existing debts as they mature.
- The firm is likely to need additional financing.
- Unexpected obligations can be met.
- The firm can take advantage of new business opportunities as they arise.

LOS 27.a: Compare cash flows from operating, investing, and financing activities and classify cash flow items as relating to one of those three categories given a description of the items.

CFA® Program Curriculum, Volume 3, page 253

Items on the cash flow statement come from two sources: (1) income statement items and (2) changes in balance sheet accounts. A firm's cash receipts and payments are classified on the cash flow statement as either operating, investing, or financing activities.

Cash flow from operating activities (CFO), sometimes referred to as "cash flow from operations" or "operating cash flow," consists of the inflows and outflows of cash resulting from transactions that affect a firm's net income.

Cash flow from investing activities (CFI) consists of the inflows and outflows of cash resulting from the acquisition or disposal of long-term assets and certain investments.

Cash flow from financing activities (CFF) consists of the inflows and outflows of cash resulting from transactions affecting a firm's capital structure.

Examples of each cash flow classification, in accordance with U.S. GAAP, are presented in Figure 1.

Figure 1: U.S. GAAP Cash Flow Classifications

Operating Activities	
Inflows	*Outflows*
Cash collected from customers	Cash paid to employees and suppliers
Interest and dividends received	Cash paid for other expenses
Sale proceeds from trading securities	Acquisition of trading securities
	Interest paid
	Taxes paid

Investing Activities	
Inflows	*Outflows*
Sale proceeds from fixed assets	Acquisition of fixed assets
Sale proceeds from debt and equity investments	Acquisition of debt and equity investments
Principal received from loans made to others	Loans made to others

Financing Activities	
Inflows	*Outflows*
Principal amounts of debt issued	Principal paid on debt
Proceeds from issuing stock	Payments to reacquire stock
	Dividends paid to shareholders

Note that the acquisition of debt and equity investments (other than trading securities) and loans made to others are reported as investing activities; however, the income from these investments (interest and dividends received) is reported as an operating activity. Also, note that principal amounts borrowed from others are reported as financing activities; however, the interest paid is reported as an operating activity. Finally, note that dividends paid to the firm's shareholders are financing activities.

 Professor's Note: Don't confuse dividends received and dividends paid. Under U.S. GAAP, dividends received are operating cash flows and dividends paid are financing cash flows.

©2012 Kaplan, Inc.

LOS 27.b: Describe how non-cash investing and financing activities are reported.

CFA® Program Curriculum, Volume 3, page 255

Noncash investing and financing activities are not reported in the cash flow statement since they do not result in inflows or outflows of cash.

For example, if a firm acquires real estate with financing provided by the seller, the firm has made an investing and financing decision. This transaction is the equivalent of borrowing the purchase price. However, since no cash is involved in the transaction, it is not reported as an investing and financing activity in the cash flow statement.

Another example of a noncash transaction is an exchange of debt for equity. Such an exchange results in a reduction of debt and an increase in equity. However, since no cash is involved in the transaction, it is not reported as a financing activity in the cash flow statement.

Noncash transactions must be disclosed in either a footnote or supplemental schedule to the cash flow statement. Analysts should be aware of the firm's noncash transactions, incorporate them into analysis of past and current performance, and include their effects in estimating future cash flows.

LOS 27.c: Contrast cash flow statements prepared under International Financial Reporting Standards (IFRS) and U.S. generally accepted accounting principles (U.S. GAAP).

CFA® Program Curriculum, Volume 3, page 255

Recall from Figure 1 that under U.S. GAAP, dividends paid to the firm's shareholders are reported as financing activities while interest paid is reported in operating activities. Interest received and dividends received from investments are also reported as operating activities.

International Financial Reporting Standards (IFRS) allow more flexibility in the classification of cash flows. Under IFRS, interest and dividends received may be classified as either operating *or* investing activities. Dividends paid to the company's shareholders and interest paid on the company's debt may be classified as either operating *or* financing activities.

Another important difference relates to income taxes paid. Under U.S. GAAP, all taxes paid are reported as operating activities, even taxes related to investing and financing transactions. Under IFRS, income taxes are also reported as operating activities unless the expense is associated with an investing or financing transaction.

For example, consider a company that sells land that was held for investment for $1 million. Income taxes on the sale total $160,000. Under U.S. GAAP, the firm reports an inflow of cash from investing activities of $1 million and an outflow of cash from operating activities of $160,000. Under IFRS, the firm can report a net inflow of $840,000 from investing activities.

LOS 27.d: Distinguish between the direct and indirect methods of presenting cash from operating activities and describe the arguments in favor of each method.

CFA® Program Curriculum, Volume 3, page 256

There are two methods of presenting the cash flow statement: the direct method and the indirect method. Both methods are permitted under U.S. GAAP and IFRS. The use of the direct method, however, is encouraged by both standard setters. Regrettably, most firms use the indirect method. The difference between the two methods relates to the presentation of cash flow from operating activities. The presentation of cash flows from investing activities and financing activities is exactly the same under both methods.

Direct Method

Under the **direct method**, each line item of the accrual-based income statement is converted into cash receipts or cash payments. Recall that under the accrual method of accounting, the timing of revenue and expense recognition may differ from the timing of the related cash flows. Under cash-basis accounting, revenue and expense recognition occur when cash is received or paid. Simply stated, the direct method converts an accrual-basis income statement into a cash-basis income statement.

Figure 2 contains an example of a presentation of operating cash flow for Seagraves Supply Company using the direct method.

Figure 2: Direct Method of Presenting Operating Cash Flow

Seagraves Supply Company *Operating Cash Flow – Direct Method* *For the year ended December 31, 20X7*	
Cash collections from customers	$429,980
Cash paid to suppliers	(265,866)
Cash paid for operating expenses	(124,784)
Cash paid for interest	(4,326)
Cash paid for taxes	(14,956)
Operating cash flow	$20,048

Notice the similarities of the direct method cash flow presentation and an income statement. The direct method begins with cash inflows from customers and then deducts cash outflows for purchases, operating expenses, interest, and taxes.

Indirect Method

Under the **indirect method**, net income is converted to operating cash flow by making adjustments for transactions that affect net income but are not cash transactions. These adjustments include eliminating noncash expenses (e.g., depreciation and amortization), nonoperating items (e.g., gains and losses), and changes in balance sheet accounts resulting from accrual accounting events.

Figure 3 contains an example of a presentation of operating cash flow for Seagraves Supply Company under the indirect method.

©2012 Kaplan, Inc.

Figure 3: Indirect Method of Presenting Operating Cash Flow

Seagraves Supply Company *Operating Cash Flow – Indirect Method* *For the year ended December 31, 20X7*	
Net income	$18,788
Adjustments to reconcile net income to cash flow provided by operating activities:	
Depreciation and amortization	7,996
Deferred income taxes	416
Increase in accounts receivable	(1,220)
Increase in inventory	(20,544)
Decrease in prepaid expenses	494
Increase in accounts payable	13,406
Increase in accrued liabilities	712
Operating cash flow	$20,048

Notice that under the indirect method, the starting point is net income, the "bottom line" of the income statement. Under the direct method, the starting point is the top of the income statement, revenues, adjusted to show cash received from customers. Total cash flow from operating activities is exactly the same under both methods, only the presentation methods differ.

Arguments in Favor of Each Method

The primary advantage of the direct method is that it presents the firm's operating cash receipts and payments, while the indirect method only presents the net result of these receipts and payments. Therefore, the direct method provides more information than the indirect method. This knowledge of past receipts and payments is useful in estimating future operating cash flows.

The main advantage of the indirect method is that it focuses on the differences in net income and operating cash flow. This provides a useful link to the income statement when forecasting future operating cash flow. Analysts forecast net income and then derive operating cash flow by adjusting net income for the differences between accrual accounting and the cash basis of accounting.

Disclosure Requirements

Under U.S. GAAP, a direct method presentation must also disclose the adjustments necessary to reconcile net income to cash flow from operating activities. This disclosure is the same information that is presented in an indirect method cash flow statement. This reconciliation is not required under IFRS.

Under IFRS, payments for interest and taxes must be disclosed separately in the cash flow statement under either method (direct or indirect). Under U.S. GAAP, payments for interest and taxes can be reported in the cash flow statement or disclosed in the footnotes.

LOS 27.e: Describe how the cash flow statement is linked to the income statement and the balance sheet.

CFA® Program Curriculum, Volume 3, page 266

The cash flow statement reconciles the beginning and ending balances of cash over an accounting period. The change in cash is a result of the firm's operating, investing, and financing activities as follows:

	Operating cash flow
+	Investing cash flow
+	Financing cash flow
=	Change in cash balance
+	Beginning cash balance
=	Ending cash balance

With a few exceptions, operating activities relate to the firm's current assets and current liabilities. Investing activities typically relate to the firm's noncurrent assets, and financing activities typically relate to the firm's noncurrent liabilities and equity.

Transactions for which the timing of revenue or expense recognition differs from the receipt or payment of cash are reflected in changes in balance sheet accounts. For example, when revenues (sales) exceed cash collections, the firm has sold items on credit and accounts receivable (an asset) increase. The opposite occurs when customers repay more on their outstanding accounts than the firm extends in new credit: cash collections exceed revenues and accounts receivable decrease. When purchases from suppliers exceed cash payments, accounts payable (a liability) increase. When cash payments exceed purchases, payables decrease.

It is helpful to understand how transactions affect each balance sheet account. For example, accounts receivable are increased by sales and decreased by cash collections. We can summarize this relationship as follows:

	Beginning accounts receivable
+	Sales
–	Cash collections
=	Ending accounts receivable

Knowing three of the four variables, we can solve for the fourth. For example, if beginning accounts receivable are €10,000, ending accounts receivable are €15,000, and sales are €68,000, then cash collections must equal €63,000.

Understanding these interrelationships is not only useful in preparing the cash flow statement, but is also helpful in uncovering accounting shenanigans.

©2012 Kaplan, Inc.

LOS 27.f: Describe the steps in the preparation of direct and indirect cash flow statements, including how cash flows can be computed using income statement and balance sheet data.

CFA® Program Curriculum, Volume 3, page 267

Professor's Note: Throughout the discussion of the direct and indirect methods, remember the following points:

- *CFO is calculated differently, but the result is the same under both methods.*
- *The calculation of CFI and CFF is identical under both methods.*
- *There is an inverse relationship between changes in assets and changes in cash flows. In other words, an increase in an asset account is a use of cash, and a decrease in an asset account is a source of cash.*
- *There is a direct relationship between changes in liabilities and changes in cash flow. In other words, an increase in a liability account is a source of cash, and a decrease in a liability is a use of cash.*
- *Sources of cash are positive numbers (cash inflows) and uses of cash are negative numbers (cash outflows).*

Direct Method

The direct method of presenting a firm's statement of cash flows shows only cash payments and cash receipts over the period. The sum of these inflows and outflows is the company's CFO. The direct method gives the analyst more information than the indirect method. The analyst can see the actual amounts that went to each use of cash and that were received from each source of cash. This information can help the analyst to better understand the firm's performance over time and to forecast future cash flows.

The following are common components of cash flow that appear on a statement of cash flow presented under the direct method:

- Cash collected from customers, typically the main component of CFO.
- Cash used in the production of goods and services (cash inputs).
- Cash operating expenses.
- Cash paid for interest.
- Cash paid for taxes.

Professor's Note: A common "trick" in direct method questions is to provide information on depreciation expense along with other operating cash flow components. When using the direct method, ignore depreciation expense—it's a noncash charge. We'll see later that we do consider depreciation expense in indirect method computations, but we do this solely because depreciation expense and other noncash expenses have been subtracted in calculating net income (our starting point) and need to be added back to get cash flow.

Investing cash flows (CFI) are calculated by examining the change in the gross asset accounts that result from investing activities, such as property, plant, and equipment, intangible assets, and investment securities. Related accumulated depreciation or amortization accounts are ignored since they do not represent cash expenses.

 Professor's Note: In this context, "gross" simply means an amount that is presented on the balance sheet before deducting any accumulated depreciation or amortization.

When calculating cash paid for a new asset, it is necessary to determine whether old assets were sold. If assets were sold during the period, you must use the following formula:

cash paid for new asset = ending gross assets + gross cost of old assets sold – beginning gross assets

 Professor's Note: It may be easier to think in terms of the account reconciliation format discussed earlier. That is, beginning gross assets + cash paid for new assets – gross cost of assets sold = ending gross assets. Given three of the variables, simply solve for the fourth.

When calculating the cash flow from an asset that has been sold, it is necessary to consider any gain or loss from the sale using the following formula:

cash from asset sold = book value of the asset + gain (or – loss) on sale

Financing cash flows (CFF) are determined by measuring the cash flows occurring between the firm and its suppliers of capital. Cash flows between the firm and its creditors result from new borrowings (positive CFF) and debt principal repayments (negative CFF). Note that interest paid is technically a cash flow to creditors, but it is included in CFO under U.S. GAAP. Cash flows between the firm and its shareholders occur when equity is issued, shares are repurchased, or dividends are paid. CFF is the sum of these two measures:

net cash flows from creditors = new borrowings – principal amounts repaid

net cash flows from shareholders = new equity issued – share repurchases – cash dividends paid

Cash dividends paid can be calculated from dividends declared and any changes in dividends payable.

Finally, total cash flow is equal to the sum of CFO, CFI, and CFF. If calculated correctly, the total cash flow will equal the change in cash from one balance sheet to the next.

©2012 Kaplan, Inc.

Indirect Method

Cash flow from operations is presented differently under the indirect method, but the amount of CFO is the same under either method. Cash flow from financing and cash flow from investing are presented in the same way on cash flow statements prepared under both the direct and indirect methods of presenting the statement of cash flows.

Under the indirect method of presenting CFO, we begin with net income and adjust it for differences between accounting items and actual cash receipts and cash disbursements. Depreciation, for example, is deducted in calculating net income, but requires no cash outlay in the current period. Therefore, we must add depreciation (and amortization) to net income for the period in calculating CFO.

Another adjustment to net income on an indirect statement of cash flows is to subtract gains on the disposal of assets. Proceeds from the sale of fixed assets are an investing cash flow. Since gains are a portion of such proceeds, we need to subtract them from net income in calculating CFO under the indirect method. Conversely, a loss would be added back to net income in calculating CFO under the indirect method.

Under the indirect method, we also need to adjust net income for change in balance sheet accounts. If, for example, accounts receivable went up during the period, we know that sales during the period were greater than the cash collected from customers. Since sales were used to calculate net income under the accrual method, we need to reduce net income to reflect the fact that credit sales, rather than cash collected were used in calculating net income.

A change in accounts payable indicates a difference between purchases and the amount paid to suppliers. An increase in accounts payable, for example, results when purchases are greater than cash paid to suppliers. Since purchases were subtracted in calculating net income, we need to add any increase in accounts payable to net income so that CFO reflects the actual cash disbursements for purchases (rather than total purchases).

The steps in calculating CFO under the indirect method can be summarized as follows:

Step 1: Begin with net income.

Step 2: Subtract gains or add losses that resulted from financing or investing cash flows (such as gains from sale of land).

Step 3: Add back all noncash charges to income (such as depreciation and amortization) and subtract all noncash components of revenue.

Step 4: Add or subtract changes to balance sheet operating accounts as follows:
- Increases in the operating asset accounts (uses of cash) are subtracted, while decreases (sources of cash) are added.
- Increases in the operating liability accounts (sources of cash) are added, while decreases (uses of cash) are subtracted.

Example: Statement of cash flows using the indirect method

Use the following balance sheet and income statement to prepare a statement of cash flows under the indirect method.

Income Statement for 20X7

Sales	$100,000
Expense	
Cost of goods sold	40,000
Wages	5,000
Depreciation	7,000
Interest	500
Total expenses	$52,500
Income from continuing operations	$47,500
Gain from sale of land	10,000
Pretax income	57,500
Provision for taxes	20,000
Net income	$37,500
Common dividends declared	$8,500

Balance Sheets for 20X7 and 20X6

	20X7	20X6
Assets		
Current assets		
Cash	$33,000	$9,000
Accounts receivable	10,000	9,000
Inventory	5,000	7,000
Noncurrent assets		
Land	$35,000	$40,000
Gross plant and equipment	85,000	60,000
less: Accumulated depreciation	(16,000)	(9,000)
Net plant and equipment	$69,000	$51,000
Goodwill	10,000	10,000
Total assets	$162,000	$126,000

©2012 Kaplan, Inc.

Liabilities

Current liabilities		
Accounts payable	$9,000	$5,000
Wages payable	4,500	8,000
Interest payable	3,500	3,000
Taxes payable	5,000	4,000
Dividends payable	6,000	1,000
Total current liabilities	28,000	21,000
Noncurrent liabilities		
Bonds	$15,000	$10,000
Deferred tax liability	20,000	15,000
Total liabilities	$63,000	$46,000
Stockholders' equity		
Common stock	$40,000	$50,000
Retained earnings	59,000	30,000
Total equity	$99,000	$80,000
Total liabilities and stockholders' equity	$162,000	$126,000

Any discrepancies between the changes in accounts reported on the balance sheet and those reported in the statement of cash flows are typically due to business combinations and changes in exchange rates.

Answer:

Operating Cash Flow:

Step 1: Start with net income of $37,500.
Step 2: Subtract gain from sale of land of $10,000.
Step 3: Add back noncash charges of depreciation of $7,000.
Step 4: Subtract increases in receivables and inventories and add increases of payables and deferred taxes.

Net income	$37,500
Gain from sale of land	(10,000)
Depreciation	7,000
Subtotal	$34,500
Changes in operating accounts	
Increase in receivables	($1,000)
Decrease in inventories	2,000
Increase in accounts payable	4,000
Decrease in wages payable	(3,500)
Increase in interest payable	500
Increase in taxes payable	1,000
Increase in deferred taxes	5,000
Cash flow from operations	$42,500

Investing cash flow:

In this example, we have two components of investing cash flow: the sale of land and the change in gross plant and equipment (P&E).

cash from sale of land = decrease in asset + gain on sale = $5,000 + $10,000 = $15,000 (source)

  beginning land + land purchased – gross cost of land sold = ending land = $40,000 + $0 – $5,000 = $35,000

Note: If the land had been sold at a loss, we would have subtracted the loss amount from the decrease in land.

P&E purchased = ending gross P&E + gross cost of P&E sold – beginning gross P&E
        = $85,000 + $0 – $60,000 = $25,000 (use)

  beginning gross P&E + P&E purchased – gross cost of P&E sold = ending P&E = $60,000 + $25,000 – $0 = $85,000

Cash from sale of land	$15,000
Purchase of plant and equipment	(25,000)
Cash flow from investments	($10,000)

Financing cash flow:

cash from bond issue = ending bonds payable + bonds repaid – beginning bonds payable = $15,000 + $0 – $10,000 = $5,000 (source)

  beginning bonds payable + bonds issued – bonds repaid = ending bonds payable = $10,000 + $5,000 – $0 = $15,000

cash to reacquire stock = beginning common stock + stock issued – ending common stock = $50,000 + $0 – $40,000 = $10,000 (use, or a net share repurchase of $10,000)

  beginning common stock + stock issued – stock reacquired = ending common stock = $50,000 + $0 – $10,000 = $40,000

cash dividends = – dividend declared + increase in dividends payable
        = –$8,500* + $5,000 = –$3,500 (use)

  beginning dividends payable + dividends declared – dividends paid = ending dividends payable = $1,000 + $8,500 – $3,500 = $6,000

Note: If the dividend declared amount is not provided, you can calculate the amount as follows: dividends declared = beginning retained earnings + net income – ending retained earnings. Here, $30,000 + $37,500 – $59,000 = $8,500.

©2012 Kaplan, Inc.

Sale of bonds	$5,000
Repurchase of stock	(10,000)
Cash dividends	(3,500)
Cash flow from financing	($8,500)

Total cash flow:

Cash flow from operations	$42,500
Cash flow from investments	(10,000)
Cash flow from financing	(8,500)
Total cash flow	$24,000

The total cash flow of $24,000 is equal to the increase in the cash account. The difference between beginning cash and ending cash should be used as a check figure to ensure that the total cash flow calculation is correct.

Both IFRS and U.S. GAAP encourage the use of a statement of cash flows in the direct format. Under U.S. GAAP, a statement of cash flows under the direct method must include footnote disclosure of the indirect method. Most companies however, report cash flows using the indirect method, which requires no additional disclosure. The next LOS illustrates the method an analyst will use to create a statement of cash flows in the direct method format when the company reports using the indirect method.

LOS 27.g: Convert cash flows from the indirect to direct method.

CFA® Program Curriculum, Volume 3, page 267

The only difference between the indirect and direct methods of presentation is in the cash flow from operations (CFO) section. CFO under the direct method can be computed using a combination of the income statement and a statement of cash flows prepared under the indirect method.

There are two major sections in CFO under the direct method: cash inflows (receipts) and cash outflows (payments). We will illustrate the conversion process using some frequently used accounts. Please note that the list below is for illustrative purposes only and is far from all-inclusive of what may be encountered in practice. The general principle here is to adjust each income statement item for its corresponding balance sheet accounts and to eliminate noncash and nonoperating transactions.

Cash collections from customers:

1. Begin with net sales from the income statement.

2. Subtract (add) any increase (decrease) in the accounts receivable balance as reported in the indirect method. If the company has sold more on credit than has been collected from customers, accounts receivable will increase and cash collections will be less than net sales.

3. Add (subtract) an increase (decrease) in unearned revenue. Unearned revenue includes cash advances from customers. Cash received from customers when the goods or services have yet to be delivered is not included in net sales, so the advances must be added to net sales in order to calculate cash collections.

Cash payments to suppliers:

1. Begin with cost of goods sold (COGS) as reported in the income statement.

2. If depreciation and/or amortization have been included in COGS (they increase COGS), these noncash expenses must be added back when computing the cash paid to suppliers.

3. Reduce (increase) COGS by any increase (decrease) in the accounts payable balance as reported in the indirect method. If payables have increased, then more was spent on credit purchases during the period than was paid on existing payables, so cash payments are reduced by the amount of the increase in payables.

4. Add (subtract) any increase (decrease) in the inventory balance as disclosed in the indirect method. Increases in inventory are not included in COGS for the period but still represent the purchase of inputs, so they increase cash paid to suppliers.

5. Subtract an inventory write-off that occurred during the period. An inventory write-off, as a result of applying the lower of cost or market rule, will reduce ending inventory and increase COGS for the period. However, no cash flow is associated with the write-off.

Other items in a direct method cash flow statement follow the same principles. Cash taxes paid, for example, can be derived by starting with income tax expense on the income statement. Adjustment must be made for changes in related balance sheet accounts (deferred tax assets and liabilities, and income taxes payable).

Cash operating expense is equal to selling, general, and administrative expense (SG&A) from the income statement, increased (decreased) for any increase (decrease) in prepaid expenses. Any increase in prepaid expenses is a cash outflow that is not included in SG&A for the current period.

©2012 Kaplan, Inc.

Example: Direct method for computing CFO

Prepare a cash flow statement using the direct method, based on the indirect statement of cash flows, balance sheet, and income statement from the previous example.

Answer:

Professor's Note: There are many ways to think about these calculations and lots of sources and uses and pluses and minuses to keep track of. It's easier if you use a "+" sign for net sales and a "−" sign for cost of goods sold and other cash expenses used as the starting points. Doing so will allow you to consistently follow the rule that an increase in assets or decrease in liabilities is a use of cash and a decrease in assets or an increase in liabilities is a source. We'll use this approach in the answer to the example. Remember, sources are always + and uses are always −.

The calculations that follow include a reconciliation of each account, analyzing the transactions that increase and decrease the account for the period. As previously discussed, this reconciliation is useful in understanding the interrelationships between the balance sheet, income statement, and cash flow statement.

Cash from operations:

Keep track of the balance sheet items used to calculate CFO by marking them off the balance sheet. They will not be needed again when determining CFI and CFF.

cash collections = sales − increase in accounts receivable = $100,000 − $1,000 = $99,000

> beginning receivables + sales − cash collections = ending receivables = $9,000 + $100,000 − $99,000 = $10,000

cash paid to suppliers = −COGS + decrease in inventory + increase in accounts payable = −$40,000 + $2,000 + $4,000 = −$34,000

> beginning inventory + purchases − COGS = ending inventory = $7,000 + $38,000 (not provided) − $40,000 = $5,000

> beginning accounts payable + purchases − cash paid to suppliers = ending accounts payable = $5,000 + $38,000 (not provided) − $34,000 = $9,000

cash wages = −wages − decrease in wages payable = −$5,000 − $3,500 = −$8,500

> beginning wages payable + wages expense − wages paid = ending wages payable = $8,000 + $5,000 − $8,500 = $4,500

cash interest = −interest expense + increase in interest payable = −$500 + $500 = 0

> beginning interest payable + interest expense − interest paid = ending interest payable = $3,000 + $500 − $0 = $3,500

cash taxes = –tax expense + increase in taxes payable + increase in deferred tax liability

= –$20,000 + $1,000 + $5,000 = –$14,000

beginning taxes payable + beginning deferred tax liability + tax expense – taxes paid = ending taxes payable + ending deferred tax liability = $4,000 + $15,000 + $20,000 – $14,000 = $5,000 + $20,000

Cash collections	$99,000
Cash to suppliers	(34,000)
Cash wages	(8,500)
Cash interest	0
Cash taxes	(14,000)
Cash flow from operations	$42,500

LOS 27.h: Analyze and interpret both reported and common-size cash flow statements.

CFA® Program Curriculum, Volume 3, page 279

Major Sources and Uses of Cash

Cash flow analysis begins with an evaluation of the firm's sources and uses of cash from operating, investing, and financing activities. Sources and uses of cash change as the firm moves through its life cycle. For example, when a firm is in the early stages of growth, it may experience negative operating cash flow as it uses cash to finance increases in inventory and receivables. This negative operating cash flow is usually financed externally by issuing debt or equity securities. These sources of financing are not sustainable. Eventually, the firm must begin generating positive operating cash flow or the sources of external capital may no longer be available. Over the long term, successful firms must be able to generate operating cash flows that exceed capital expenditures and provide a return to debt and equity holders.

Operating Cash Flow

An analyst should identify the major determinants of operating cash flow. Positive operating cash flow can be generated by the firm's earnings-related activities. However, positive operating cash flow can also be generated by decreasing noncash working capital, such as liquidating inventory and receivables or increasing payables. Decreasing noncash working capital is not sustainable, since inventories and receivables cannot fall below zero and creditors will not extend credit indefinitely unless payments are made when due.

Operating cash flow also provides a check of the quality of a firm's earnings. A stable relationship of operating cash flow and net income is an indication of quality earnings. (This relationship can also be affected by the business cycle and the firm's life cycle.) Earnings that significantly exceed operating cash flow may be an indication of aggressive (or even improper) accounting choices such as recognizing revenues too soon or delaying the recognition of expenses. The variability of net income and operating cash flow should also be considered.

Investing Cash Flow

The sources and uses of cash from investing activities should be examined. Increasing capital expenditures, a use of cash, is usually an indication of growth. Conversely, a firm may reduce capital expenditures or even sell capital assets in order to save or generate cash. This may result in higher cash outflows in the future as older assets are replaced or growth resumes. As mentioned above, generating operating cash flow that exceeds capital expenditures is a desirable trait.

Financing Cash Flow

The financing activities section of the cash flow statement reveals information about whether the firm is generating cash flow by issuing debt or equity. It also provides information about whether the firm is using cash to repay debt, reacquire stock, or pay dividends. For example, an analyst would certainly want to know if a firm issued debt and used the proceeds to reacquire stock or pay dividends to shareholders.

Common-Size Cash Flow Statement

Like the income statement and balance sheet, common-size analysis can be used to analyze the cash flow statement.

The cash flow statement can be converted to common-size format by expressing each line item as a percentage of revenue. Alternatively, each inflow of cash can be expressed as a percentage of total cash inflows, and each outflow of cash can be expressed as a percentage of total cash outflows.

A revenue based common-size cash flow statement is useful in identifying trends and forecasting future cash flow. Since each line item of the cash flow statement is stated in terms of revenue, once future revenue is forecast, cash flows can be estimated for those items that are tied to revenue.

Example: Common-size cash flow statement analysis

Triple Y Corporation's common-size cash flow statement is shown in the table below. Explain the decrease in Triple Y's total cash flow as a percentage of revenues.

Triple Y Corporation

Cash Flow Statement (Percent of Revenues)

Year	20X9	20X8	20X7
Net income	13.4%	13.4%	13.5%
Depreciation	4.0%	3.9%	3.9%
Accounts receivable	–0.6%	–0.6%	–0.5%
Inventory	–10.3%	–9.2%	–8.8%
Prepaid expenses	0.2%	–0.2%	0.1%
Accrued liabilities	5.5%	5.5%	5.6%
Operating cash flow	12.2%	12.8%	13.8%
Cash from sale of fixed assets	0.7%	0.7%	0.7%
Purchase of plant and equipment	–12.3%	–12.0%	–11.7%
Investing cash flow	–11.6%	–11.3%	–11.0%
Sale of bonds	2.6%	2.5%	2.6%
Cash dividends	–2.1%	–2.1%	–2.1%
Financing cash flow	0.5%	0.4%	0.5%
Total cash flow	1.1%	1.9%	3.3%

Answer:

Operating cash flow has decreased as a percentage of revenues. This appears to be due largely to accumulating inventories. Investing activities, specifically purchases of plant and equipment, have also required an increasing percentage of the firm's cash flow.

LOS 27.i: Calculate and interpret free cash flow to the firm, free cash flow to equity, and performance and coverage cash flow ratios.

CFA® Program Curriculum, Volume 3, page 287

Free cash flow is a measure of cash that is available for discretionary purposes. This is the cash flow that is available once the firm has covered its capital expenditures. This is a fundamental cash flow measure and is often used for valuation. There are several measures of free cash flow. Two of the more common measures are free cash flow to the firm and free cash flow to equity.

Free Cash Flow to the Firm

Free cash flow to the firm (FCFF) is the cash available to all investors, both equity owners and debt holders. FCFF can be calculated by starting with either net income or operating cash flow.

FCFF is calculated from net income as:

$$FCFF = NI + NCC + [Int \times (1 - \text{tax rate})] - FCInv - WCInv$$

where:
NI = net income
NCC = noncash charges (depreciation and amortization)
Int = interest expense
FCInv = fixed capital investment (net capital expenditures)
WCInv = working capital investment

 Professor's Note: Fixed capital investment is cash spent on fixed assets minus cash received from selling fixed assets. It is not the same as CFI, which includes cash flows from fixed investments, investments in securities, and repaid principal from loans made.

Note that interest expense, net of tax, is added back to net income. This is because FCFF is the cash flow available to stockholders and debt holders. Since interest is paid to (and therefore "available to") the debt holders, it must be included in FCFF.

FCFF can also be calculated from operating cash flow as:

$$FCFF = CFO + [Int \times (1 - \text{tax rate})] - FCInv$$

where:
CFO = cash flow from operations
Int = interest expense
FCInv = fixed capital investment (net capital expenditures)

It is not necessary to adjust for noncash charges and changes in working capital when starting with CFO, since they are already reflected in the calculation of CFO. For firms that follow IFRS, it is not necessary to adjust for interest expense that is included as a part of financing activities. Additionally, firms that follow IFRS can report dividends paid as operating activities. In this case, the dividends paid would be added back to CFO. Again, the goal is to calculate the cash flow that is available to the shareholders and debt holders. It is not necessary to adjust dividends for taxes since dividends paid are not tax deductible.

Free Cash Flow to Equity

Free cash flow to equity (FCFE) is the cash flow that would be available for distribution to common shareholders. FCFE can be calculated as follows:

$$FCFE = CFO - FCInv + \text{net borrowing}$$

where:
CFO = cash flow from operations
FCInv = fixed capital investment (net capital expenditures)
net borrowing = debt issued – debt repaid

Professor's Note: If net borrowing is negative (debt repaid exceeds debt issued), we would subtract net borrowing in calculating FCFE.

If firms that follow IFRS have subtracted dividends paid in calculating CFO, dividends must be added back when calculating FCFE.

Other Cash Flow Ratios

Just as with the income statement and balance sheet, the cash flow statement can be analyzed by comparing the cash flows either over time or to those of other firms. Cash flow ratios can be categorized as performance ratios and coverage ratios.

Performance Ratios

The **cash flow-to-revenue ratio** measures the amount of operating cash flow generated for each dollar of revenue.

$$\text{cash flow-to-revenue} = \frac{\text{CFO}}{\text{net revenue}}$$

The **cash return-on-assets ratio** measures the return of operating cash flow attributed to all providers of capital.

$$\text{cash return-on-assets} = \frac{\text{CFO}}{\text{average total assets}}$$

The **cash return-on-equity ratio** measures the return of operating cash flow attributed to shareholders.

$$\text{cash return-on-equity} = \frac{\text{CFO}}{\text{average total equity}}$$

The **cash-to-income ratio** measures the ability to generate cash from firm operations.

$$\text{cash-to-income} = \frac{\text{CFO}}{\text{operating income}}$$

 Professor's Note: A similar ratio, the "cash flow to earnings index" (CFO / net income), appears in our topic review of Financial Reporting Quality.

Cash flow per share is a variation of basic earnings per share measured by using CFO instead of net income.

$$\text{cash flow per share} = \frac{\text{CFO} - \text{preferred dividends}}{\text{weighted average number of common shares}}$$

Note: If common dividends were classified as operating activities under IFRS, they should be added back to CFO for purposes of calculating cash flow per share.

 ©2012 Kaplan, Inc.

Coverage Ratios

The **debt coverage ratio** measures financial risk and leverage.

$$\text{debt coverage} = \frac{\text{CFO}}{\text{total debt}}$$

The **interest coverage ratio** measures the firm's ability to meet its interest obligations.

$$\text{interest coverage} = \frac{\text{CFO + interest paid + taxes paid}}{\text{interest paid}}$$

Note: If interest paid was classified as a financing activity under IFRS, no interest adjustment is necessary.

The **reinvestment ratio** measures the firm's ability to acquire long-term assets with operating cash flow.

$$\text{reinvestment} = \frac{\text{CFO}}{\text{cash paid for long-term assets}}$$

The **debt payment ratio** measures the firm's ability to satisfy long-term debt with operating cash flow.

$$\text{debt payment} = \frac{\text{CFO}}{\text{cash long-term debt repayment}}$$

The **dividend payment ratio** measures the firm's ability to make dividend payments from operating cash flow.

$$\text{dividend payment} = \frac{\text{CFO}}{\text{dividends paid}}$$

The **investing and financing ratio** measures the firm's ability to purchase assets, satisfy debts, and pay dividends.

$$\text{investing and financing} = \frac{\text{CFO}}{\text{cash outflows from investing and financing activities}}$$

KEY CONCEPTS

LOS 27.a

Cash flow from operating activities (CFO) consists of the inflows and outflows of cash resulting from transactions that affect a firm's net income.

Cash flow from investing activities (CFI) consists of the inflows and outflows of cash resulting from the acquisition or disposal of long-term assets and certain investments.

Cash flow from financing activities (CFF) consists of the inflows and outflows of cash resulting from transactions affecting a firm's capital structure, such as issuing or repaying debt and issuing or repurchasing stock.

LOS 27.b

Noncash investing and financing activities, such as taking on debt to the seller of a purchased asset, are not reported in the cash flow statement but must be disclosed in the footnotes or a supplemental schedule.

LOS 27.c

Under U.S. GAAP, dividends paid are financing cash flows. Interest paid, interest received, and dividends received are operating cash flows. All taxes paid are operating cash flows.

Under IFRS, dividends paid and interest paid can be reported as either operating or financing cash flows. Interest received and dividends received can be reported as either operating or investing cash flows. Taxes paid are operating cash flows unless they arise from an investing or financing transaction.

LOS 27.d

Under the direct method of presenting CFO, each line item of the accrual-based income statement is adjusted to get cash receipts or cash payments. The main advantage of the direct method is that it presents clearly the firm's operating cash receipts and payments.

Under the indirect method of presenting CFO, net income is adjusted for transactions that affect net income but do not affect operating cash flow, such as depreciation and gains or losses on asset sales, and for changes in balance sheet items. The main advantage of the indirect method is that it focuses on the differences between net income and operating cash flow. This provides a useful link to the income statement when forecasting future operating cash flow.

LOS 27.e

Operating activities typically relate to the firm's current assets and current liabilities. Investing activities typically relate to noncurrent assets. Financing activities typically relate to noncurrent liabilities and equity.

Timing of revenue or expense recognition that differs from the receipt or payment of cash is reflected in changes in balance sheet accounts.

©2012 Kaplan, Inc.

LOS 27.f

The direct method of calculating CFO is to sum cash inflows and cash outflows for operating activities.

- Cash collections from customers—sales adjusted for changes in receivables and unearned revenue.
- Cash paid for inputs—COGS adjusted for changes in inventory and accounts payable.
- Cash operating expenses—SG&A adjusted for changes in related accrued liabilities or prepaid expenses.
- Cash interest paid—interest expense adjusted for the change in interest payable.
- Cash taxes paid—income tax expense adjusted for changes in taxes payable and changes in deferred tax assets and liabilities.

The indirect method of calculating CFO begins with net income and adjusts it for gains or losses related to investing or financing cash flows, noncash charges to income, and changes in balance sheet operating items.

CFI is calculated by determining the changes in asset accounts that result from investing activities. The cash flow from selling an asset is its book value plus any gain on the sale (or minus any loss on the sale).

CFF is the sum of net cash flows from creditors (new borrowings minus principal repaid) and net cash flows from shareholders (new equity issued minus share repurchases minus cash dividends paid).

LOS 27.g

An indirect cash flow statement can be converted to a direct cash flow statement by adjusting each income statement account for changes in associated balance sheet accounts and by eliminating noncash and non-operating items.

LOS 27.h

An analyst should determine whether a company is generating positive operating cash flow over time that is greater than its capital spending needs and whether the company's accounting policies are causing reported earnings to diverge from operating cash flow.

A common-size cash flow statement shows each item as a percentage of revenue or shows each cash inflow as a percentage of total inflows and each outflow as a percentage of total outflows.

LOS 27.i

Free cash flow to the firm (FCFF) is the cash available to all investors, both equity owners and debt holders.

- FCFF = net income + noncash charges + [interest expense × (1 – tax rate)] – fixed capital investment – working capital investment.
- FCFF = CFO + [interest expense × (1 – tax rate)] – fixed capital investment.

Free cash flow to equity (FCFE) is the cash flow that is available for distribution to the common shareholders after all obligations have been paid.

FCFE = CFO – fixed capital investment + net borrowing

Cash flow performance ratios, such as cash return on equity or on assets, and cash coverage ratios, such as debt coverage or cash interest coverage, provide information about the firm's operating performance and financial strength.

©2012 Kaplan, Inc.

CONCEPT CHECKERS

1. Using the following information, what is the firm's cash flow from operations?

Net income	$120
Decrease in accounts receivable	20
Depreciation	25
Increase in inventory	10
Increase in accounts payable	7
Decrease in wages payable	5
Increase in deferred tax liabilities	15
Profit from the sale of land	2

   A. $158.
   B. $170.
   C. $174.

Assuming U.S. GAAP, use the following data to answer Questions 2 through 4.

Net income	$45
Depreciation	75
Taxes paid	25
Interest paid	5
Dividends paid	10
Cash received from sale of company building	40
Sale of preferred stock	35
Repurchase of common stock	30
Purchase of machinery	20
Issuance of bonds	50
Debt retired through issuance of common stock	45
Paid off long-term bank borrowings	15
Profit on sale of building	20

2. Cash flow from operations is:
   A. $70.
   B. $100.
   C. $120.

3. Cash flow from investing activities is:
    A. –$30.
    B. $20.
    C. $50.

4. Cash flow from financing activities is:
    A. $30.
    B. $55.
    C. $75.

5. Given the following:

Sales	$1,500
Increase in inventory	100
Depreciation	150
Increase in accounts receivable	50
Decrease in accounts payable	70
After-tax profit margin	25%
Gain on sale of machinery	$30

Cash flow from operations is:
A. $115.
B. $275.
C. $375.

6. Which of the following items is *least likely* considered a cash flow from financing activity under U.S. GAAP?
    A. Receipt of cash from the sale of bonds.
    B. Payment of cash for dividends.
    C. Payment of interest on debt.

7. Which of the following would be *least likely* to cause a change in investing cash flow?
    A. The sale of a division of the company.
    B. The purchase of new machinery.
    C. An increase in depreciation expense.

8. Which of the following is *least likely* a change in cash flow from operations under U.S. GAAP?
    A. A decrease in notes payable.
    B. An increase in interest expense.
    C. An increase in accounts payable.

©2012 Kaplan, Inc.

9.   Where are dividends paid to shareholders reported in the cash flow statement under U.S. GAAP and IFRS?

	U.S. GAAP	IFRS
A.	Operating or financing activities	Operating or financing activities
B.	Financing activities	Operating or financing activities
C.	Operating activities	Financing activities

10.   Sales of inventory would be classified as:
A.   operating cash flow.
B.   investing cash flow.
C.   financing cash flow.

11.   Issuing bonds would be classified as:
A.   investing cash flow.
B.   financing cash flow.
C.   no cash flow impact.

12.   Sale of land would be classified as:
A.   operating cash flow.
B.   investing cash flow.
C.   financing cash flow.

13.   Under U.S. GAAP, taxes paid would be classified as:
A.   operating cash flow.
B.   financing cash flow.
C.   no cash flow impact.

14.   An increase in notes payable would be classified as:
A.   investing cash flow.
B.   financing cash flow.
C.   no cash flow impact.

15.   Under U.S. GAAP, interest paid would be classified as:
A.   operating cash flow.
B.   financing cash flow.
C.   no cash flow impact.

16.   Continental Corporation reported sales revenue of $150,000 for the current year. If accounts receivable decreased $10,000 during the year and accounts payable increased $4,000 during the year, cash collections were:
A. $154,000.
B. $160,000.
C. $164,000.

17.   The write-off of obsolete equipment would be classified as:
A.   operating cash flow.
B.   investing cash flow.
C.   no cash flow impact.

18. Sale of obsolete equipment would be classified as:
    A. operating cash flow.
    B. investing cash flow.
    C. financing cash flow.

19. Under IFRS, interest expense would be classified as:
    A. either operating cash flow or financing cash flow.
    B. operating cash flow only.
    C. financing cash flow only.

20. Depreciation expense would be classified as:
    A. operating cash flow.
    B. investing cash flow.
    C. no cash flow impact.

21. Under U.S. GAAP, dividends received from investments would be classified as:
    A. operating cash flow.
    B. investing cash flow.
    C. financing cash flow.

22. Torval, Inc. retires debt securities by issuing equity securities. This is considered a:
    A. cash flow from investing.
    B. cash flow from financing.
    C. noncash transaction.

23. Net income for Monique, Inc. for the year ended December 31, 20X7 was $78,000. Its accounts receivable balance at December 31, 20X7 was $121,000, and this balance was $69,000 at December 31, 20X6. The accounts payable balance at December 31, 20X7 was $72,000 and was $43,000 at December 31, 20X6. Depreciation for 20X7 was $12,000, and there was an unrealized gain of $15,000 included in 20X7 income from the change in value of trading securities. Which of the following amounts represents Monique's cash flow from operations for 20X7?
    A. $52,000.
    B. $67,000.
    C. $82,000.

24. Martin, Inc. had the following transactions during 20X7:
- Purchased new fixed assets for $75,000.
- Converted $70,000 worth of preferred shares to common shares.
- Received cash dividends of $12,000. Paid cash dividends of $21,000.
- Repaid mortgage principal of $17,000.

Assuming Martin follows U.S. GAAP, which of the following amounts represents Martin's cash flows from investing and cash flows from financing in 20X7, respectively?

	Cash flows from investing	Cash flows from financing
A.	($5,000)	($21,000)
B.	($75,000)	($21,000)
C.	($75,000)	($38,000)

©2012 Kaplan, Inc.

25. In preparing a common-size cash flow statement, each cash flow is expressed as a percentage of:
   A. total assets.
   B. total revenues.
   C. the change in cash.

CHALLENGE PROBLEMS

Assuming U.S. GAAP, use the following data to answer Questions A through F.

Balance Sheet Data

Assets	20X7	20X6
Cash	$290	$100
Accounts receivable	250	200
Inventory	740	800
Property, plant, and equipment	920	900
Accumulated depreciation	(290)	(250)
Total assets	$1,910	$1,750
Liabilities and Equity		
Accounts payable	$470	$450
Interest payable	15	10
Dividends payable	10	5
Mortgage	535	585
Bank note	100	0
Common stock	430	400
Retained earnings	350	300
Total liabilities and equity	$1,910	$1,750

Income Statement for the Year 20X7	20X7
Sales	$1,425
Cost of goods sold	1,200
Depreciation	100
Interest Expense	30
Gain on sale of old machine	10
Taxes	45
Net income	$60

Notes:

- Dividends declared to shareholders were $10.
- New common shares were sold at par for $30.
- Fixed assets were sold for $30. Original cost of these assets was $80, and $60 of accumulated depreciation has been charged to their original cost.
- The firm borrowed $100 on a 10-year bank note—the proceeds of the loan were used to pay for new fixed assets.
- Depreciation for the year was $100 (accumulated depreciation up $40 and depreciation on sold assets $60).

A.   Calculate cash flow from operations using the *indirect* method.

B.   Calculate total cash collections, cash paid to suppliers, and other cash expenses.

C.   Calculate cash flow from operations using the *direct* method.

D.   Calculate cash flow from financing, cash flow from investing, and total cash flow.

E.   Calculate free cash flow to equity owners.

F.   What would the impact on investing cash flow and financing cash flow have been if the company leased the new fixed assets instead of borrowing the money and purchasing the equipment?

©2012 Kaplan, Inc.

ANSWERS – CONCEPT CHECKERS

1. **B**   Net income – profits from sale of land + depreciation + decrease in receivables – increase in inventories + increase in accounts payable – decrease in wages payable + increase in deferred tax liabilities = 120 – 2 + 25 + 20 – 10 + 7 – 5 + 15 = $170. Note that the profit on the sale of land should be subtracted from net income because this transaction is classified as investing, not operating.

2. **B**   Net income – profit on sale of building + depreciation = 45 – 20 + 75 = $100. Note that taxes and interest are already deducted in calculating net income, and that the profit on the sale of the building should be subtracted from net income.

3. **B**   Cash from sale of building – purchase of machinery = 40 – 20 = $20.

4. **A**   Sale of preferred stock + issuance of bonds – principal payments on bank borrowings – repurchase of common stock – dividends paid = 35 + 50 – 15 – 30 – 10 = $30. Note that we did not include $45 of debt retired through issuance of common stock since this was a noncash transaction. Knowing how to handle noncash transactions is important.

5. **B**   Net income = $1,500 × 0.25 = $375, and cash flow from operations = net income – gain on sale of machinery + depreciation – increase in accounts receivable – increase in inventory – decrease in accounts payable = 375 – 30 + 150 – 50 – 100 – 70 = $275.

6. **C**   The payment of interest on debt is an *operating* cash flow under U.S. GAAP.

7. **C**   Depreciation does not represent a cash flow. To the extent that it affects the firm's taxes, an increase in depreciation changes operating cash flows, but not investing cash flows.

8. **A**   A change in notes payable is a financing cash flow.

9. **B**   Under U.S. GAAP, dividends paid are reported as financing activities. Under IFRS, dividends paid can be reported as either operating or financing activities.

10. **A**   Sales of inventory would be classified as operating cash flow.

11. **B**   Issuing bonds would be classified as financing cash flow.

12. **B**   Sale of land would be classified as investing cash flow.

13. **A**   Taxes paid are an operating cash flow under U.S. GAAP.

14. **B**   Increase in notes payable would be classified as financing cash flow.

15. **A**   Interest paid is classified as operating cash flow under U.S. GAAP.

16. **B** $150,000 sales + $10,000 decrease in accounts receivable = $160,000 cash collections. The change in accounts payable does not affect cash collections. Accounts payable result from a firm's purchases from its suppliers.

17. **C**   Write-off of obsolete equipment has no cash flow impact.

18. **B**   Sale of obsolete equipment would be classified as investing cash flow.

19. **A**   Under IFRS, interest expense can be classified as either an operating cash flow or financing cash flow.

20. **C**   Depreciation expense would be classified as no cash flow impact.

21. **A**   Dividends received from investments would be classified as operating cash flow under U.S. GAAP.

22. **C**   The exchange of debt securities for equity securities is a noncash transaction.

23. **A**

Net income	$78,000
Depreciation	12,000
Unrealized gain	(15,000)
Increase in accounts receivable	(52,000)
Increase in accounts payable	29,000
Cash flow from operations	$52,000

24. **C**   Purchased new fixed assets for $75,000 – cash <u>outflow</u> from investing
Converted $70,000 of preferred shares to common shares – noncash transaction
Received dividends of $12,000 – cash <u>inflow</u> from operations
Paid dividends of $21,000 – cash <u>outflow</u> from financing
Mortgage repayment of $17,000 – cash <u>outflow</u> from financing
CFI = –75,000
CFF = –21,000 – 17,000 = –$38,000

25. **B**   The cash flow statement can be converted to common-size format by expressing each line item as a percentage of revenue.

ANSWERS – CHALLENGE PROBLEMS

A.   Net income – gain on sale of machinery + depreciation – increase in receivables + decrease in inventories + increase in accounts payable + increase in interest payable = 60 – 10 + 100 – 50 + 60 + 20 + 5 = $185.

B.   Cash collections = sales – increase in receivables = 1,425 – 50 = $1,375.

Cash paid to suppliers = –cost of goods sold + decrease in inventory + increase in accounts payable = –1,200 + 60 + 20 = –$1,120. (Note that the question asks for cash paid to suppliers, so no negative sign is needed in the answer.)

Other cash expenses = –interest expense + increase in interest payable – tax expense = –30 + 5 – 45 = –$70. (Note that the question asks for cash expenses so no negative sign is needed in the answer.)

C.   CFO cash collections – cash to suppliers – other cash expenses = 1,375 – 1,120 – 70 = $185. This must match the answer to Question A, because CFO using the direct method will be the same as CFO under the indirect method.

©2012 Kaplan, Inc.

D.   CFF = sale of stock + new bank note – payment of mortgage – dividends + increase in dividends payable = 30 + 100 – 50 – 10 + 5 = $75.

CFI = sale of fixed assets – new fixed assets = 30 – 100 = –$70. Don't make this difficult. We sold assets for 30 and bought assets for 100. Assets sold had an original cost of 80, so (gross) PP&E only went up by 20.

The easiest way to determine total cash flow is to simply take the change in cash from the balance sheet. However, adding the three components of cash flow will yield 185 – 70 + 75 = $190.

E.   FCFE = cash flow from operations – capital spending + sale of fixed assets + debt issued – debt repaid = $185 – 100 + 30 + 100 – 50 = $165. No adjustment is necessary for interest since FCFE includes debt service.

F.   Investing cash flow would be higher and financing cash flow would be lower. The company would spend less on investments but would not have inflows from the borrowing.

The following is a review of the Financial Reporting and Analysis principles designed to address the learning outcome statements set forth by CFA Institute. This topic is also covered in:

FINANCIAL ANALYSIS TECHNIQUES

EXAM FOCUS

This topic review presents a "tool box" for an analyst. It would be nice if you could calculate all these ratios, but it is imperative that you understand what firm characteristic each one is measuring, and even more important, that you know whether a higher or lower ratio is better in each instance. Different analysts calculate some ratios differently. It would be helpful if analysts were always careful to distinguish between total liabilities, total interest-bearing debt, long-term debt, and creditor and trade debt, but they do not. Some analysts routinely add deferred tax liabilities to debt or exclude goodwill when calculating assets and equity; others do not. Statistical reporting services almost always disclose how each of the ratios they present was calculated. So do not get too tied up in the details of each ratio, but understand what each one represents and what factors would likely lead to significant changes in a particular ratio. The DuPont formulas have been with us a long time and were in the curriculum when I took the exams back in the 1980s. Decomposing ROE into its components is an important analytic technique and it should definitely be in your tool box.

LOS 28.a: Describe tools and techniques used in financial analysis, including their uses and limitations.

CFA® Program Curriculum, Volume 3, page 304

Various tools and techniques are used to convert financial statement data into formats that facilitate analysis. These include ratio analysis, common-size analysis, graphical analysis, and regression analysis.

Ratio Analysis

Ratios are useful tools for expressing relationships among data that can be used for internal comparisons and comparisons across firms. They are often most useful in identifying questions that need to be answered, rather than answering questions directly. Specifically, ratios can be used to do the following:

- Project future earnings and cash flow.
- Evaluate a firm's flexibility (the ability to grow and meet obligations even when unexpected circumstances arise).
- Assess management's performance.
- Evaluate changes in the firm and industry over time.
- Compare the firm with industry competitors.

©2012 Kaplan, Inc.

Analysts must also be aware of the limitations of ratios, including the following:

- Financial ratios are not useful when viewed in isolation. They are only informative when compared to those of other firms or to the company's historical performance.
- Comparisons with other companies are made more difficult by different accounting treatments. This is particularly important when comparing U.S. firms to non-U.S. firms.
- It is difficult to find comparable industry ratios when analyzing companies that operate in multiple industries.
- Conclusions cannot be made by calculating a single ratio. All ratios must be viewed relative to one another.
- Determining the target or comparison value for a ratio is difficult, requiring some range of acceptable values.

It is important to understand that the definitions of ratios can vary widely among the analytical community. For example, some analysts use all liabilities when measuring leverage, while other analysts only use interest-bearing obligations. Consistency is paramount. Analysts must also understand that reasonable values of ratios can differ among industries.

Common-Size Analysis

Common-size statements normalize balance sheets and income statements and allow the analyst to more easily compare performance across firms and for a single firm over time.

- A vertical common-size balance sheet expresses all balance sheet accounts as a percentage of total assets.
- A vertical common-size income statement expresses all income statement items as a percentage of sales.

In addition to comparisons of financial data across firms and time, common-size analysis is appropriate for quickly viewing certain financial ratios. For example, the gross profit margin, operating profit margin, and net profit margin are all clearly indicated within a common-size income statement. Vertical common-size income statement ratios are especially useful for studying trends in costs and profit margins.

$$\text{vertical common-size income statement ratios} = \frac{\text{income statement account}}{\text{sales}}$$

Balance sheet accounts can also be converted to common-size ratios by dividing each balance sheet item by total assets.

$$\text{vertical common-size balance-sheet ratios} = \frac{\text{balance sheet account}}{\text{total assets}}$$

Study Session 8

Example: Constructing common-size statements

The common-size statements in Figure 1 show balance sheet items as percentages of assets, and income statement items as percentages of sales.

- You can convert all asset and liability amounts to their actual values by multiplying the percentages listed below by their total assets of $57,100; $55,798; and $52,071, respectively for 20X6, 20X5, and 20X4 (data is USD millions).
- Also, all income statement items can be converted to their actual values by multiplying the given percentages by total sales, which were $29,723; $29,234; and $22,922, respectively, for 20X6, 20X5, and 20X4.

Figure 1: Vertical Common-Size Balance Sheet and Income Statement

Balance Sheet, fiscal year-end	20X6	20X5	20X4
Assets			
Cash & cash equivalents	0.38%	0.29%	0.37%
Accounts receivable	5.46%	5.61%	6.20%
Inventories	5.92%	5.42%	5.84%
Deferred income taxes	0.89%	0.84%	0.97%
Other current assets	0.41%	0.40%	0.36%
Total current assets	13.06%	12.56%	13.74%
Gross fixed assets	25.31%	23.79%	25.05%
Accumulated depreciation	8.57%	7.46%	6.98%
Net gross fixed assets	16.74%	16.32%	18.06%
Other long-term assets	70.20%	71.12%	68.20%
Total assets	100.00%	100.00%	100.00%
Liabilities			
Accounts payable	3.40%	3.40%	3.79%
Short-term debt	1.00%	2.19%	1.65%
Other current liabilities	8.16%	10.32%	9.14%
Total current liabilities	12.56%	15.91%	14.58%
Long-term debt	18.24%	14.58%	5.18%
Other long-term liabilities	23.96%	27.44%	53.27%
Total liabilities	54.76%	57.92%	73.02%
Preferred equity	0.00%	0.00%	0.00%
Common equity	45.24%	42.08%	26.98%
Total liabilities & equity	100.00%	100.00%	100.00%

©2012 Kaplan, Inc.

Income Statement, fiscal year	20X6	20X5	20X4
Revenues	100.00%	100.00%	100.00%
Cost of goods sold	59.62%	60.09%	60.90%
Gross profit	40.38%	39.91%	39.10%
Selling, general & administrative	16.82%	17.34%	17.84%
Depreciation	2.39%	2.33%	2.18%
Amortization	0.02%	3.29%	2.33%
Other operating expenses	0.58%	0.25%	-0.75%
Operating income	20.57%	16.71%	17.50%
Interest and other debt expense	2.85%	4.92%	2.60%
Income before taxes	17.72%	11.79%	14.90%
Provision for income taxes	6.30%	5.35%	6.17%
Net income	11.42%	6.44%	8.73%

Even a cursory inspection of the income statement in Figure 1 can be quite instructive. Beginning at the bottom, we can see that the profitability of the company has increased nicely in 20X6 after falling slightly in 20X5. We can examine the 20X6 income statement values to find the source of this greatly improved profitability. Cost of goods sold seems to be stable, with an improvement (decrease) in 20X6 of only 0.48%. SG&A was down approximately one-half percent as well.

These improvements from (relative) cost reduction, however, only begin to explain the 5% increase in the net profit margin for 20X6. Improvements in two items, "amortization" and "interest and other debt expense," appear to be the most significant factors in the firm's improved profitability in 20X6. Clearly the analyst must investigate further in both areas to learn whether these improvements represent permanent improvements or whether these items can be expected to return to previous percentage-of-sales levels in the future.

We can also note that interest expense as a percentage of sales was approximately the same in 20X4 and 20X6. We must investigate the reasons for the higher interest costs in 20X5 to determine whether the current level of 2.85% can be expected to continue into the next period. In addition, more than 3% of the 5% increase in net profit margin in 20X6 is due to a decrease in amortization expense. Since this is a noncash expense, the decrease may have no implications for cash flows looking forward.

This discussion should make clear that common-size analysis doesn't tell an analyst the whole story about this company, but can certainly point the analyst in the right direction to find out the circumstances that led to the increase in the net profit margin and to determine the effects, if any, on firm cash flow going forward.

Another way to present financial statement data that is quite useful when analyzing trends over time is a **horizontal common-size balance sheet or income statement**. The divisor here is the first-year values, so they are all standardized to 1.0 by construction. Figure 2 illustrates this approach.

Figure 2: Horizontal Common-Size Balance Sheet Data

	20X4	20X5	20X6
Inventory	1.0	1.1	1.4
Cash and marketable securities	1.0	1.3	1.2
Long-term debt	1.0	1.6	1.8
PP&E (net of depreciation)	1.0	0.9	0.8

Trends in the values of these items, as well as the relative growth in these items, are readily apparent from a horizontal common-size balance sheet.

Professor's Note: We have presented data in Figure 1 with information for the most recent period on the left, and in Figure 2 we have presented the historical values from left to right. Both presentation methods are common, and on the exam you should pay special attention to which method is used in the data presented for any question.

We can view the values in the common-size financial statements as ratios. Net income is shown on the common-size income statement as net income/revenues, which is the net profit margin, and tells the analyst the percentage of each dollar of sales that remains for shareholders after all expenses related to the generation of those sales are deducted. One measure of financial leverage, long-term debt to total assets, can be read directly from the vertical common-size financial statements. Specific ratios commonly used in financial analysis and interpretation of their values are covered in detail in this review.

Graphical Analysis

Graphs can be used to visually present performance comparisons and composition of financial statement elements over time.

A **stacked column graph** (also called a *stacked bar graph*) shows the changes in items from year to year in graphical form. Figure 3 presents such data for a hypothetical corporation.

©2012 Kaplan, Inc.

Figure 3: Stacked Column (Stacked Bar) Graph

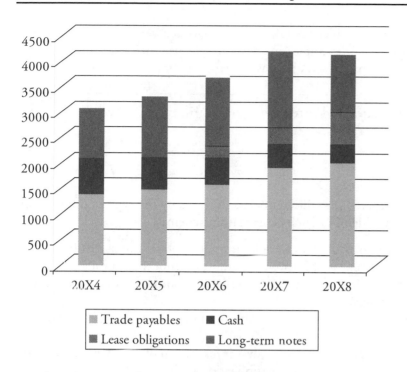

Another alternative for graphic presentation of data is a **line graph**. Figure 4 presents the same data as Figure 3, but as a line graph. The increase in trade payables and the decrease in cash are evident in either format and would alert the analyst to potential liquidity problems that require further investigation and analysis.

Figure 4: Line Graph

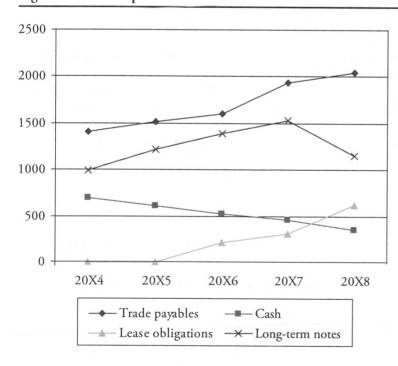

Regression Analysis

Regression analysis can be used to identify relationships between variables. The results are often used for forecasting. For example, an analyst might use the relationship between GDP and sales to prepare a sales forecast.

LOS 28.b: Classify, calculate, and interpret activity, liquidity, solvency, profitability, and valuation ratios.

CFA® Program Curriculum, Volume 3, page 319

Financial ratios can be segregated into different classifications by the type of information about the company they provide. One such classification scheme is:

- **Activity ratios.** This category includes several ratios also referred to asset utilization or turnover ratios (e.g., inventory turnover, receivables turnover, and total assets turnover). They often give indications of how well a firm utilizes various assets such as inventory and fixed assets.
- **Liquidity ratios.** Liquidity here refers to the ability to pay short-term obligations as they come due.
- **Solvency ratios.** Solvency ratios give the analyst information on the firm's financial leverage and ability to meet its longer-term obligations.
- **Profitability ratios.** Profitability ratios provide information on how well the company generates operating profits and net profits from its sales.
- **Valuation ratios.** Sales per share, earnings per share, and price to cash flow per share are examples of ratios used in comparing the relative valuation of companies.

 Professor's Note: We examine valuation ratios in another LOS concerning equity analysis later in this review, and in the Study Session on equity investments.

It should be noted that these categories are not mutually exclusive. An activity ratio such as payables turnover may also provide information about the liquidity of a company, for example. There is no one standard set of ratios for financial analysis. Different analysts use different ratios and different calculation methods for similar ratios. Some ratios are so commonly used that there is very little variation in how they are defined and calculated. We will note some alternative treatments and alternative terms for single ratios as we detail the commonly used ratios in each category.

ACTIVITY RATIOS

Activity ratios (also known as asset utilization ratios or operating efficiency ratios) measure how efficiently the firm is managing its assets.

- A measure of accounts receivable turnover is *receivables turnover:*

$$\text{receivables turnover} = \frac{\text{annual sales}}{\text{average receivables}}$$

©2012 Kaplan, Inc.

Professor's Note: In most cases when a ratio compares a balance sheet account (such as receivables) with an income or cash flow item (such as sales), the balance sheet item will be the average of the account instead of simply the end-of-year balance. Averages are calculated by adding the beginning-of-year account value to the end-of-year account value, then dividing the sum by two.

It is considered desirable to have a receivables turnover figure close to the industry norm.

- The inverse of the receivables turnover times 365 is the *average collection period,* or *days of sales outstanding,* which is the average number of days it takes for the company's customers to pay their bills:

$$\text{days of sales oustanding} = \frac{365}{\text{receivables turnover}}$$

It is considered desirable to have a collection period (and receivables turnover) close to the industry norm. The firm's credit terms are another important benchmark used to interpret this ratio. A collection period that is too high might mean that customers are too slow in paying their bills, which means too much capital is tied up in assets. A collection period that is too low might indicate that the firm's credit policy is too rigorous, which might be hampering sales.

- A measure of a firm's efficiency with respect to its processing and inventory management is *inventory turnover:*

$$\text{inventory turnover} = \frac{\text{cost of goods sold}}{\text{average inventory}}$$

Professor's Note: Pay careful attention to the numerator in the turnover ratios. For inventory turnover, be sure to use cost of goods sold, not sales.

- The inverse of the inventory turnover times 365 is the *average inventory processing period, number of days of inventory,* or *days of inventory on hand:*

$$\text{days of inventory on hand} = \frac{365}{\text{inventory turnover}}$$

As is the case with accounts receivable, it is considered desirable to have days of inventory on hand (and inventory turnover) close to the industry norm. A processing period that is too high might mean that too much capital is tied up in inventory and could mean that the inventory is obsolete. A processing period that is too low might indicate that the firm has inadequate stock on hand, which could hurt sales.

- A measure of the use of trade credit by the firm is the *payables turnover* ratio:

$$\text{payables turnover} = \frac{\text{purchases}}{\text{average trade payables}}$$

Professor's Note: You can use the inventory equation to calculate purchases from the financial statements. Purchases = ending inventory − beginning inventory + cost of goods sold.

- The inverse of the payables turnover ratio multiplied by 365 is the *payables payment period* or *number of days of payables*, which is the average amount of time it takes the company to pay its bills:

$$\text{number of days of payables} = \frac{365}{\text{payables turnover ratio}}$$

Professor's Note: We have shown days calculations for payables, receivables, and inventory based on annual turnover and a 365-day year. If turnover ratios are for a quarter rather than a year, the number of days in the quarter should be divided by the quarterly turnover ratios in order to get the "days" form of these ratios.

- The effectiveness of the firm's use of its total assets to create revenue is measured by its *total asset turnover*:

$$\text{total asset turnover} = \frac{\text{revenue}}{\text{average total assets}}$$

Different types of industries might have considerably different turnover ratios. Manufacturing businesses that are capital-intensive might have asset turnover ratios near one, while retail businesses might have turnover ratios near 10. As was the case with the current asset turnover ratios discussed previously, it is desirable for the total asset turnover ratio to be close to the industry norm. Low asset turnover ratios might mean that the company has too much capital tied up in its asset base. A turnover ratio that is too high might imply that the firm has too few assets for potential sales, or that the asset base is outdated.

- The utilization of fixed assets is measured by the *fixed asset turnover* ratio:

$$\text{fixed asset turnover} = \frac{\text{revenue}}{\text{average net fixed assets}}$$

As was the case with the total asset turnover ratio, it is desirable to have a fixed asset turnover ratio close to the industry norm. Low fixed asset turnover might mean that the company has too much capital tied up in its asset base or is using the assets it has inefficiently. A turnover ratio that is too high might imply that the firm has obsolete equipment, or at a minimum, that the firm will probably have to incur capital expenditures in the near future to increase capacity to support growing revenues. Since "net" here refers to net of accumulated depreciation, firms with more recently acquired assets will typically have lower fixed asset turnover ratios.

©2012 Kaplan, Inc.

- How effectively a company is using its working capital is measured by the *working capital turnover* ratio:

$$\text{working capital turnover} = \frac{\text{revenue}}{\text{average working capital}}$$

Working capital (sometimes called *net* working capital) is current assets minus current liabilities. The working capital turnover ratio gives us information about the utilization of working capital in terms of dollars of sales per dollar of working capital. Some firms may have very low working capital if outstanding payables equal or exceed inventory and receivables. In this case the working capital turnover ratio will be very large, may vary significantly from period to period, and is less informative about changes in the firm's operating efficiency.

LIQUIDITY RATIOS

Liquidity ratios are employed by analysts to determine the firm's ability to pay its short-term liabilities.

- The *current ratio* is the best-known measure of liquidity:

$$\text{current ratio} = \frac{\text{current assets}}{\text{current liabilities}}$$

The higher the current ratio, the more likely it is that the company will be able to pay its short-term bills. A current ratio of less than one means that the company has negative working capital and is probably facing a liquidity crisis. Working capital equals current assets minus current liabilities.

- The *quick ratio* is a more stringent measure of liquidity because it does not include inventories and other assets that might not be very liquid:

$$\text{quick ratio} = \frac{\text{cash + marketable securities + receivables}}{\text{current liabilities}}$$

The higher the quick ratio, the more likely it is that the company will be able to pay its short-term bills. Marketable securities are short-term debt instruments, typically liquid and of good credit quality.

- The most conservative liquidity measure is the *cash ratio:*

$$\text{cash ratio} = \frac{\text{cash + marketable securities}}{\text{current liabilities}}$$

The higher the cash ratio, the more likely it is that the company will be able to pay its short-term bills.

The current, quick, and cash ratios differ only in the assumed liquidity of the current assets that the analyst projects will be used to pay off current liabilities.

- The *defensive interval ratio* is another measure of liquidity that indicates the number of days of average cash expenditures the firm could pay with its current liquid assets:

$$\text{defensive interval} = \frac{\text{cash} + \text{marketable securities} + \text{receivables}}{\text{average daily expenditures}}$$

Expenditures here include cash expenses for costs of goods, SG&A, and research and development. If these items are taken from the income statement, noncash charges such as depreciation should be added back just as in the preparation of a statement of cash flows by the indirect method.

- The *cash conversion cycle* is the length of time it takes to turn the firm's cash investment in inventory back into cash, in the form of collections from the sales of that inventory. The cash conversion cycle is computed from days sales outstanding, days of inventory on hand, and number of days of payables:

$$\text{cash conversion cycle} = \left(\begin{array}{c} \text{days sales} \\ \text{outstanding} \end{array} \right) + \left(\begin{array}{c} \text{days of inventory} \\ \text{on hand} \end{array} \right) - \left(\begin{array}{c} \text{number of days} \\ \text{of payables} \end{array} \right)$$

High cash conversion cycles are considered undesirable. A conversion cycle that is too high implies that the company has an excessive amount of capital investment in the sales process.

SOLVENCY RATIOS

Solvency ratios measure a firm's financial leverage and ability to meet its long-term obligations. Solvency ratios include various **debt ratios** that are based on the balance sheet and **coverage ratios** that are based on the income statement.

- A measure of the firm's use of fixed-cost financing sources is the *debt-to-equity* ratio:

$$\text{debt-to-equity} = \frac{\text{total debt}}{\text{total shareholders' equity}}$$

Increases and decreases in this ratio suggest a greater or lesser reliance on debt as a source of financing.

Total debt is calculated differently by different analysts and different providers of financial information. Here, we will define it as long-term debt plus interest-bearing short-term debt.

Some analysts include the present value of lease obligations and/or non-interest-bearing current liabilities, such as trade payables.

©2012 Kaplan, Inc.

- Another way of looking at the usage of debt is the *debt-to-capital* ratio:

$$\text{debt-to-capital} = \frac{\text{total debt}}{\text{total debt} + \text{total shareholders' equity}}$$

Capital equals all short-term and long-term debt plus preferred stock and equity. Increases and decreases in this ratio suggest a greater or lesser reliance on debt as a source of financing.

- A slightly different way of analyzing debt utilization is the *debt-to-assets* ratio:

$$\text{debt-to-assets} = \frac{\text{total debt}}{\text{total assets}}$$

Increases and decreases in this ratio suggest a greater or lesser reliance on debt as a source of financing.

- Another measure that is used as an indicator of a company's use of debt financing is the *financial leverage* ratio (or leverage ratio):

$$\text{financial leverage} = \frac{\text{average total assets}}{\text{average total equity}}$$

Average here means the average of the values at the beginning and at the end of the period. Greater use of debt financing increases financial leverage and, typically, risk to equity holders and bondholders alike.

- The remaining risk ratios help determine the firm's ability to repay its debt obligations. The first of these is the *interest coverage ratio*:

$$\text{interest coverage} = \frac{\text{earnings before interest and taxes}}{\text{interest payments}}$$

The lower this ratio, the more likely it is that the firm will have difficulty meeting its debt payments.

- A second ratio that is an indicator of a company's ability to meet its obligations is the *fixed charge coverage* ratio:

$$\text{fixed charge coverage} = \frac{\text{earnings before interest and taxes} + \text{lease payments}}{\text{interest payments} + \text{lease payments}}$$

Here, lease payments are added back to operating earnings in the numerator and also added to interest payments in the denominator. Significant lease obligations will reduce this ratio significantly compared to the interest coverage ratio. Fixed charge coverage is the more meaningful measure for companies that lease a large portion of their assets, such as some airlines.

Professor's Note: With all solvency ratios, the analyst must consider the variability of a firm's cash flows when determining the reasonableness of the ratios. Firms with stable cash flows are usually able to carry more debt.

PROFITABILITY RATIOS

Profitability ratios measure the overall performance of the firm relative to revenues, assets, equity, and capital.

* The *net profit margin* is the ratio of net income to revenue:

$$\text{net profit margin} = \frac{\text{net income}}{\text{revenue}}$$

Analysts should be concerned if this ratio is too low. The net profit margin should be based on net income from continuing operations, because analysts should be primarily concerned about future expectations, and below-the-line items such as discontinued operations will not affect the company in the future.

Operating profitability ratios look at how good management is at turning their efforts into profits. Operating ratios compare the top of the income statement (sales) to profits. The different ratios are designed to isolate specific costs.

Know these terms:

gross profits	= net sales – COGS
operating profits	= earnings before interest and taxes = EBIT
net income	= earnings after taxes but before dividends
total capital	= long-term debt + short-term debt + common and preferred equity
total capital	= total assets

Professor's Note: The difference between these two definitions of total capital is working capital liabilities, such as accounts payable. Some analysts consider these liabilities a source of financing for a firm and include them in total capital. Other analysts view total capital as the sum of a firm's debt and equity.

©2012 Kaplan, Inc.

How they relate in the income statement:

	Net sales
–	Cost of goods sold
	Gross profit
–	Operating expenses
	Operating profit (EBIT)
–	Interest
	Earnings before taxes (EBT)
–	Taxes
	Earnings after taxes (EAT)
+/–	Below the line items adjusted for tax
	Net income
–	Preferred dividends
	Income available to common

- The *gross profit margin* is the ratio of gross profit (sales less cost of goods sold) to sales:

$$\text{gross profit margin} = \frac{\text{gross profit}}{\text{revenue}}$$

An analyst should be concerned if this ratio is too low. Gross profit can be increased by raising prices or reducing costs. However, the ability to raise prices may be limited by competition.

- The *operating profit margin* is the ratio of operating profit (gross profit less selling, general, and administrative expenses) to sales. Operating profit is also referred to as earnings before interest and taxes (EBIT):

$$\text{operating profit margin} = \frac{\text{operating income}}{\text{revenue}} \text{ or } \frac{\text{EBIT}}{\text{revenue}}$$

Strictly speaking, EBIT includes some nonoperating items, such as gains on investment. The analyst, as with other ratios with various formulations, must be consistent in his calculation method and know how published ratios are calculated. Analysts should be concerned if this ratio is too low. Some analysts prefer to calculate the operating profit margin by adding back depreciation and any amortization expense to arrive at earnings before interest, taxes, depreciation, and amortization (EBITDA).

- Sometimes profitability is measured using earnings before tax (EBT), which can be calculated by subtracting interest from EBIT or from operating earnings. The *pretax margin* is calculated as:

$$\text{pretax margin} = \frac{\text{EBT}}{\text{revenue}}$$

- Another set of profitability ratios measure profitability relative to funds invested in the company by common stockholders, preferred stockholders, and suppliers of debt financing. The first of these measures is the *return on assets* (ROA). Typically, ROA is calculated using net income:

$$\text{return on assets (ROA)} = \frac{\text{net income}}{\text{average total assets}}$$

This measure is a bit misleading, however, because interest is excluded from net income but total assets include debt as well as equity. Adding interest adjusted for tax back to net income puts the returns to both equity and debt holders in the numerator. The interest expense that should be added back is gross interest expense, not net interest expense (which is gross interest expense less interest income). This results in an alternative calculation for ROA:

$$\text{return on assets (ROA)} = \frac{\text{net income} + \text{interest expense} (1 - \text{tax rate})}{\text{average total assets}}$$

- A measure of return on assets that includes both taxes and interest in the numerator is the *operating return on assets*:

$$\text{operating return on assets} = \frac{\text{operating income}}{\text{average total assets}} \text{ or } \frac{\text{EBIT}}{\text{average total assets}}$$

- The *return on total capital* (ROTC) is the ratio of net income before interest and taxes to total capital:

$$\text{return on total capital} = \frac{\text{EBIT}}{\text{average total capital}}$$

Total capital includes short- and long-term debt, preferred equity, and common equity. Analysts should be concerned if this ratio is too low.

An alternative method for computing ROTC is to include the present value of operating leases on the balance sheet as a fixed asset and as a long-term liability. This adjustment is especially important for firms that are dependent on operating leases as a major form of financing. Calculations related to leasing will be discussed in the next Study Session.

- The *return on equity* (ROE) is the ratio of net income to average total equity (including preferred stock):

$$\text{return on equity} = \frac{\text{net income}}{\text{average total equity}}$$

Analysts should be concerned if this ratio is too low. It is sometimes called return on total equity.

©2012 Kaplan, Inc.

- A similar ratio to the return on equity is the *return on common equity:*

$$\text{return on common equity} = \frac{\text{net income} - \text{preferred dividends}}{\text{average common equity}}$$

$$= \frac{\text{net income available to common}}{\text{average common equity}}$$

This ratio differs from the return on total equity in that it only measures the accounting profits available to, and the capital invested by, common stockholders, instead of common and preferred stockholders. That is why preferred dividends are deducted from net income in the numerator. Analysts should be concerned if this ratio is too low.

The return on common equity is often more thoroughly analyzed using the DuPont decomposition, which is described later in this topic review.

LOS 28.c: Describe the relationships among ratios and evaluate a company using ratio analysis.

CFA® Program Curriculum, Volume 3, page 339

Example: Using ratios to evaluate a company

A balance sheet and income statement for a hypothetical company are shown below for this year and the previous year.

Using the company information provided, calculate the current year ratios. Discuss how these ratios compare with the company's performance last year and with the industry's performance.

Sample Balance Sheet

Year	Current year	Previous year
Assets		
Cash and marketable securities	$105	$95
Receivables	205	195
Inventories	310	290
Total current assets	620	580
Gross property, plant, and equipment	1,800	$1,700
Accumulated depreciation	360	340
Net property, plant, and equipment	1,440	1,360
Total assets	$2,060	$1,940
Liabilities		
Payables	$110	$90
Short-term debt	160	140
Current portion of long-term debt	55	45
Current liabilities	325	$275
Long-term debt	610	$690
Deferred taxes	105	95
Common stock	300	300
Additional paid in capital	400	400
Retained earnings	320	180
Common shareholders equity	1,020	880
Total liabilities and equity	$2,060	$1,940

Sample Income Statement

Year	Current year
Sales	$4,000
Cost of goods sold	3,000
Gross profit	1,000
Operating expenses	650
Operating profit	350
Interest expense	50
Earnings before taxes	300
Taxes	100
Net income	200
Common dividends	60

©2012 Kaplan, Inc.

Financial Ratio Template

	Current Year	Last Year	Industry
Current ratio		2.1	1.5
Quick ratio		1.1	0.9
Days of sales outstanding		18.9	18.0
Inventory turnover		10.7	12.0
Total asset turnover		2.3	2.4
Working capital turnover		14.5	11.8
Gross profit margin		27.4%	29.3%
Net profit margin		5.8%	6.5%
Return on total capital		21.1%	22.4%
Return on common equity		24.1%	19.8%
Debt-to-equity		99.4%	35.7%
Interest coverage		5.9	9.2

Answer:

- current ratio = $\dfrac{\text{current assets}}{\text{current liabilities}}$

$$\text{current ratio} = \frac{620}{325} = 1.9$$

The current ratio indicates lower liquidity levels when compared to last year and more liquidity than the industry average.

- quick ratio = $\dfrac{\text{cash + receivables + marketable securities}}{\text{current liabilities}}$

$$\text{quick ratio} = \frac{(105 + 205)}{325} = 0.95$$

The quick ratio is lower than last year and is in line with the industry average.

- DSO (days of sales outstanding) = $\dfrac{365}{\text{revenue}/\text{average receivables}}$

$$\text{DSO} = \frac{365}{4{,}000 \big/ [(205 + 195)/2]} = 18.25$$

The DSO is a bit lower relative to the company's past performance but slightly higher than the industry average.

- inventory turnover = $\dfrac{\text{cost of goods sold}}{\text{average inventories}}$

$$\text{inventory turnover} = \frac{3{,}000}{(310 + 290)/2} = 10.0$$

Inventory turnover is much lower than last year and the industry average. This suggests that the company is not managing inventory efficiently and may have obsolete stock.

©2012 Kaplan, Inc.

- total asset turnover = $\dfrac{\text{revenue}}{\text{average assets}}$

total asset turnover = $\dfrac{4,000}{(2,060 + 1,940) / 2} = 2.0$

Total asset turnover is slightly lower than last year and the industry average.

- working capital turnover = $\dfrac{\text{revenue}}{\text{average working capital}}$

beginning working capital = 580 – 275 = 305

ending working capital = 620 – 325 = 295

working capital turnover = $\dfrac{4,000}{(305 + 295) / 2} = 13.3$

Working capital turnover is lower than last year, but still above the industry average.

- gross profit margin = $\dfrac{\text{gross profit}}{\text{revenue}}$

gross profit margin = $\dfrac{1,000}{4,000} = 25.0\%$

The gross profit margin is lower than last year and much lower than the industry average.

- net profit margin = $\dfrac{\text{net income}}{\text{revenue}}$

net profit margin = $\dfrac{200}{4,000} = 5.0\%$

The net profit margin is lower than last year and much lower than the industry average.

- return on total capital = $\dfrac{\text{EBIT}}{\text{short- and long-term debt + equity}}$

beginning total capital = 140 + 45 + 690 + 880 = 1,755

ending total capital = 160 + 55 + 610 + 1,020 = 1,845

return on total capital = $\dfrac{350}{(1,755 + 1,845) / 2}$ = 19.4%

The return on total capital is below last year and below the industry average. This suggests a problem stemming from the low asset turnover and low profit margin.

- return on common equity = $\dfrac{\text{net income} - \text{preferred dividends}}{\text{average common equity}}$

return on common equity = $\dfrac{200}{(1,020 + 880) / 2}$ = 21.1%

The return on equity is lower than last year but better than the industry average. The reason it is higher than the industry average is probably because of greater use of leverage.

- debt-to-equity ratio = $\dfrac{\text{total debt}}{\text{total equity}}$

debt-to-equity ratio = $\dfrac{610 + 160 + 55}{1,020}$ = 80.9%

Note that preferred equity would be included in the denominator if there were any, and that we have included short-term debt and the current portion of long-term debt in calculating total (interest-bearing) debt.

The debt-to-equity ratio is lower than last year but still much higher than the industry average. This suggests the company is trying to get its debt level more in line with the industry.

- interest coverage = $\dfrac{\text{EBIT}}{\text{interest payments}}$

interest coverage = $\dfrac{350}{50}$ = 7.0

The interest coverage is better than last year but still worse than the industry average. This, along with the slip in profit margin and return on assets, might cause some concern.

©2012 Kaplan, Inc.

LOS 28.d: Demonstrate the application of DuPont analysis of return on equity, and calculate and interpret the effects of changes in its components.

CFA® Program Curriculum, Volume 3, page 342

The **DuPont system of analysis** is an approach that can be used to analyze return on equity (ROE). It uses basic algebra to break down ROE into a function of different ratios, so an analyst can see the impact of leverage, profit margins, and turnover on shareholder returns. There are two variants of the DuPont system: The original three-part approach and the extended five-part system.

For the **original approach**, start with ROE defined as:

$$\text{return on equity} = \left(\frac{\text{net income}}{\text{equity}}\right)$$

Average or year-end values for equity can be used. Multiplying ROE by (revenue/revenue) and rearranging terms produces:

$$\text{return on equity} = \left(\frac{\text{net income}}{\text{revenue}}\right)\left(\frac{\text{revenue}}{\text{equity}}\right)$$

The first term is the profit margin, and the second term is the equity turnover:

$$\text{return on equity} = \left(\frac{\text{net profit}}{\text{margin}}\right)\left(\frac{\text{equity}}{\text{turnover}}\right)$$

We can expand this further by multiplying these terms by (assets/assets), and rearranging terms:

$$\text{return on equity} = \left(\frac{\text{net income}}{\text{sales}}\right)\left(\frac{\text{sales}}{\text{assets}}\right)\left(\frac{\text{assets}}{\text{equity}}\right)$$

 Professor's Note: For the exam, remember that (net income / sales) × (sales / assets) = return on assets (ROA).

The first term is still the profit margin, the second term is now asset turnover, and the third term is a financial leverage ratio that will increase as the use of debt financing increases:

$$\text{return on equity} = \left(\frac{\text{net profit}}{\text{margin}}\right)\left(\frac{\text{asset}}{\text{turnover}}\right)\left(\frac{\text{leverage}}{\text{ratio}}\right)$$

 Professor's Note: The leverage ratio is sometimes called the "equity multiplier."

This is the original DuPont equation. It is arguably the most important equation in ratio analysis, since it breaks down a very important ratio (ROE) into three key components. If ROE is relatively low, it must be that at least one of the following is true: The company has a poor profit margin, the company has poor asset turnover, or the firm has too little leverage.

Professor's Note: Often candidates get confused and think the DuPont method is a way to calculate ROE. While you can calculate ROE given the components of either the original or extended DuPont equations, this isn't necessary if you have the financial statements. If you have net income and equity, you can calculate ROE. The DuPont method is a way to decompose ROE, to better see what changes are driving the changes in ROE.

Example: Decomposition of ROE with original DuPont

Staret, Inc. has maintained a stable and relatively high ROE of approximately 18% over the last three years. Use traditional DuPont analysis to decompose this ROE into its three components and comment on trends in company performance.

Staret, Inc. Selected Balance Sheet and Income Statement Items (Millions)

Year	20X3	20X4	20X5
Net Income	21.5	22.3	21.9
Sales	305	350	410
Equity	119	124	126
Assets	230	290	350

Answer:

ROE 20X3: 21.5 / 119 = 18.1%

20X4: 22.3 / 124 = 18.0%

20X5: 21.9 / 126 = 17.4%

DuPont 20X3: 7.0% × 1.33 × 1.93

20X4: 6.4% × 1.21 × 2.34

20X5: 5.3% × 1.17 × 2.78

(some rounding in values)

While the ROE has dropped only slightly, both the total asset turnover and the net profit margin have declined. The effects of declining net margins and turnover on ROE have been offset by a significant increase in leverage. The analyst should be concerned about the net margin and find out what combination of pricing pressure and/or increasing expenses have caused this. Also, the analyst must note that the company has become more risky due to increased debt financing.

©2012 Kaplan, Inc.

Example: Computing ROE using original DuPont

A company has a net profit margin of 4%, asset turnover of 2.0, and a debt-to-assets ratio of 60%. What is the ROE?

Answer:

Debt-to-assets = 60%, which means equity to assets is 40%; this implies assets to equity (the leverage ratio) is 1 / 0.4 = 2.5

$$\text{ROE} = \left(\frac{\text{net profit}}{\text{margin}}\right)\left(\frac{\text{total asset}}{\text{turnover}}\right)\left(\frac{\text{assets}}{\text{equity}}\right) = (0.04)(2.00)(2.50) = 0.20, \text{ or } 20\%$$

The **extended (5-way) DuPont equation** takes the net profit margin and breaks it down further.

$$\text{ROE} = \left(\frac{\text{net income}}{\text{EBT}}\right)\left(\frac{\text{EBT}}{\text{EBIT}}\right)\left(\frac{\text{EBIT}}{\text{revenue}}\right)\left(\frac{\text{revenue}}{\text{total assets}}\right)\left(\frac{\text{total assets}}{\text{total equity}}\right)$$

Note that the first term in the 3-part DuPont equation, net profit margin, has been decomposed into three terms:

$\dfrac{\text{net income}}{\text{EBT}}$ is called the *tax burden* and is equal to $(1 - \text{tax rate})$.

$\dfrac{\text{EBT}}{\text{EBIT}}$ is called the *interest burden.*

$\dfrac{\text{EBIT}}{\text{revenue}}$ is called the *EBIT margin.*

We then have:

$$\text{ROE} = \left(\frac{\text{tax}}{\text{burden}}\right)\left(\frac{\text{interest}}{\text{burden}}\right)\left(\frac{\text{EBIT}}{\text{margin}}\right)\left(\frac{\text{asset}}{\text{turnover}}\right)\left(\frac{\text{financial}}{\text{leverage}}\right)$$

An increase in interest expense as proportion of EBIT will increase the interest burden (i.e., decrease the interest burden ratio). Increases in either the tax burden or the interest burden (i.e., decreases in the ratios) will tend to decrease ROE.

EBIT in the second two expressions can be replaced by operating earnings. In this case, we have the operating margin rather than the EBIT margin. The interest burden term would then show the effects of nonoperating income as well as the effect of interest expense.

Note that in general, high profit margins, leverage, and asset turnover will lead to high levels of ROE. However, this version of the formula shows that more leverage *does not always* lead to higher ROE. As leverage rises, so does the interest burden. Hence, the positive effects of leverage can be offset by the higher interest payments that accompany more debt. Note that higher taxes will always lead to lower levels of ROE.

Example: Extended DuPont analysis

An analyst has gathered data from two companies in the same industry. Calculate the ROE for both companies and use the extended DuPont analysis to explain the critical factors that account for the differences in the two companies' ROEs.

Selected Income and Balance Sheet Data

	Company A	Company B
Revenues	$500	$900
EBIT	35	100
Interest expense	5	0
EBT	30	100
Taxes	10	40
Net income	20	60
Total assets	250	300
Total debt	100	50
Owners' equity	$150	$250

Answer:

EBIT = EBIT / revenue
   Company A: EBIT margin = 35 / 500 = 7.0%
   Company B: EBIT margin = 100 / 900 = 11.1%

asset turnover = revenue / assets
   Company A: asset turnover = 500 / 250 = 2.0
   Company B: asset turnover = 900 / 300 = 3.0

interest burden = EBT / EBIT
   Company A: interest burden = 30 / 35 = 85.7%
   Company B: interest burden = 100 / 100 = 1

financial leverage = assets / equity
   Company A: financial leverage = 250 / 150 = 1.67
   Company B: financial leverage = 300 / 250 = 1.2

tax burden = net income / EBT
   Company A: tax burden = 20 / 30 = 66.7%
   Company B: tax burden = 60 / 100 = 60.0%

Company A: ROE = $0.667 \times 0.857 \times 0.07 \times 2.0 \times 1.67 = 13.4\%$

Company B: ROE = $0.608 \times 1.0 \times 0.111 \times 3.0 \times 1.2 = 24\%$

©2012 Kaplan, Inc.

Company B has a higher tax burden but a lower interest burden (a lower ratio indicates a higher burden). Company B has better EBIT margins and better asset utilization (perhaps management of inventory, receivables, or payables, or a lower cost basis in its fixed assets due to their age), and less leverage. Its higher EBIT margins and asset turnover are the main factors leading to its significantly higher ROE, which it achieves with less leverage than Company A.

LOS 28.e: Calculate and interpret ratios used in equity analysis, credit analysis, and segment analysis.

CFA® Program Curriculum, Volume 3, page 347

Valuation ratios are used in analysis for investment in common equity. The most widely used valuation ratio is the *price-to-earnings* (P/E) ratio, the ratio of the current market price of a share of stock divided by the company's earnings per share. Related measures based on price per share are the *price-to-cash flow*, the *price-to-sales*, and the *price-to-book value* ratios.

 Professor's Note: The use of the above valuation ratios is covered in detail in the Study Session on equity securities.

Per-share valuation measures include *earnings per share* (EPS). *Basic EPS* is net income available to common divided by the weighted average number of common shares outstanding.

Diluted EPS is a "what if" value. It is calculated to be the lowest possible EPS that could have been reported if all firm securities that can be converted into common stock, and that would decrease basic EPS if they had been, were converted. That is, if all dilutive securities had been converted. Potentially dilutive securities include convertible debt and convertible preferred stock, as well as options and warrants issued by the company. The numerator of diluted EPS is increased by the after-tax interest savings on any dilutive debt securities and by the dividends on any dilutive convertible preferred stock. The denominator is increased by the common shares that would result from conversion or exchange of dilutive securities into common shares.

 Professor's Note: Refer back to our topic review of Understanding Income Statements for details and examples of how to calculate basic and diluted EPS.

Other per-share measures include *cash flow per share, EBIT per share,* and *EBITDA per share*. Per share measures are not comparable because the number of outstanding shares differ among firms. For example, assume Firm A and Firm B both report net income of $100. If Firm A has 100 shares outstanding, its EPS is $1 per share. If Firm B has 20 shares outstanding, its EPS is $5 per share.

Dividends

Dividends are declared on a per-common-share basis. Total dividends on a firm-wide basis are referred to as *dividends declared*. Neither EPS nor net income is reduced by the payment of common stock dividends. Net income minus dividends declared is retained earnings, the earnings that are used to grow the corporation rather than being distributed to equity holders. The proportion of a firm's net income that is retained to fund growth is an important determinant of the firm's *sustainable growth rate*.

To estimate the sustainable growth rate for a firm, the rate of return on resources is measured as the return on equity capital, or the ROE. The proportion of earnings reinvested is known as the *retention rate* (RR).

- The formula for the sustainable growth rate, which is how fast the firm can grow without additional external equity issues while holding leverage constant, is:

$$g = RR \times ROE$$

- The calculation of the retention rate is:

$$\text{retention rate} = \frac{\text{net income available to common} - \text{dividends declared}}{\text{net income available to common}}$$

$$= 1 - \text{dividend payout ratio}$$

where:

$$\text{dividend payout ratio} = \frac{\text{dividends declared}}{\text{net income available to common}}$$

Example: Calculating sustainable growth

The following figure provides data for three companies.

Growth Analysis Data

Company	A	B	C
Earnings per share	$3.00	$4.00	$5.00
Dividends per share	1.50	1.00	2.00
Return on equity	14%	12%	10%

Calculate the sustainable growth rate for each company.

Answer:

RR = 1 – (dividends / earnings)

Company A: RR = 1 – (1.50 / 3.00) = 0.500
Company B: RR = 1 – (1.00 / 4.00) = 0.750
Company C: RR = 1 – (2.00 / 5.00) = 0.600

g = RR × ROE

Company A: g = 0.500 × 14% = 7.0%
Company B: g = 0.750 × 12% = 9.0%
Company C: g = 0.600 × 10% = 6.0%

Some ratios have specific applications in certain industries.

Net income per employee and *sales per employee* are used in the analysis and valuation of service and consulting companies.

Growth in same-store sales is used in the restaurant and retail industries to indicate growth without the effects of new locations that have been opened. It is a measure of how well the firm is doing at attracting and keeping existing customers and, in the case of locations with overlapping markets, may indicate that new locations are taking customers from existing ones.

Sales per square foot is another metric commonly used in the retail industry.

Business Risk

The standard deviation of revenue, standard deviation of operating income, and the standard deviation of net income are all indicators of the variation in and the uncertainty about a firm's performance. Since they all depend on the size of the firm to a great extent, analysts employ a size-adjusted measure of variation. The **coefficient of variation** for a variable is its standard deviation divided by its expected value.

 Professor's Note: We saw this before as a measure of portfolio risk in Quantitative Methods.

Certainly, different industries have different levels of uncertainty about revenues, expenses, taxes, and nonoperating items. Comparing coefficients of variation for a firm across time, or among a firm and its peers, can aid the analyst in assessing both the relative and absolute degree of risk a firm faces in generating income for its investors.

$$\text{CV sales} = \frac{\text{standard deviation of sales}}{\text{mean sales}}$$

$$\text{CV operating income} = \frac{\text{standard deviation of operating income}}{\text{mean operating income}}$$

$$\text{CV net income} = \frac{\text{standard deviation of net income}}{\text{mean net income}}$$

Banks, insurance companies, and other financial firms carry their own challenges for analysts. Part of the challenge is to understand the commonly used terms and the ratios they represent.

Capital adequacy typically refers to the ratio of some dollar measure of the risk, both operational and financial, of the firm to its equity capital. Other measures of capital are also used. A common measure of capital risk is *value-at-risk*, which is an estimate of the dollar size of the loss that a firm will exceed only some specific percent of the time, over a specific period of time.

Banks are subject to minimum *reserve requirements*. Their ratios of various liabilities to their central bank reserves must be above the minimums. The ratio of a bank's liquid assets to certain liabilities is called the *liquid asset requirement.*

The performance of financial companies that lend funds is often summarized as the *net interest margin,* which is simply interest income divided by the firm's interest-earning assets.

Credit Analysis

Credit analysis is based on many of the ratios that we have already covered in this review. In assessing a company's ability to service and repay its debt, analysts use interest coverage ratios (calculated with EBIT or EBITDA), return on capital, and debt-to-assets ratios. Other ratios focus on various measures of cash flow to total debt.

Ratios have been used to analyze and predict firm bankruptcies. Altman (2000)[1] developed a Z-score that is useful in predicting firm bankruptcies (a low score indicates high probability of failure). The predictive model was based on a firm's working capital to assets, retained earnings to assets, EBIT to assets, market to book value of a share of stock, and revenues to assets.

Segment Analysis

A **business segment** is a portion of a larger company that accounts for more than 10% of the company's revenues or assets, and is distinguishable from the company's other lines of business in terms of the risk and return characteristics of the segment. **Geographic segments** are also identified when they meet the size criterion above and the geographic

---

1. Edward I. Altman, "Predicting Financial Distress of Companies: Revisiting the Z-Score and Zeta® Models," July 2000.

©2012 Kaplan, Inc.

unit has a business environment that is different from that of other segments or the remainder of the company's business.

Both U.S. GAAP and IFRS require companies to report segment data, but the required disclosure items are only a subset of the required disclosures for the company as a whole. Nonetheless, an analyst can prepare a more detailed analysis and forecast by examining the performance of business or geographic segments separately. Segment profit margins, asset utilization (turnover), and return on assets can be very useful in gaining a clear picture of a firm's overall operations. For forecasting, growth rates of segment revenues and profits can be used to estimate future sales and profits and to determine the changes in company characteristics over time.

Figure 5 illustrates how Boeing broke down its results into business segments in its 2010 annual report (source: Boeing.com).

Figure 5: Boeing, Inc. Segment Reporting

(Dollars in millions) Year ended December 31	2010	2009	2008
Revenues:			
Commercial Airplanes	$31,834	$34,051	$28,263
Boeing Defense, Space & Security:			
Boeing Military Aircraft	14,238	14,304	13,445
Network & Space Systems	9,455	10,877	11,346
Global Services & Support	8,250	8,480	7,256
Total Boeing Defense, Space & Security	31,943	33,661	32,047
Boeing Capital Corporation	639	660	703
Other segment	138	165	567
Unallocated items and eliminations	(248)	(256)	(671)
Total revenues	$64,306	$68,281	$60,909
Earnings/(loss) from operations:			
Commercial Airplanes	$ 3,006	$ (583)	$ 1,186
Boeing Defense, Space & Security:			
Boeing Military Aircraft	1,258	1,528	1,294
Network & Space Systems	711	839	1,034
Global Services & Support	906	932	904
Total Boeing Defense, Space & Security	2,875	3,299	3,232
Boeing Capital Corporation	152	126	162
Other segment	(327)	(152)	(307)
Unallocated items and eliminations	(735)	(594)	(323)
Earnings from operations	4,971	2,096	3,950
Other income/(expense), net	52	(26)	247
Interest and debt expense	(516)	(339)	(202)
Earnings before income taxes	4,507	1,731	3,995
Income tax expense	(1,196)	(396)	(1,341)
Net earnings from continuing operations	3,311	1,335	2,654
Net (loss)/gain on disposal of discontinued operations, net of taxes of $2, $13 and ($10)	(4)	(23)	18
Net earnings	$3,307	$ 1,312	$ 2,672

Study Session 8

LOS 28.f: Describe how ratio analysis and other techniques can be used to model and forecast earnings.

CFA® Program Curriculum, Volume 3, page 358

Ratio analysis can be used in preparing pro forma financial statements that provide estimates of financial statement items for one or more future periods. The preparation of pro forma financial statements and related forecasts is covered in some detail in the Study Session on corporate finance. Here, some examples will suffice.

A forecast of financial results that begins with an estimate of a firm's next-period revenues might use the most recent COGS, or an average of COGS, from a common-size income statement. On a common-size income statement, COGS is calculated as a percentage of revenue. If the analyst has no reason to believe that COGS in relation to sales will change for the next period, the COGS percentage from a common-size income statement can be used in constructing a pro forma income statement for the next period based on the estimate of sales.

Similarly, the analyst may believe that certain ratios will remain the same or change in one direction or the other for the next period. In the absence of any information indicating a change, an analyst may choose to incorporate the operating profit margin from the prior period into a pro forma income statement for the next period. Beginning with an estimate of next-period sales, the estimated operating profit margin can be used to forecast operating profits for the next period.

Rather than point estimates of sales and net and operating margins, the analyst may examine possible changes in order to create a range of possible values for key financial variables.

Three methods of examining the variability of financial outcomes around point estimates are: *sensitivity analysis, scenario analysis*, and *simulation*. Sensitivity analysis is based on "what if" questions such as: What will be the effect on net income if sales increase by 3% rather than the estimated 5%? Scenario analysis is based on specific scenarios (a specific set of outcomes for key variables) and will also yield a range of values for financial statement items. Simulation is a technique in which probability distributions for key variables are selected and a computer is used to generate a distribution of values for outcomes based on repeated random selection of values for the key variables.

©2012 Kaplan, Inc.

KEY CONCEPTS

LOS 28.a
Ratios can be used to project earnings and future cash flow, evaluate a firm's flexibility, assess management's performance, evaluate changes in the firm and industry over time, and compare the firm with industry competitors.

Vertical common-size data are stated as a percentage of sales for income statements or as a percentage of total assets for balance sheets. Horizontal common-size data present each item as a percentage of its value in a base year.

Ratio analysis has limitations. Ratios are not useful when viewed in isolation and require adjustments when different companies use different accounting treatments. Comparable ratios may be hard to find for companies that operate in multiple industries. Ratios must be analyzed relative to one another, and determining the range of acceptable values for a ratio can be difficult.

LOS 28.b
Activity ratios indicate how well a firm uses its assets. They include receivables turnover, days of sales outstanding, inventory turnover, days of inventory on hand, payables turnover, payables payment period, and turnover ratios for total assets, fixed assets, and working capital.

Liquidity ratios indicate a firm's ability to meet its short-term obligations. They include the current, quick, and cash ratios, the defensive interval, and the cash conversion cycle.

Solvency ratios indicate a firm's ability to meet its long-term obligations. They include the debt-to-equity, debt-to-capital, debt-to-assets, financial leverage, interest coverage, and fixed charge coverage ratios.

Profitability ratios indicate how well a firm generates operating income and net income. They include net, gross, and operating profit margins, pretax margin, return on assets, operating return on assets, return on total capital, return on total equity, and return on common equity.

Valuation ratios are used to compare the relative values of stocks. They include earnings per share and price-to-earnings, price-to-sales, price-to-book value, and price-to-cash-flow ratios.

LOS 28.c
An analyst should use an appropriate combination of different ratios to evaluate a company over time and relative to comparable companies. The interpretation of an increase in ROE, for example, may be quite different for a firm that has significantly increased its financial leverage compared to one that has maintained or decreased its financial leverage.

LOS 28.d
Basic DuPont equation:

$$ROE = \left(\frac{\text{net income}}{\text{sales}}\right)\left(\frac{\text{sales}}{\text{assets}}\right)\left(\frac{\text{assets}}{\text{equity}}\right)$$

Extended DuPont equation:

$$ROE = \left(\frac{\text{net income}}{\text{EBT}}\right)\left(\frac{\text{EBT}}{\text{EBIT}}\right)\left(\frac{\text{EBIT}}{\text{revenue}}\right)\left(\frac{\text{revenue}}{\text{total assets}}\right)\left(\frac{\text{total assets}}{\text{total equity}}\right)$$

LOS 28.e
Ratios used in equity analysis include price-to-earnings, price-to-cash flow, price-to-sales, and price-to-book value ratios, and basic and diluted earnings per share. Other ratios are relevant to specific industries such as retail and financial services.

Credit analysis emphasizes interest coverage ratios, return on capital, debt-to-assets ratios, and cash flow to total debt.

Firms are required to report some items for significant business and geographic segments. Profitability, leverage, and turnover ratios by segment can give the analyst a better understanding of the performance of the overall business.

LOS 28.f
Ratio analysis in conjunction with other techniques can be used to construct pro forma financial statements based on a forecast of sales growth and assumptions about the relation of changes in key income statement and balance sheet items to growth of sales.

©2012 Kaplan, Inc.

CONCEPT CHECKERS

1. To study trends in a firm's cost of goods sold (COGS), the analyst should standardize the cost of goods sold numbers to a common-sized basis by dividing COGS by:
   A. assets.
   B. sales.
   C. net income.

2. Which of the following is *least likely* a limitation of financial ratios?
   A. Data on comparable firms are difficult to acquire.
   B. Determining the target or comparison value for a ratio requires judgment.
   C. Different accounting treatments require the analyst to adjust the data before comparing ratios.

3. An analyst who is interested in a company's long-term solvency would *most likely* examine the:
   A. return on total capital.
   B. defensive interval ratio.
   C. fixed charge coverage ratio.

4. RGB, Inc.'s purchases during the year were $100,000. The balance sheet shows an average accounts payable balance of $12,000. RGB's payables payment period is *closest* to:
   A. 37 days.
   B. 44 days.
   C. 52 days.

5. RGB, Inc. has a gross profit of $45,000 on sales of $150,000. The balance sheet shows average total assets of $75,000 with an average inventory balance of $15,000. RGB's total asset turnover and inventory turnover are *closest* to:

	Asset turnover	Inventory turnover
A.	7.00 times	2.00 times
B.	2.00 times	7.00 times
C.	0.50 times	0.33 times

6. If RGB, Inc. has annual sales of $100,000, average accounts payable of $30,000, and average accounts receivable of $25,000, RGB's receivables turnover and average collection period are *closest* to:

	Receivables turnover	Average collection period
A.	2.1 times	174 days
B.	3.3 times	111 days
C.	4.0 times	91 days

Study Session 8

7. A company's current ratio is 1.9. If some of the accounts payable are paid off from the cash account, the:
    A. numerator would decrease by a greater percentage than the denominator, resulting in a lower current ratio.
    B. denominator would decrease by a greater percentage than the numerator, resulting in a higher current ratio.
    C. numerator and denominator would decrease proportionally, leaving the current ratio unchanged.

8. A company's quick ratio is 1.2. If inventory were purchased for cash, the:
    A. numerator would decrease more than the denominator, resulting in a lower quick ratio.
    B. denominator would decrease more than the numerator, resulting in a higher current ratio.
    C. numerator and denominator would decrease proportionally, leaving the current ratio unchanged.

9. All other things held constant, which of the following transactions will increase a firm's current ratio if the ratio is greater than one?
    A. Accounts receivable are collected and the funds received are deposited in the firm's cash account.
    B. Fixed assets are purchased from the cash account.
    C. Accounts payable are paid with funds from the cash account.

10. RGB, Inc.'s receivable turnover is ten times, the inventory turnover is five times, and the payables turnover is nine times. RGB's cash conversion cycle is *closest* to:
    A. 69 days.
    B. 104 days.
    C. 150 days.

11. RGB, Inc.'s income statement shows sales of $1,000, cost of goods sold of $400, pre-interest operating expense of $300, and interest expense of $100. RGB's interest coverage ratio is *closest* to:
    A. 2 times.
    B. 3 times.
    C. 4 times.

12. Return on equity using the traditional DuPont formula equals:
    A. (net profit margin) (interest component) (solvency ratio).
    B. (net profit margin) (total asset turnover) (tax retention rate).
    C. (net profit margin) (total asset turnover) (financial leverage multiplier).

13. RGB, Inc. has a net profit margin of 12%, a total asset turnover of 1.2 times, and a financial leverage multiplier of 1.2 times. RGB's return on equity is *closest* to:
    A. 12.0%.
    B. 14.2%.
    C. 17.3%.

©2012 Kaplan, Inc.

14. Use the following information for RGB, Inc.:
    - EBIT / revenue = 10%
    - Tax retention rate = 60%
    - Revenue / assets = 1.8 times
    - Current ratio = 2 times
    - EBT / EBIT = 0.9 times
    - Assets / equity = 1.9 times

    RGB, Inc.'s return on equity is *closest* to:
    A. 10.5%.
    B. 14.0%.
    C. 18.5%.

15. Which of the following equations *least accurately* represents return on equity?
    A. (net profit margin)(equity turnover).
    B. (net profit margin)(total asset turnover)(assets / equity).
    C. (ROA)(interest burden)(tax retention rate).

16. Paragon Co. has an operating profit margin (EBIT / revenue) of 11%; an asset turnover ratio of 1.2; a financial leverage multiplier of 1.5 times; an average tax rate of 35%; and an interest burden of 0.7. Paragon's return on equity is *closest* to:
    A. 9%.
    B. 10%.
    C. 11%.

17. A firm has a dividend payout ratio of 40%, a net profit margin of 10%, an asset turnover of 0.9 times, and a financial leverage multiplier of 1.2 times. The firm's sustainable growth rate is *closest* to:
    A. 4.3%.
    B. 6.5%.
    C. 8.0%.

18. An analyst who needs to model and forecast a company's earnings for the next three years would be *least likely* to:
    A. assume that key financial ratios will remain unchanged for the forecast period.
    B. use common-size financial statements to estimate expenses as a percentage of net income.
    C. examine the variability of the predicted outcomes by performing a sensitivity or scenario analysis.

CHALLENGE PROBLEMS

A. The following table lists partial financial statement data for Alpha Company:

Alpha Company

Sales	$5,000
Cost of goods sold	2,500
Average	
Inventories	$600
Accounts receivable	450
Working capital	750
Cash	200
Accounts payable	500
Fixed assets	4,750
Total assets	$6,000
Annual purchases	$2,400

Calculate the following ratios for Alpha Company:
- Inventory turnover.
- Days of inventory on hand.
- Receivables turnover.
- Days of sales outstanding.
- Payables turnover.
- Number of days of payables.
- Cash conversion cycle.

©2012 Kaplan, Inc.

Use the following information for problems B through E.

Beta Co. has a loan covenant requiring it to maintain a current ratio of 1.5 or better. As Beta approaches year-end, current assets are $20 million ($1 million in cash, $9 million in accounts receivable, and $10 million in inventory) and current liabilities are $13.5 million.

B.   Calculate Beta's current ratio and quick ratio.

C.   Which of the following transactions would Beta Co. *most likely* enter to meet its loan covenant?

    •   Sell $1 million in inventory and deposit the proceeds in the company's checking account.

    •   Borrow $1 million short term and deposit the funds in their checking account.

    •   Sell $1 million in inventory and pay off some of its short-term creditors.

D.   If Beta sells $2 million in inventory on credit, how will this affect its current ratio?

E.   If Beta sells $1 million in inventory and pays off accounts payable, how will this affect its quick ratio?

ANSWERS – CONCEPT CHECKERS

1. **B**   With a vertical common-size income statement, all income statement accounts are divided by sales.

2. **A**   Company and industry data are widely available from numerous private and public sources. The other statements describe limitations of financial ratios.

3. **C**   Fixed charge coverage is a solvency ratio. Return on total capital is a measure of profitability and the defensive interval ratio is a liquidity measure.

4. **B**   payables turnover = (purchases / avg. AP) = 100 / 12 = 8.33
    payables payment period = 365 / 8.33 = 43.8 days

5. **B**   total asset turnover = (sales / total assets) = 150 / 75 = 2 times

    inventory turnover = (COGS / avg. inventory) = (150 – 45) / 15 = 7 times

6. **C**   receivables turnover = (S / avg. AR) = 100 / 25 = 4

    average collection period = 365 / 4 = 91.25 days

7. **B**   Current ratio = (cash + AR + inv) / AP. If cash and AP decrease by the same amount and the current ratio is greater than 1, then the denominator falls faster (in percentage terms) than the numerator, and the current ratio increases.

8. **A**   Quick ratio = (cash + AR) / AP. If cash decreases, the quick ratio will also decrease. The denominator is unchanged.

9. **C**   Current ratio = current assets / current liabilities. If CR is > 1, then if CA and CL both fall, the overall ratio will increase.

10. **A**   (365 / 10 + 365 / 5 – 365 / 9) = 69 days

11. **B**   Interest coverage ratio = EBIT / I = (1,000 – 400 – 300) / 100 = 3 times

12. **C**   This is the correct formula for the three-ratio DuPont model for ROE.

13. **C**   return on equity = $\left(\dfrac{\text{net income}}{\text{sales}}\right)\left(\dfrac{\text{sales}}{\text{assets}}\right)\left(\dfrac{\text{assets}}{\text{equity}}\right)$ = (0.12)(1.2)(1.2) = 0.1728 = 17.28%

14. **C**   Tax burden = (1 – tax rate) = tax retention rate = 0.6.

    ROE = 0.6 × 0.9 × 0.1 × 1.8 × 1.9 = 0.1847 = 18.47%.

15. **C**   (ROA)(interest burden)(tax retention rate) is not one of the DuPont models for calculating ROE.

16. **A**   Tax burden = 1 – 0.35 = 0.65.

    ROE = 0.65 × 0.7 × 0.11 × 1.2 × 1.5 = 0.0901.

©2012 Kaplan, Inc.

17. **B**   g = (retention rate)(ROE)

ROE = net profit margin × asset turnover × equity multiplier = (0.1)(0.9)(1.2) = 0.108

g = (1 − 0.4)(0.108) = 6.5%

18. **B**   An earnings forecast model would typically estimate expenses as a percentage of sales.

ANSWERS – CHALLENGE PROBLEMS

A.   inventory turnover = COGS / avg. inventory = 2500 / 600 = 4.167 times

days of inventory on hand = 365 / inventory turnover = 365 / 4.167 = 87.6 days

receivables turnover = sales / avg. account receivable = 5,000 / 450 = 11.11 times

days of sales outstanding = 365 / receivables turnover = 365 / 11.11 = 32.85 days

payables turnover = purchases / avg. payables = 2,400 / 500 = 4.8 times

number of days of payables = 365 / payables turnover = 365 / 4.8 = 76 days

cash conversion cycle = days of inventory on hand + days of sales outstanding − number of days of payables

= 33 + 88 − 76 = 45 days

B.   current ratio – current assets / current liabilities

= [(1 + 9 + 10) / 13.5] = 20 / 13.5 = 1.48 times

Quick ratio = (cash + marketable securities + receivables) / current liabilities

= (1 + 9) / 13.5 = 10 / 13.5 = 0.74 times

C.   Selling $1 million in inventory and pay off some of its short-term creditors would increase the current ratio: (20 − 1) / (13.5 − 1) = 19 / 12.5 = 1.52.

Selling $1 million in inventory and depositing the proceeds in the company's checking account would leave the ratio unchanged: (20 + 1 − 1) / 13.5 = 1.48. Borrowing $1 million short term and depositing the funds in their checking account would decrease the current ratio: (20 + 1) / (13.5 + 1) = 21 / 14.5 = 1.45.

D.   If Beta sells the inventory at a profit, receivables increase by more than inventory decreases, and current assets increase. If Beta sells the inventory for its carrying value, inventory decreases and receivables increase by the same amount, and current assets are unchanged.

E.   QR = (cash + AR) / AP. AP will decrease without any change to the numerator, thus increasing the overall ratio.

The following is a review of the Financial Reporting and Analysis principles designed to address the learning outcome statements set forth by CFA Institute. This topic is also covered in:

INVENTORIES

EXAM FOCUS

This topic review discusses the different inventory cost flow methods: FIFO, LIFO, and weighted average cost. You must understand how to calculate COGS, ending inventory, and gross profit under each of these methods. Also, you must understand the effects of each method on a firm's liquidity, profitability, activity, and solvency ratios. Be able to apply the appropriate inventory valuation method under IFRS (lower of cost or net realizable value) and U.S. GAAP (lower of cost or market), and calculate inventory losses and loss reversals, if allowed. Finally, be able to evaluate a firm's effectiveness in managing its inventory.

INTRODUCTION TO INVENTORY ACCOUNTING

Merchandising firms, such as wholesalers and retailers, purchase inventory that is ready for sale. In this case, inventory is reported in one account on the balance sheet. Manufacturing firms normally report inventory using three separate accounts: raw materials, work-in-process, and finished goods.

Cost of goods sold (COGS), also referred to as cost of sales (COS) under IFRS, is related to the beginning balance of inventory, purchases, and the ending balance of inventory. The relationship is summarized in the following equation:

COGS = beginning inventory + purchases − ending inventory

This equation can be rearranged to solve for any of the four variables:

purchases = ending inventory − beginning inventory + COGS

beginning inventory = COGS − purchases + ending inventory

ending inventory = beginning inventory + purchases − COGS

> *Professor's Note: Many candidates find the inventory equation easiest to remember in this last form. If you start with beginning inventory, add the goods that came in (purchases), and subtract the goods that went out (COGS), the result must be ending inventory.*

LOS 29.a: Distinguish between costs included in inventories and costs recognized as expenses in the period in which they are incurred.

CFA® Program Curriculum, Volume 3, page 374

Cost is the basis for most inventory valuation. The main issue involves determining the amounts that should be included in cost.

©2012 Kaplan, Inc.

The costs included in inventory are similar under IFRS and U.S. GAAP. These costs, known as **product costs**, are capitalized in the Inventories account on the balance sheet and include:

- Purchase cost less trade discounts and rebates.
- Conversion costs including labor and overhead.
- Other costs necessary to bring the inventory to its present location and condition.

By capitalizing inventory cost as an asset, expense recognition is delayed until the inventory is sold and revenue is recognized.

Not all inventory costs are capitalized; some costs are expensed in the period incurred. These costs, known as **period costs**, include:

- Abnormal waste of materials, labor, or overhead.
- Storage costs (unless required as part of production).
- Administrative overhead.
- Selling costs.

Example: Costs included in inventory

Vindaloo Company manufactures a single product. The following information was taken from the company's production and cost records last year:

Units produced	5,000
Raw materials	$15,000
Conversion cost for finished goods	$20,000
Freight-in to plant	$800
Storage cost for finished goods	$500
Abnormal waste	$100
Freight-out to customers	$1,100

Assuming no abnormal waste is included in conversion cost, calculate the capitalized cost of one unit.

Answer:

Capitalized inventory cost includes the raw materials cost, conversion cost, and freight-in to plant, as follows:

Raw materials	$15,000	
Conversion cost	$20,000	
Freight-in to plant	$800	
Total capitalized cost	$35,800	
Units produced	5,000	
Capitalized cost per unit	$7.16	($35,800 / 5,000 units)

The storage cost, abnormal waste, and the freight-out to customers are expensed as incurred.

LOS 29.b: Describe different inventory valuation methods (cost formulas).

CFA® Program Curriculum, Volume 3, page 375

If the cost of inventory remains constant over time, determining the firm's COGS and ending inventory is simple. To compute COGS, simply multiply the number of units sold by the cost per unit. Similarly, to compute ending inventory, multiply the number of units remaining by the cost per unit.

However, it is likely that the cost of purchasing or producing inventory will change over time. As a result, firms must select a cost flow method (known as the *cost flow assumption* under U.S. GAAP and *cost flow formula* under IFRS) to allocate the inventory cost to the income statement (COGS) and the balance sheet (ending inventory).

Under IFRS, the permissible methods are:

- Specific identification.
- First-in, first-out.
- Weighted average cost.

U.S. GAAP permits these same cost flow methods, as well as the last-in, first-out (LIFO) method. LIFO is not allowed under IFRS.

A firm can use one or more of the inventory cost flow methods. However, the firm must employ the same cost flow method for inventories of similar nature and use.

Under the **specific identification** method, each unit sold is matched with the unit's actual cost. Specific identification is appropriate when inventory items are not interchangeable and is commonly used by firms with a small number of costly and easily distinguishable items such as jewelry. Specific identification is also appropriate for special orders or projects outside a firm's normal course of business.

Under the **first-in, first-out** (FIFO) method, the first item purchased is assumed to be the first item sold. The advantage of FIFO is that ending inventory is valued based on the most recent purchases, arguably the best approximation of current cost. Conversely, FIFO COGS is based on the earliest purchase costs. In an inflationary environment, COGS will be understated compared to current cost. As a result, earnings will be overstated.

Under the **last-in, first-out** (LIFO) method, the item purchased most recently is assumed to be the first item sold. In an inflationary environment, LIFO COGS will be higher than FIFO COGS, and earnings will be lower. Lower earnings translate into lower income taxes, which increase cash flow. Under LIFO, ending inventory on the balance sheet is valued using the earliest costs. Therefore, in an inflationary environment, LIFO ending inventory is less than current cost.

 Professor's Note: The income tax advantages of using LIFO explain its popularity among U.S. firms. The tax savings result in the peculiar situation where lower reported earnings are associated with higher cash flow from operations.

©2012 Kaplan, Inc.

Weighted average cost is a simple and objective method. The average cost per unit of inventory is computed by dividing the total cost of goods available for sale (beginning inventory + purchases) by the total quantity available for sale. To compute COGS, the average cost per unit is multiplied by the number of units sold. Similarly, to compute ending inventory, the average cost per unit is multiplied by the number of units that remain.

During inflationary or deflationary periods, the weighted average cost method will produce an inventory value between those produced by FIFO and LIFO.

Figure 1: Inventory Cost Flow Comparison

Method	Assumption	Cost of Goods Sold Consists of...	Ending Inventory Consists of...
FIFO (U.S. and IFRS)	The items first purchased are the first to be sold.	first purchased	most recent purchases
LIFO (U.S. only)	The items last purchased are the first to be sold.	last purchased	earliest purchases
Weighted average cost (U.S. and IFRS)	Items sold are a mix of purchases.	average cost of all items	average cost of all items

LOS 29.c: Calculate cost of sales and ending inventory using different inventory valuation methods and explain the impact of the inventory valuation method choice on gross profit.

CFA® Program Curriculum, Volume 3, page 377

The following example demonstrates how to calculate COGS and ending inventory using the FIFO, LIFO, and weighted average cost flow methods.

Example: Inventory cost flow methods

Use the inventory data in the following figure to calculate the cost of goods sold and ending inventory under the FIFO, LIFO, and weighted average cost methods.

Inventory Data

January 1 (beginning inventory)	2 units @ $2 per unit =	$4
January 7 purchase	3 units @ $3 per unit =	$9
January 19 purchase	5 units @ $5 per unit =	$25
Cost of goods available	10 units	$38
Units sold during January	7 units	

Answer:

FIFO cost of goods sold. Value the seven units sold at the unit cost of the first units purchased. Start with the earliest units purchased and work down, as illustrated in the following figure.

FIFO COGS Calculation

From beginning inventory	2 units @ $2 per unit =	$4
From first purchase	3 units @ $3 per unit =	$9
From second purchase	2 units @ $5 per unit =	$10
FIFO cost of goods sold	7 units	$23
Ending inventory	3 units @$5 =	$15

LIFO cost of goods sold. Value the seven units sold at the unit cost of the last units purchased. Start with the most recently purchased units and work up, as illustrated in the following figure.

LIFO COGS Calculation

From second purchase	5 units @ $5 per unit =	$25
From first purchase	2 units @ $3 per unit =	$6
LIFO cost of goods sold	7 units	$31
Ending inventory	2 units @$2 + 1 unit @$3 =	$7

Average cost of goods sold. Value the seven units sold at the average unit cost of goods available.

Weighted Average COGS Calculation

Average unit cost	$38 / 10 =	$3.80 per unit
Weighted average cost of goods sold	7 units @ $3.80 per unit =	$26.60
Ending inventory	3 units @ $3.80 per unit =	$11.40

Summary

Inventory system	COGS	Ending Inventory
FIFO	$23.00	$15.00
LIFO	$31.00	$7.00
Average Cost	$26.60	$11.40

Note that prices and inventory levels were rising over the period and that purchases during the period were the same for all cost flow methods.

©2012 Kaplan, Inc.

During inflationary periods and with stable or increasing inventory quantities, LIFO COGS is higher than FIFO COGS. This is because the last units purchased have a higher cost than the first units purchased. Under LIFO, the more costly last units purchased are assumed to be the first units sold (to COGS). Of course, higher COGS under LIFO will result in lower gross profit and net income compared to FIFO.

Using similar logic, we can see that LIFO ending inventory is lower than FIFO ending inventory because under LIFO, ending inventory is valued using older, lower costs.

During deflationary periods and stable or increasing inventory quantities, the cost flow effects of using LIFO and FIFO will be reversed; that is, LIFO COGS will be lower and LIFO ending inventory will be higher. This makes sense because the most recent lower-cost purchases are assumed to be sold first under LIFO, and the units in ending inventory are assumed to be the earliest purchases with higher costs.

Consider the diagram in Figure 2 to help visualize the FIFO-LIFO difference during periods of rising prices and growing inventory levels.

Figure 2: LIFO and FIFO Diagram—Rising Prices and Growing Inventory Balances

INVENTORY IN

INVENTORY OUT

FIFO Inventory

FIFO COGS

LIFO COGS

LIFO Inv

FIFO = Big Inventory
CR = CA/CL – Big
WC = CA – CL = Big

LIFO = Small Inventory
CR = CA/CL = Small
WC = CA – CL = Small

INVENTORY OUT

INVENTORY IN

FIFO Income Stmt
SALES – COGS (Small)
Net Income (Big)

Higher Taxes
Lower Cash Flows

LIFO Income Stmt
SALES – COGS (Big)
Net Income (Small)

Lower Taxes
Higher Cash Flows

Remember, it's not the older or newer physical inventory units that are reported in the income statement and balance sheet; rather, it is the *costs* that are assigned to the units sold and to the units remaining in inventory.

Professor's Note: Be able to describe the effects of LIFO and FIFO, assuming inflation, in your sleep. When prices are falling, the effects are simply reversed. When you are finished with this review, take the time to look at these graphs and relationships again to solidify the concepts in your mind.

LOS 29.d: Calculate and compare cost of sales, gross profit, and ending inventory using perpetual and periodic inventory systems.

CFA® Program Curriculum, Volume 3, page 379

Firms account for changes in inventory using either a periodic or perpetual system. In a **periodic inventory system**, inventory values and COGS are determined at the end of the accounting period. No detailed records of inventory are maintained; rather, inventory acquired during the period is reported in a Purchases account. At the end of the period, purchases are added to beginning inventory to arrive at cost of goods available for sale. To calculate COGS, ending inventory is subtracted from goods available for sale.

In a **perpetual inventory system**, inventory values and COGS are updated continuously. Inventory purchased and sold is recorded directly in inventory when the transactions occur. Thus, a Purchases account is not necessary.

For the FIFO and specific identification methods, ending inventory values and COGS are the same whether a periodic or perpetual system is used. However, periodic and perpetual inventory systems can produce different values for inventory and COGS under the LIFO and weighted average cost methods.

The following example illustrates the differences.

Example: Periodic vs. perpetual inventory system

Our earlier cost flow illustration was actually an example of a periodic system. Accordingly, we waited until the end of January to calculate COGS and ending inventory. Now assume the purchases and sales occurred as follows:

January 1 (beginning inventory)	2 units @ $2 per unit
January 7 purchase	3 units @ $3 per unit
January 12 sale	4 units
January 19 purchase	5 units @ $5 per unit
January 29 sale	3 units

Recalculate COGS and ending inventory under the FIFO and LIFO cost flow methods using a perpetual inventory system.

Answer:

In the case of FIFO, ending inventory and COGS will be the same as with the periodic system illustrated in the earlier example.

FIFO Perpetual System

The January 12 sale of 4 units consists of:

Units	From		Cost
2	Jan 1 beginning inventory	2 units × $2 =	$4
2	Jan 7 purchase	2 units × $3 =	$6
			$10

The January 29 sale of 3 units consists of:

Units	From		Cost
1	Jan 7 purchase	1 unit × $3 =	$3
2	Jan 19 purchase	2 units × $5 =	$10
			$13

Total FIFO COGS for January			$23

January ending inventory consists of:

Units	From		Cost
3	Jan 19 purchase	3 units × $5 =	$15

FIFO COGS and ending inventory are the same whether a perpetual or periodic system is used because the first-in (and therefore the first-out) values are the same regardless of subsequent purchases.

In the case of LIFO, COGS and ending inventory under a periodic system will be different from those calculated under a perpetual system. In our earlier example, LIFO COGS and ending inventory for January were $31 and $7, respectively, using a periodic system. Using a perpetual system, LIFO COGS and ending inventory are $26 and $12.

LIFO Perpetual System

The January 12 sale of 4 units consists of:

Units	From		Cost
3	Jan 7 purchase	3 units × $3 =	$9
1	Jan 1 purchase	1 units × $2 =	$2
			$11

The January 29 sale of 3 units consists of:

Units	From		Cost
3	Jan 19 purchase	3 units × $5 =	$15

Total LIFO COGS for January			$26

January ending inventory consists of:

Units	From		Cost
1	Jan 1 beginning inventory	1 units × $2 =	$2
2	Jan 19 purchase	2 units × $5 =	$10
LIFO ending inventory for January			$12

A periodic system matches the total purchases for the month with the total withdrawals of inventory units for the month. Conversely, a perpetual system matches each unit withdrawn with the immediately preceding purchases.

Summary

Inventory System	FIFO COGS	LIFO COGS	FIFO Inventory	LIFO Inventory
Periodic	$23	$31	$15	$7
Perpetual	$23	$26	$15	$12

Notice the relationship of higher COGS under LIFO and lower ending inventory under LIFO (assuming inflation) still holds whether the firm uses a periodic or perpetual inventory system. The point of this example is that under a perpetual system, LIFO COGS and ending inventory will differ from those calculated under a periodic system.

LOS 29.e: Compare and contrast cost of sales, ending inventory, and gross profit using different inventory valuation methods.

CFA® Program Curriculum, Volume 3, page 381

During periods of stable prices, all three cost flow methods will yield the same results for inventory, COGS, and gross profit. During periods of trending prices (up or down), different cost flow methods may result in significant differences in these items.

 Professor's Note: The presumption in this section is that inventory quantities are stable or increasing.

©2012 Kaplan, Inc.

Ending inventory. When prices are rising or falling, FIFO provides the most useful measure of ending inventory. This is a critical point. Recall that FIFO inventory is made up of the most recent purchases. These purchase costs can be viewed as a better approximation of current cost, and thus a better approximation of economic value. LIFO inventory, by contrast, is based on older costs that may differ significantly from current economic value.

Cost of goods sold. Changing prices can also produce significant differences between COGS under LIFO and FIFO. Recall that LIFO COGS is based on the most recent purchases. As a result, when prices are rising, LIFO COGS will be higher than FIFO COGS. When prices are falling, LIFO COGS will be lower than FIFO COGS. Because LIFO COGS is based on the most recent purchases, LIFO produces a better approximation of current cost in the income statement.

When prices are changing, the weighted average cost method will produce values of COGS and ending inventory between those of FIFO and LIFO.

Gross profit. Because COGS is subtracted from revenue in calculating gross profit, gross profit is also affected by the choice of cost flow method. Assuming inflation, higher COGS under LIFO will result in lower gross profit. In fact, all profitability measures (gross profit, operating profit, income before taxes, and net income) will be affected by the choice of cost flow method.

Figure 3: Effects of Inventory Valuation Methods

	FIFO	*LIFO*
Cost of sales	Lower	Higher
Ending inventory	Higher	Lower
Gross profit	Higher	Lower

Note: Assumes increasing prices and stable or increasing inventory levels.

LOS 29.f: Describe the measurement of inventory at the lower of cost and net realisable value.

CFA® Program Curriculum, Volume 3, page 381

Under IFRS, inventory is reported on the balance sheet at the lower of cost or net realizable value. **Net realizable value** is equal to the expected sales price less the estimated selling costs and completion costs. If net realizable value is less than the balance sheet value of inventory, the inventory is "written down" to net realizable value and the loss is recognized in the income statement. If there is a subsequent recovery in value, the inventory can be "written up" and the gain is recognized in the income statement by reducing COGS by the amount of the recovery. Because inventory is valued at the lower of cost or net realizable value, inventory cannot be written up by more than it was previously written down.

Professor's Note: The writedown, or subsequent write-up, of inventory is usually accomplished through the use of a valuation allowance account. A valuation allowance account is a contra-asset account, similar to accumulated depreciation. By using a valuation allowance account, the firm is able to separate the original cost of inventory from the carrying value of the inventory.

Under U.S. GAAP, inventory is reported on the balance sheet at the **lower of cost or market**. Market is usually equal to replacement cost, but cannot be greater than net realizable value (NRV) or less than NRV minus a normal profit margin. If replacement cost exceeds NRV, then market is NRV. If replacement cost is less than NRV minus a normal profit margin, then market is NRV minus a normal profit margin.

Professor's Note: Think of lower of cost or market, where "market" cannot be outside a range of values. The range is from net realizable value minus a normal profit margin, to net realizable value. So the size of the range is the normal profit margin. "Net" means sales price less selling and completion costs.

If cost exceeds market, the inventory is written down to market on the balance sheet and a loss is recognized in the income statement. The market value becomes the new cost basis. If there is a subsequent recovery in value, no write-up is allowed under U.S. GAAP.

Example: Inventory writedown

Zoom, Inc. sells digital cameras. Per-unit cost information pertaining to Zoom's inventory is as follows:

Original cost	$210
Estimated selling price	$225
Estimated selling costs	$22
Net realizable value	$203
Replacement cost	$197
Normal profit margin	$12

What are the per-unit carrying values of Zoom's inventory under IFRS and under U.S. GAAP?

©2012 Kaplan, Inc.

Answer:

Under IFRS, inventory is reported on the balance sheet at the lower of cost or net realizable value. Since original cost of $210 exceeds net realizable value ($225 − $22 = $203), the inventory is written down to the net realizable value of $203 and a $7 loss ($203 net realizable value − $210 original cost) is reported in the income statement.

Under U.S. GAAP, inventory is reported at the lower of cost or market. In this case, market is equal to replacement cost of $197, since net realizable value of $203 is greater than replacement cost, and net realizable value minus a normal profit margin ($203 − $12 = $191) is less than replacement cost. Since original cost exceeds market (replacement cost), the inventory is written down to $197 and a $13 loss ($197 replacement cost − $210 original cost) is reported in the income statement.

Example: Inventory write-up

Assume that in the year after the writedown in the previous example, net realizable value and replacement cost both increase by $10. What is the impact of the recovery under IFRS and under U.S. GAAP?

Answer:

Under IFRS, Zoom will write up inventory to $210 per unit and recognize a $7 gain in its income statement. The write-up (gain) is limited to the original writedown of $7. The carrying value cannot exceed original cost.

Under U.S. GAAP, no write-up is allowed. The per-unit carrying value will remain at $197. Zoom will simply recognize higher profit when the inventory is sold.

Recall that LIFO ending inventory is based on older, lower costs (assuming inflation) than under FIFO. Because cost is the basis for determining whether an impairment has occurred, LIFO firms are less likely to recognize inventory writedowns than firms using FIFO or weighted average cost.

Analysts must understand how an inventory writedown or write-up affects a firm's ratios. For example, a writedown may significantly affect inventory turnover in current and future periods. Thus, comparability of ratios across periods may be an issue.

In certain industries, reporting inventory above historical cost is permitted under IFRS and U.S. GAAP. This exception applies primarily to producers and dealers of commodity-like products, such as agricultural and forest products, mineral ores, and precious metals. Under this exception, inventory is reported at net realizable value and any unrealized gains and losses from changing market prices are recognized in the income statement. If an active market exists for the commodity, the quoted market price is used to value the inventory. Otherwise, recent market transactions are used.

LOS 29.g: Describe the financial statement presentation of and disclosures relating to inventories.

CFA® Program Curriculum, Volume 3, page 383

Inventory disclosures, usually found in the financial statement footnotes, are useful in evaluating the firm's inventory management. The disclosures are also useful in making adjustments to facilitate comparisons with other firms in the industry.

 Professor's Note: Analyst adjustments to inventory are addressed in our topic review of Financial Statement Analysis—Applications.

Required inventory disclosures are similar under U.S. GAAP and IFRS and include:

- The cost flow method (LIFO, FIFO, etc.) used.
- Total carrying value of inventory, with carrying value by classification (raw materials, work-in-process, and finished goods) if appropriate.
- Carrying value of inventories reported at fair value less selling costs.
- The cost of inventory recognized as an expense (COGS) during the period.
- Amount of inventory writedowns during the period.
- Reversals of inventory writedowns during the period, including a discussion of the circumstances of reversal (IFRS only because U.S. GAAP does not allow reversals).
- Carrying value of inventories pledged as collateral.

Inventory Changes

Although rare, a firm can change inventory cost flow methods. In most cases, the change is made retrospectively; that is, the prior years' financial statements are recast based on the new cost flow method. The cumulative effect of the change is reported as an adjustment to the beginning retained earnings of the earliest year presented.

Under IFRS, the firm must demonstrate that the change will provide reliable and more relevant information. Under U.S. GAAP, the firm must explain why the change in cost flow method is preferable.

An exception to retrospective application applies when a firm changes *to LIFO* from another cost flow method. In this case, the change is applied prospectively; no adjustments are made to the prior periods. With prospective application, the carrying value of inventory under the old method simply becomes the first layer of inventory under LIFO in the period of the change.

LOS 29.h: Calculate and interpret ratios used to evaluate inventory management.

CFA® Program Curriculum, Volume 3, page 384

A firm's choice of inventory cost flow method can have a significant impact on profitability, liquidity, activity, and solvency ratios.

Professor's Note: The presumption in this section is that prices are rising and inventory quantities are stable or increasing.

Profitability. As compared to FIFO, LIFO produces higher COGS in the income statement and will result in lower earnings. Any profitability measure that includes COGS will be lower under LIFO. For example, higher COGS will result in lower gross, operating, and net profit margins as compared to FIFO.

Liquidity. Compared to FIFO, LIFO results in a lower inventory value on the balance sheet. Because inventory (a current asset) is lower under LIFO, the current ratio, a popular measure of liquidity, is also lower under LIFO than under FIFO. Working capital is lower under LIFO as well, because current assets are lower. The quick ratio is unaffected by the firm's inventory cost flow method because inventory is excluded from its numerator.

Activity. Inventory turnover (COGS / average inventory) is higher for firms that use LIFO compared to firms that use FIFO. Under LIFO, COGS is valued at more recent, higher costs (higher numerator), while inventory is valued at older, lower costs (lower denominator). Higher turnover under LIFO will result in lower days of inventory on hand (365 / inventory turnover).

Solvency. LIFO results in lower total assets compared to FIFO because LIFO inventory is lower. Lower total assets under LIFO result in lower stockholders' equity (assets – liabilities). Because total assets and stockholders' equity are lower under LIFO, the debt ratio and the debt-to-equity ratio are higher under LIFO compared to FIFO.

 Professor's Note: Another way of thinking about the impact of LIFO on stockholders' equity is that because LIFO COGS is higher, net income is lower. Lower net income will result in lower stockholders' equity (retained earnings) compared to stockholders' equity under FIFO.

Inventory Management

Analysts can use ratio analysis, inventory disclosures, and industry average ratios to evaluate how efficiently the firm is managing its inventory.

For example, the inventory turnover ratio measures how quickly a firm is selling its inventory. Inventory turnover that is too low may be an indication of slow-selling or even obsolete products. Carrying too much inventory is costly, as the firm incurs storage costs, insurance, and inventory taxes. Excessive inventory also ties up cash that might be used more effectively somewhere else.

 Professor's Note: Recall that inventory turnover is measured in turns per period. Alternatively, we can measure inventory turnover in terms of days of inventory on hand. There is an inverse relationship between inventory turnover and days of inventory on hand. That is, low inventory turnover will result in high days of inventory on hand and vice versa. In either case, the inventory measures should be compared to industry averages and to their values over time.

Generally, high inventory turnover (low days of inventory on hand) is desirable. However, inventory turnover can be too high. A firm with an inventory turnover ratio that is too high may not be carrying enough inventory to satisfy customers' needs, which can cause the firm to lose sales. High inventory turnover may also indicate that inventory writedowns have occurred. Writedowns are usually the result of poor inventory management.

To further assess the explanation for high inventory turnover, we can look at inventory turnover relative to sales growth within the firm and industry. High turnover together with slower growth may be an indication of inadequate inventory quantities. Alternatively, sales growth at or above the industry average supports the conclusion that high inventory turnover reflects greater efficiency.

We can also examine gross profit margin (gross profit / revenue). Gross profit margin measures the relationship between the unit sales price and the cost per unit sold. Gross profit margins are usually lower in highly competitive industries as firms experience downward pressure on sales prices.

Gross profit margin is also a function of the product type. For example, firms are usually able to realize greater gross margins on specialty or luxury products. On the other hand, firms selling specialty or luxury products will usually have lower inventory turnover ratios.

Many of a firm's ratios are directly affected by its choice of inventory cost flow method. Thus, when evaluating a firm's performance, or when comparing the firm to its industry peers, the analyst must understand the differences that result from differences in cost flow assumptions.

Example: Inventory analysis

Viper Corp. is a high-performance bicycle manufacturer. Viper reports its inventory using the first-in, first-out (FIFO) cost flow method. Selected ratios compiled from Viper's financial statements for the year ended 20X6 are shown in the following table.

Ratio Analysis

Year ended 20X6	Viper Corp.	Peer Group
Current ratio	2.2	1.7
Inventory turnover	7.6	9.8
Long-term debt-to-equity	0.6	0.6
Gross profit margin	25.3%	32.1%
Sales growth	5.4%	6.5%
Return on assets	10.4%	11.2%

Discuss Viper's performance relative to its peer group in terms of liquidity, activity, solvency, and profitability. Had Viper used the last-in, first-out (LIFO) cost flow method instead of FIFO, how would Viper's results have differed assuming rising prices and stable inventory quantities?

©2012 Kaplan, Inc.

Answer:

Liquidity—Viper's current ratio exceeds its peer group, indicating greater liquidity. Additional analysis of the components of current assets, primarily inventory and receivables, is needed to determine the effectiveness of Viper's current asset management. Because no receivables data are provided, we will focus on inventory.

Activity—Viper's inventory turnover is less than that of its peer group, indicating that Viper takes longer to sell its goods. In terms of inventory days (365 / inventory turnover), Viper has 48.0 days of inventory on hand while the peer group has 37.2 days of inventory on average. Too much inventory is costly, as we noted previously, and can indicate slow-moving or obsolete inventory.

Solvency—Viper's adjusted long-term debt-to-equity ratio of 0.6 is in line with its peer group.

Profitability—Viper's gross profit margin is significantly less than its peer group average. Coupled with lower inventory turnover, Viper's lower gross profit margin may be an indication that Viper has reduced prices in order to sell its inventory. This is another indication that some of Viper's inventory may be obsolete. As previously discussed, obsolete (impaired) inventory must be written down.

Results under LIFO—Had Viper used the LIFO cost flow method instead of FIFO, we would be unable to compare Viper's results to its peer group without making adjustments to inventory, total assets, shareholders' equity, cost of goods sold, gross profit, and net income.

Under LIFO, Viper's ending inventory would have been based on older, lower costs. As a result, ending inventory would have been lower under LIFO compared to FIFO. Lower inventory under LIFO would reduce the current ratio (numerator), total assets, and shareholders' equity.

Viper's COGS would have been higher under LIFO because LIFO COGS reflects more recent, higher costs. Higher COGS reduces gross profit, operating profit, and net profit.

A lower ending inventory value under LIFO increases the inventory turnover ratio (lower days of inventory on hand) compared to the ratio under FIFO.

KEY CONCEPTS

LOS 29.a

Costs included in inventory on the balance sheet include purchase cost, conversion costs, and other costs necessary to bring the inventory to its present location and condition. All of these costs for inventory acquired or produced in the current period are added to beginning inventory value and then allocated either to cost of goods sold for the period or to ending inventory.

Period costs, such as abnormal waste, most storage costs, administrative costs, and selling costs, are expensed as incurred.

LOS 29.b

Inventory cost flow methods:
- FIFO: The cost of the first item purchased is the cost of the first item sold. Ending inventory is based on the cost of the most recent purchases, thereby approximating current cost.
- LIFO: The cost of the last item purchased is the cost of the first item sold. Ending inventory is based on the cost of the earliest items purchased. LIFO is prohibited under IFRS.
- Weighted average cost: COGS and inventory values are between their FIFO and LIFO values.
- Specific identification: Each unit sold is matched with the unit's actual cost.

LOS 29.c

Under LIFO, cost of sales reflects the most recent purchase or production costs, and balance sheet inventory values reflect older outdated costs.

Under FIFO, cost of sales reflects the oldest purchase or production costs for inventory, and balance sheet inventory values reflect the most recent costs.

Under the weighted average cost method, cost of sales and balance sheet inventory values are between those of LIFO and FIFO.

When purchase or production costs are rising, LIFO cost of sales is higher than FIFO cost of sales, and LIFO gross profit is lower than FIFO gross profit as a result. LIFO inventory is lower than FIFO inventory.

When purchase or production costs are falling, LIFO cost of sales is lower than FIFO cost of sales, and LIFO gross profit is higher than FIFO gross profit as a result. LIFO inventory is higher than FIFO inventory.

In either case, LIFO cost of sales and FIFO inventory values better represent economic reality (replacement costs).

©2012 Kaplan, Inc.

LOS 29.d

In a periodic system, inventory values and COGS are determined at the end of the accounting period. In a perpetual system, inventory values and COGS are updated continuously.

In the case of FIFO and specific identification, ending inventory values and COGS are the same whether a periodic or perpetual system is used. LIFO and weighted average cost, however, can produce different inventory values and COGS depending on whether a periodic or perpetual system is used.

LOS 29.e

When prices are rising and inventory quantities are stable or increasing:

LIFO results in:	*FIFO results in:*
higher COGS	lower COGS
lower gross profit	higher gross profit
lower inventory balances	higher inventory balances
higher inventory turnover	lower inventory turnover

The weighted average cost method results in values between those of LIFO and FIFO.

LOS 29.f

Under IFRS, inventories are valued at the lower of cost or net realizable value. Inventory write-ups are allowed, but only to the extent that a previous writedown to net realizable value was recorded.

Under U.S. GAAP, inventories are valued at the lower of cost or market. Market is usually equal to replacement cost but cannot exceed net realizable value or be less than net realizable value minus a normal profit margin. No subsequent write-up is allowed.

LOS 29.g

Required inventory disclosures:

- The cost flow method (LIFO, FIFO, etc.) used.
- Total carrying value of inventory and carrying value by classification (raw materials, work-in-process, and finished goods) if appropriate.
- Carrying value of inventories reported at fair value less selling costs.
- The cost of inventory recognized as an expense (COGS) during the period.
- Amount of inventory writedowns during the period.
- Reversals of inventory writedowns during the period (IFRS only because U.S. GAAP does not allow reversals).
- Carrying value of inventories pledged as collateral.

LOS 29.h

Inventory turnover, days of inventory on hand, and gross profit margin can be used to evaluate the quality of a firm's inventory management.

Inventory turnover that is too low (high days of inventory on hand) may be an indication of slow-moving or obsolete inventory.

High inventory turnover together with low sales growth relative to the industry may indicate inadequate inventory levels and lost sales because customer orders could not be fulfilled.

High inventory turnover together with high sales growth relative to the industry average suggests that high inventory turnover reflects greater efficiency rather than inadequate inventory.

©2012 Kaplan, Inc.

CONCEPT CHECKERS

1. Which of the following is *most likely* included in a firm's ending inventory?
    A. Storage costs of finished goods.
    B. Variable production overhead.
    C. Selling and administrative costs.

2. Under which inventory cost flow assumption does inventory on the balance sheet *best* approximate its current cost?
    A. First-in, first-out.
    B. Weighted average cost.
    C. Last-in, first-out.

3. During the year, a firm's inventory purchases were as follows:

Quarter	Units Purchased	Cost per Unit	Total
1	400	$3.30	$1,320
2	100	3.60	360
3	200	3.90	780
4	50	4.20	210
	750		$2,670

    • The firm uses a periodic inventory system and calculates inventory and COGS at the end of the year.
    • Beginning inventory was 200 units at $3 per unit = $600.
    • Sales for the year were 600 units.

    Compute COGS for the year under FIFO and LIFO.

	FIFO	LIFO
A.	$1,920	$2,175
B.	$1,920	$1,850
C.	$2,070	$2,175

4. During May, a firm's inventory account included the following transactions:

May 1	Inventory	25 units @ $4.00
May 12	Purchased	60 units @ $4.20
May 16	Sold	40 units @ $6.00
May 27	Purchased	30 units @ $4.25
May 29	Sold	40 units @ $6.10

    Assuming periodic FIFO inventory costing, gross profit for May was:
    A. $132.
    B. $147.
    C. $153.

5.   In periods of rising prices and stable inventory quantities, which of the following *best* describes the effect on gross profit of using LIFO as compared to using FIFO?
     A. Lower.
     B. Higher.
     C. The same.

6.   Kamp, Inc., sells specialized bicycle shoes. At year-end, due to a sudden increase in manufacturing costs, the replacement cost per pair of shoes is $55. The original cost is $43, and the current selling price is $50. The normal profit margin is 10% of the selling price, and the selling costs are $3 per pair. According to U.S. GAAP, which of the following amounts should each pair of shoes be reported on Kamp's year-end balance sheet?
     A. $42.
     B. $43.
     C. $47.

7.   Which of the following inventory disclosures would *least likely* be found in the footnotes of a firm following IFRS?
     A. The amount of loss reversals, from previously written-down inventory, recognized during the period.
     B. The carrying value of inventories that collateralize a short-term loan.
     C. The separate carrying values of raw materials, work-in-process, and finished goods computed under the LIFO cost flow method.

8.   Which of the following is *most likely* for a firm with high inventory turnover and lower sales growth than the industry average? The firm:
     A. is managing its inventory effectively.
     B. may have obsolete inventory that requires a writedown.
     C. may be losing sales by not carrying enough inventory.

©2012 Kaplan, Inc.

ANSWERS – CONCEPT CHECKERS

1. **B**   Variable production overhead is capitalized as a part of inventory. Storage costs not related to the production process, and selling and administrative costs are expensed as incurred.

2. **A**   Under FIFO, ending inventory is made up of the most recent purchases, thereby providing a closer approximation of current cost.

3. **A**   FIFO COGS

   200 units from beginning inventory × $3.00 = $600
   400 units from 1st quarter × $3.30   = __1,320__
                                                 $1,920

   LIFO COGS

   50 units from 4th quarter × $4.20   = $210
   200 units from 3rd quarter × $3.90 = 780
   100 units from 2nd quarter × $3.60 = 360
   250 units from 1st quarter × $3.30 = __825__
                                         $2,175

   Note the shortcut. Once FIFO COGS of $1,920 is calculated, look at the LIFO column. We know that during inflation and stable or increasing inventory quantities, LIFO COGS is higher than FIFO. Only LIFO COGS of $2,175 meets this condition.

4. **C**   Under FIFO, the first units purchased are the first units sold. FIFO COGS is the same under a periodic system and a perpetual system.

   Revenue $484 (40 units × $6.00) + (40 units × $6.10)
   COGS $331 (25 units × $4.00) + (55 units × $4.20)
   Gross profit $153

5. **A**   Compared to FIFO, COGS calculated under LIFO will be higher because the most recent, higher cost units are assumed to be the first units sold. Higher COGS under LIFO will result in lower gross profit (revenue – COGS).

6. **B**   Market is equal to the replacement cost as long as replacement cost is within a specific range. The upper bound is net realizable value (NRV) which is equal to the selling price ($50) less selling costs ($3) for a NRV of $47. The lower bound is NRV ($47) less normal profit margin (10% of selling price = $5) for a net amount of $42. Because replacement cost is greater than NRV ($47), market equals NRV ($47). Additionally, we have to use the lower of cost ($43) or market ($47) principle, so the shoes should be recorded at a cost of $43.

7. **C**   While the separate carrying values of raw materials, work-in-process, and finished goods are required disclosure for some firms, LIFO is not permitted under IFRS.

8. **C**   High inventory turnover coupled with low sales growth relative to the industry may be an indication of inadequate inventory levels. In this case, the firm may be losing sales by not carrying enough inventory.

The following is a review of the Financial Reporting and Analysis principles designed to address the learning outcome statements set forth by CFA Institute. This topic is also covered in:

LONG-LIVED ASSETS

EXAM FOCUS

Long-lived assets include tangible assets, intangible assets, and financial assets. Firms make many estimates and choices in accounting for long-lived assets that affect the firms' profits, ratios, and cash flow classifications. You must understand the effects of and issues concerning capitalization versus immediate expensing of various costs, including construction interest, research and development, and software costs. For capitalized costs, you must be familiar with the effects of the different depreciation and amortization methods and be able to determine if an asset is impaired. Finally, you must be familiar with the revaluation (fair value) model under IFRS and the disclosure requirements for financial reporting.

LOS 30.a: Distinguish between costs that are capitalized and costs that are expensed in the period in which they are incurred.

CFA® Program Curriculum, Volume 3, page 404

When a firm makes an expenditure, it can either **capitalize** the cost as an asset on the balance sheet or **expense** the cost in the income statement in the period incurred. As a general rule, an expenditure that is expected to provide a future economic benefit over multiple accounting periods is capitalized; however, if the future economic benefit is unlikely or highly uncertain, the expenditure is expensed in the period incurred.

An expenditure that is capitalized is initially recorded as an asset on the balance sheet at cost, typically its fair value at acquisition plus any costs necessary to prepare the asset for use. Except for land and intangible assets with indefinite lives (such as acquisition goodwill), the cost is then allocated to the income statement over the life of the asset as **depreciation** expense (for tangible assets) or **amortization** expense (for intangible assets with finite lives).

Alternatively, if an expenditure is immediately expensed, current period pretax income is reduced by the amount of the expenditure.

Once an asset is capitalized, subsequent related expenditures that provide more future economic benefits (e.g., rebuilding the asset) are also capitalized. Subsequent expenditures that merely sustain the usefulness of the asset (e.g., regular maintenance) are expensed when incurred.

©2012 Kaplan, Inc.

Example: Capitalizing versus expensing

Northwood Corp. purchased new equipment to be used in its manufacturing plant. The cost of the equipment was $250,000 including $5,000 freight and $12,000 of taxes. In addition to the equipment cost, Northwood paid $10,000 to install the equipment and $7,500 to train its employees to use the equipment. Over the asset's life, Northwood paid $35,000 for repair and maintenance. At the end of five years, Northwood extended the life of the asset by rebuilding the equipment's motors at a cost of $85,000.

What amounts should be capitalized on Northwood's balance sheet and what amounts should be expensed in the period incurred?

Answer:

Northwood should capitalize all costs that provide future economic benefits, including the costs that are necessary to get the asset ready for use. Rebuilding the equipment's motors extended its life and thus increased its future benefits.

Capitalized Costs
Purchase price	$250,000 (including freight & taxes)
Installation costs	10,000
Rebuilt motors	85,000
	$345,000

Costs that do not provide future economic benefits are expensed in the period incurred. The initial training costs are not necessary to get the asset ready for use. Rather, the training costs are necessary to get the employees ready to use the asset. Thus, the training costs are immediately expensed. Repair and maintenance costs are operating expenditures that do not extend the life of the equipment.

Costs Expensed When Incurred
Initial training costs	$7,500
Repair and maintenance	35,000
	$42,500

Although it may make no operational difference, the choice between capitalizing costs and expensing them will affect net income, shareholders' equity, total assets, cash flow from operations, cash flow from investing, and numerous financial ratios.

Net Income

Capitalizing an expenditure delays the recognition of an expense in the income statement. Thus, in the period that an expenditure is capitalized, the firm will report higher net income compared to immediately expensing. In subsequent periods, the firm will report lower net income compared to expensing, as the capitalized expenditure is allocated to the income statement through depreciation expense. This allocation process reduces the variability of net income by spreading the expense over multiple periods.

Professor's Note: For growing firms, capitalizing expenditures may result in earnings that are higher over many periods compared to an otherwise identical expensing firm. This is because the amount of depreciation from previously capitalized expenditures is less than the amount of additional costs that are being newly capitalized each period.

Conversely, if a firm expenses an expenditure in the current period, net income is reduced by the after-tax amount of the expenditure. In subsequent periods, no allocation of cost is necessary. Thus, net income in future periods is higher than if the expenditure had been capitalized.

Over the life of an asset, *total* net income is identical whether the asset's cost is capitalized or expensed. Timing of the expense recognition in the income statement is the only difference.

Shareholders' Equity

Because capitalization results in higher net income in the period of the expenditure compared to expensing, it also results in higher shareholders' equity because retained earnings are greater. Total assets are greater with capitalization and liabilities are unaffected, so the accounting equation (A = L + E) remains balanced. As the cost is allocated to the income statement in subsequent periods, net income, retained earnings, and shareholders' equity will be reduced.

If the expenditure is immediately expensed, retained earnings and shareholders' equity will reflect the entire reduction in net income in the period of the expenditure.

Cash Flow From Operations

A capitalized expenditure is usually reported in the cash flow statement as an outflow from investing activities. If immediately expensed, the expenditure is reported as an outflow from operating activities. Thus, capitalizing an expenditure will result in higher operating cash flow and lower investing cash flow compared to expensing. Assuming no differences in tax treatment, *total* cash flow will be the same. The classification of the cash flow is the only difference.

Recall that when an expenditure is capitalized, depreciation expense is recognized in subsequent periods. Depreciation is a noncash expense and, aside from any tax effects, does not affect operating cash flow.

 Professor's Note: If the tax treatment is changed to match the financial reporting treatment of the expenditure, expensing will result in higher operating cash flow in the first year because of the tax savings. However, if the tax treatment is independent of the financial reporting treatment, taxes, and therefore cash flows, are unaffected by the choice.

©2012 Kaplan, Inc.

Financial Ratios

Capitalizing an expenditure initially results in higher assets and higher equity compared to expensing. Thus, both the debt-to-assets ratio and the debt-to-equity ratio are lower (they have larger denominators) with capitalization.

Capitalizing an expenditure will *initially* result in higher return on assets (ROA) and higher return on equity (ROE). This is the result of higher net income in the first year. In subsequent years, ROA and ROE will be lower for a capitalizing firm because net income is reduced by the depreciation expense.

Because an expensing firm recognizes the entire expense in the first year, ROA and ROE will be lower in the first year and higher in the subsequent years. After the first year, net income (numerator) is higher, and assets and equity (denominators) are lower, than they would be if the firm had capitalized the expenditure. Analysts must be careful when comparing firms because immediately expensing an expenditure gives the appearance of growth after the first year.

Capitalized Interest

When a firm constructs an asset for its own use or, in limited circumstances, for resale, the interest that accrues during the construction period is capitalized as a part of the asset's cost. The reasons for capitalizing interest are to accurately measure the cost of the asset and to better match the cost with the revenues generated by the constructed asset. The treatment of construction interest is similar under U.S. GAAP and IFRS.

The interest rate used to capitalize interest is based on debt specifically related to the construction of the asset. If no construction debt is outstanding, the interest rate is based on existing unrelated borrowings. Only interest on the construction costs is capitalized; interest costs are expensed on general corporate debt in excess of project construction costs.

Under IFRS, income earned by temporarily investing borrowed funds reduces the interest that is eligible for capitalization. There is no such reduction of capitalized interest under U.S. GAAP.

Capitalized interest is not reported in the income statement as interest expense. Once construction interest is capitalized, the interest cost is allocated to the income statement through depreciation expense (if the asset is held for use), or COGS (if the asset is held for sale).

Generally, capitalized interest is reported in the cash flow statement as an outflow from investing activities, while interest expense is reported as an outflow from operating activities.

 Professor's Note: Interest expense can be reported on the cash flow statement as either an operating activity or financing activity under IFRS.

The interest coverage ratio (EBIT / interest expense) measures a firm's ability to make required interest payments on its debt. In the year of the expenditure, capitalizing interest results in lower interest expense compared to expensing. The result is a higher interest coverage ratio (smaller denominator) when interest is capitalized.

Many analysts calculate the interest coverage ratio based on total interest expense, including capitalized interest. Because the interest is a required payment, this may be a better measure of the firm's solvency. Treating the capitalized interest as interest expense for analytical purposes reduces the interest coverage ratio. Bond rating agencies often make this adjustment.

The financial effects of capitalizing versus expensing are summarized in Figure 1.

Figure 1: Financial Statement Effects of Capitalizing vs. Expensing

	Capitalizing	*Expensing*
Total assets	Higher	Lower
Shareholders' equity	Higher	Lower
Income variability	Lower	Higher
Net income (first year)	Higher	Lower
Net income (subsequent years)	Lower	Higher
Cash flow from operations	Higher	Lower
Cash flow from investing	Lower	Higher
Debt ratio & Debt-to-equity	Lower	Higher
Interest coverage (first year)	Higher	Lower
Interest coverage (subsequent years)	Lower	Higher

LOS 30.b: Compare the financial reporting of the following classifications of intangible assets: purchased, internally developed, acquired in a business combination.

CFA® Program Curriculum, Volume 3, page 408

Intangible assets are long-term assets that lack physical substance, such as patents, brand names, copyrights, and franchises. Some intangible assets have finite lives while others have indefinite lives.

The cost of a finite-lived intangible asset is amortized over its useful life. Indefinite-lived intangible assets are not amortized, but are tested for impairment at least annually. If impaired, the reduction in value is recognized in the income statement as a loss in the period in which the impairment is recognized.

Intangible assets are also considered either identifiable or unidentifiable. Under IFRS, an **identifiable intangible asset** must be:

- Capable of being separated from the firm or arise from a contractual or legal right.
- Controlled by the firm.
- Expected to provide future economic benefits.

©2012 Kaplan, Inc.

In addition, the future economic benefits must be probable and the asset's cost must be reliably measurable.

An **unidentifiable intangible asset** is one that cannot be purchased separately and may have an indefinite life. The most common example of an unidentifiable intangible asset is goodwill. Goodwill is the excess of purchase price over the fair value of the identifiable assets (net of liabilities) acquired in a business combination.

Not all intangible assets are reported on the balance sheet. Accounting for an intangible asset depends on whether the asset was created internally, purchased externally, or obtained as part of a business combination.

Intangible Assets Created Internally

With some exceptions, costs to create intangible assets are expensed as incurred. Important exceptions are research and development costs (under IFRS) and software development costs.

Research and development costs. Under IFRS, **research costs**, which are costs aimed at the discovery of new scientific or technical knowledge and understanding, are expensed as incurred. However, **development costs** are capitalized. Development costs are incurred to translate research findings into a plan or design of a new product or process.

Under U.S. GAAP, both research and development costs are generally expensed as incurred. One exception is software development costs.

Software development costs. Costs incurred to develop software for sale to others are expensed as incurred until the product's technological feasibility has been established, after which costs are capitalized under both IFRS and U.S. GAAP. Judgment is involved in determining technological feasibility.

Under IFRS, treatment is the same whether the software is developed for sale or for a firm's own use. Under U.S. GAAP, all research and development costs are capitalized when a firm develops software for its own use.

> **Example: Software development costs**
>
> Over a 10-month period, Royal Manufacturing Company expended $2,500 per month to develop software for its own use. For the first three months, Royal could not estimate the probable future benefits of the expenditures. Over the remaining seven months, the expenditures met the capitalization criteria for identifiable intangible assets in accordance with IFRS. The software was completed on time and is in use today.
>
> What amount of the software expenditures should Royal capitalize under IFRS and U.S. GAAP?

Answer:

Under IFRS, Royal can only capitalize the software expenditures that meet the capitalization criteria. The expenditures made before the criteria were met are expensed in the period incurred. Thus, Royal will expense $7,500 ($2,500 per month × 3 months) over the first three months, and capitalize $17,500 ($2,500 per month × 7 months) over the last seven months.

Under U.S. GAAP, Royal will capitalize all of the expenditures for software developed for its own use. Thus, Royal will capitalize $25,000 ($2,500 per month × 10 months).

Purchased Intangible Assets

Like tangible assets, an intangible asset purchased from another party is initially recorded on the balance sheet at cost, typically its fair value at acquisition.

If the intangible asset is purchased as part of a group, the total purchase price is allocated to each asset on the basis of its fair value. For analytical purposes, an analyst is usually more interested in the type of asset acquired rather than the value assigned on the balance sheet. For example, recently acquired franchise rights may provide insight into the firm's future operating performance. In this case, the allocation of cost is not as important.

The financial statement effects of capitalizing intangible assets are the same as the effects of capitalizing other expenditures. Capitalizing results in higher net income in the first year and lower net income in the subsequent years. Similarly, assets, equity, and operating cash flow are all higher when expenditures are capitalized.

Intangible Assets Obtained in a Business Combination

The **acquisition method** is used to account for business combinations. Under the acquisition method, the purchase price is allocated to the identifiable assets and liabilities of the acquired firm on the basis of fair value. Any remaining amount of the purchase price is recorded as **goodwill**. Goodwill is said to be an unidentifiable asset that cannot be separated from the business itself.

Only goodwill created in a business combination is capitalized on the balance sheet. The costs of any internally generated "goodwill" are expensed in the period incurred.

©2012 Kaplan, Inc.

LOS 30.c: Describe the different depreciation methods for property, plant, and equipment, the effect of the choice of depreciation method on the financial statements, and the effects of assumptions concerning useful life and residual value on depreciation expense.

LOS 30.d: Calculate depreciation expense.

CFA® Program Curriculum, Volume 3, page 413

Depreciation is the systematic allocation of an asset's cost over time. Two important terms are:

- **Carrying (book) value.** The net value of an asset or liability on the balance sheet. For property, plant, and equipment, carrying value equals historical cost minus accumulated depreciation.
- **Historical cost.** The original purchase price of the asset including installation and transportation costs. Historical cost is also known as *gross investment in the asset.*

Depreciation is a real and significant operating expense. Even though depreciation doesn't require current cash expenditures (the cash outflow was made in the past when the asset was purchased), it is an expense nonetheless and cannot be ignored.

The analyst must decide whether the reported depreciation expense is more or less than *economic depreciation,* which is the actual decline in the value of the asset over the period. One chain of video rental stores was found to be overstating income by depreciating its stock of movies by equal amounts each year. In fact, a greater portion of the decrease in the value of newly released movies occurs in the first year. Depreciating the rental assets by a greater amount during the first year would have better approximated economic depreciation and reduced reported income.

Depreciation Methods

Depreciation of a capitalized cost (asset) may be reported using straight-line, accelerated, or units-of-production methods.

Straight-line depreciation is the predominant method of computing depreciation for financial reporting. Depreciation is the same amount each year over the asset's estimated life:

$$\text{depreciation expense} = \frac{\text{original cost} - \text{salvage value}}{\text{depreciable life}}$$

With an **accelerated depreciation** method, more depreciation expense is recognized in the early years of an asset's life and less depreciation expense in the later years. Thus, accelerated depreciation results in lower net income in the early years of an asset's life and higher net income in the later years, compared to straight-line depreciation. One often-used accelerated depreciation method is the **double-declining balance** (DDB) method:

DDB depreciation in year x =

$$\frac{2}{\text{depreciable life in years}} \times \text{book value at beginning of year } x$$

Note that salvage value is not in the formula for double-declining balance depreciation. However, once the carrying (book) value of the asset reaches the salvage value, no additional depreciation expense is recognized.

Depreciation under the **units-of-production method** is based on usage rather than time. Depreciation expense is higher in periods of high usage.

units-of-production depreciation =

$$\frac{\text{original cost} - \text{salvage value}}{\text{life in output units}} \times \text{output units in the period}$$

 Professor's Note: The units-of-production method applied to natural resources is referred to as depletion.

The following example illustrates the differences in depreciation, net income, and reported net profit margin for the three methods.

Example: Effect of depreciation methods on net income

Sackett Laboratories purchases chemical processing machinery for $550,000. The equipment has an estimated useful life of five years and an estimated salvage value of $50,000. The company expects to produce 20,000 units of output using this machinery, with 6,000 units in each of the first two years, 3,000 units in the next two years, and 2,000 units in the fifth year. The company's effective tax rate is 30%. Revenues are $600,000 per year, and expenses other than depreciation are $300,000 in each year. Calculate Sackett's net income and net profit margin if the company depreciates the machinery using (a) the straight-line method, (b) the double declining balance method, changing to the straight-line method after two years, and (c) the units of production method.

©2012 Kaplan, Inc.

Answer:

Using the *straight-line method*, depreciation expense in each year is
($550,000 – $50,000) / 5 = $100,000.

Using the *double declining balance method*, each year's depreciation is 2 / 5 of the book value. In year 1, depreciation expense is $550,000 × 2 / 5 = $220,000, and in year 2, depreciation expense is ($550,000 – $220,000) × 2 / 5 = $132,000.
Straight-line depreciation expense for the remaining three years is
($550,000 – $220,000 – $132,000 – $50,000) / 3 = $49,333.

Using the *units of production method*, depreciation expense in the first two years is (6,000 / 20,000) × ($550,000 – $50,000) = $150,000, in the next two years is (3,000 / 20,000) × ($550,000 – $50,000) = $75,000, and in the fifth year is (2,000 / 20,000) × ($550,000 – $50,000) = $50,000.

Straight-line depreciation:

	Year 1	Year 2	Year 3	Year 4	Year 5	Total
Revenue	600,000	600,000	600,000	600,000	600,000	3,000,000
Other expenses	300,000	300,000	300,000	300,000	300,000	1,500,000
Depreciation expense	100,000	100,000	100,000	100,000	100,000	500,000
Pretax income	200,000	200,000	200,000	200,000	200,000	1,000,000
Tax expense	60,000	60,000	60,000	60,000	60,000	300,000
Net income	140,000	140,000	140,000	140,000	140,000	700,000
Net profit margin	23.3%	23.3%	23.3%	23.3%	23.3%	23.3%

Double-declining balance:

	Year 1	Year 2	Year 3	Year 4	Year 5	Total
Revenue	600,000	600,000	600,000	600,000	600,000	3,000,000
Other expenses	300,000	300,000	300,000	300,000	300,000	1,500,000
Depreciation expense	220,000	132,000	49,333	49,333	49,333	500,000
Pretax income	80,000	168,000	250,667	250,667	250,667	1,000,000
Tax expense	24,000	50,400	75,200	75,200	75,200	300,000
Net income	56,000	117,600	175,467	175,467	175,467	700,000
Net profit margin	9.3%	19.6%	29.2%	29.2%	29.2%	23.3%

Units of production:

	Year 1	Year 2	Year 3	Year 4	Year 5	Total
Revenue	600,000	600,000	600,000	600,000	600,000	3,000,000
Other expenses	300,000	300,000	300,000	300,000	300,000	1,500,000
Depreciation expense	150,000	150,000	75,000	75,000	50,000	500,000
Pretax income	150,000	150,000	225,000	225,000	250,000	1,000,000
Tax expense	45,000	45,000	67,500	67,500	75,000	300,000
Net income	105,000	105,000	157,500	157,500	175,000	700,000
Net profit margin	17.5%	17.5%	26.3%	26.3%	29.2%	23.3%

The accelerated depreciation methods result in pretax income, tax expense, net income, and net profit margins that are lower in the early years and higher in the later years, compared to straight-line depreciation. Over the entire period, however, depreciation expense, tax expense, pretax income, net income, and net profit margin are unaffected by the depreciation method chosen.

Useful Lives and Salvage Values

Calculating depreciation expense requires estimating an asset's useful life and its salvage (residual) value. Firms can manipulate depreciation expense, and therefore net income, by increasing or decreasing either of these estimates.

A longer estimated useful life decreases annual depreciation and increases reported net income, while a shorter estimated useful life will have the opposite effect. A higher estimate of the salvage value will also decrease depreciation and increase net income, while a lower estimate of the salvage value will increase depreciation and decrease net income.

A change in an accounting estimate, such as useful life or salvage value, is put into effect in the current period and prospectively. That is, the change in estimate is applied to the asset's carrying (book) value and depreciation is calculated going forward using the new estimate. The previous periods are not affected by the change.

Example: Change in depreciation estimate

Alpine Company purchased machinery for $20,000 with an estimated useful life of five years and a salvage value of $4,000. Alpine uses the straight-line depreciation method. At the beginning of the third year, Alpine reduces its salvage value estimate to $1,600. Determine the depreciation expense for each year.

©2012 Kaplan, Inc.

Answer:

For the first two years, straight-line depreciation expense is [($20,000 original cost – $4,000 salvage value) / 5-year life] = $3,200 each year. At the beginning of the third year, the asset's carrying value on the balance sheet is $20,000 original cost – $6,400 accumulated depreciation = $13,600.

To calculate straight-line depreciation expense for the remaining years, simply begin with the carrying value and depreciate over the remaining useful life using the new salvage value estimate. Depreciation expense for the last three years is [($13,600 carrying value – $1,600 revised salvage value) / 3 years remaining life] = $4,000 each year.

Estimates are also involved when a manufacturing firm allocates depreciation expense between COGS and SG&A. While the allocation does not affect a firm's operating margin, it affects the firm's gross margin (which is computed before SG&A expense) and operating expenses.

Component Depreciation

IFRS requires firms to depreciate the components of an asset separately, thereby requiring useful life estimates for each component. For example, a building is made up of a roof, walls, flooring, electrical systems, plumbing, and many other components. Under **component depreciation**, the useful life of each component is estimated and depreciation expense is computed separately for each.

Component depreciation is allowed under U.S. GAAP but is seldom used.

Example: Component depreciation

Global Airlines purchased a new airplane with an all-inclusive cost of $50 million. The estimated life of the airplane is 30 years and the estimated salvage value is $5 million. Global expects to replace the interior of the aircraft after 15 years. The component cost of the interior is estimated at $3 million.

Calculate depreciation expense in Year 1 using the straight-line method, both assuming the interior is a separate component and assuming the component method is not used.

Answer:

Straight-line depreciation using the component method:

Total aircraft cost	$50,000,000
Interior cost	(3,000,000)
Aircraft component	$47,000,000

Depreciation expense:
Aircraft component $1,400,000   ($47,000,000 – 5,000,000) / 30 years
Interior component   200,000   ($3,000,000 / 15 years)
Year 1 expense $1,600,000

Straight-line depreciation without the component method:

Year 1 expense   ($50,000,000 – 5,000,000) / 30 years = $1,500,000

Depreciation expense is lower by $100,000 each year ($1,600,000 – $1,500,000) for the first 15 years without the component method. However, at the end of Year 15, Global will spend $3,000,000 to replace the interior. Thus, additional depreciation expense of $3,000,000 / 15 years = $200,000 each year is required for the last 15 years of the asset's life.

Under both scenarios, Global will have expended a total of $53,000,000 and recognized $48,000,000 of depreciation expense over the airplane's life:

Component method $1,600,000 × 30 years = $48,000,000

Non-component method   ($1,500,000 × 30 years) + ($200,000 × 15 years)
                                = $48,000,000

LOS 30.e: Describe the different amortization methods for intangible assets with finite lives, the effect of the choice of amortization method on the financial statements, and the effects of assumptions concerning useful life and residual value on amortization expense.

CFA® Program Curriculum, Volume 3, page 420

Only intangible assets with finite lives are amortized over their useful lives. Amortization is identical to the depreciation of tangible assets. The same methods, straight-line, accelerated, and units-of-production, are permitted. Likewise, it is necessary to estimate useful lives and salvage values. However, estimating useful lives is complicated by many legal, regulatory, contractual, competitive, and economic factors that may limit the use of the intangible assets.

As with depreciation, the total amount of amortization is the same under all of the methods. Timing of the amortization expense in the income statement is the only difference.

Intangible assets with indefinite lives are not amortized. Rather, they are tested for impairment at least annually. As noted earlier, goodwill created as a result of a business combination is a common example of an unidentifiable intangible asset with an indefinite life.

©2012 Kaplan, Inc.

An example of an identifiable intangible asset with an indefinite life is a trademark that may have a specific expiration date, but can be renewed at minimal cost. In this case, the trademark is considered to have an indefinite life and no amortization is required.

LOS 30.f: Calculate amortization expense.

CFA® Program Curriculum, Volume 3, page 420

Example: Calculating amortization expense

At the beginning of this year, Brandon Corporation entered into business acquisition. As a result of the acquisition, Brandon reported the following intangible assets:

Patent	$480,000
Franchise agreement	$350,000
Copyright	$150,000
Goodwill	$550,000
	$1,530,000

The patent expires in 12 years. The franchise agreement expires in 7 years but can be renewed indefinitely at a minimal cost. The copyright is expected to be sold at the end of 20 years for $30,000. Use the straight-line amortization method to calculate the total carrying value of Brandon's intangible assets at the end of the year.

Answer:

Goodwill is an indefinite-lived asset and is not amortized. Because the franchise agreement can be renewed indefinitely at minimal cost, it is also considered an indefinite-lived asset and is not amortized.

Using the straight-line method, amortization expense is $46,000 as follows:

Patent	$40,000	= $480,000 / 12 years
Copyright	6,000	= ($150,000 – 30,000) / 20 years
Amortization expense	$46,000	

Thus, the carrying value at the end of the first year is $1,484,000 as follows:

Intangible assets, at cost	$1,530,000
Accumulated amortization	(46,000)
Intangible assets, net	$1,484,000

LOS 30.g: Describe the revaluation model.

CFA® Program Curriculum, Volume 3, page 422

Under U.S. GAAP, most long-lived assets are reported on the balance sheet at depreciated cost (original cost less accumulated depreciation and any impairment charges).

There is no fair value alternative for asset reporting under U.S. GAAP. Under IFRS, most long-lived assets are also reported at depreciated cost (the *cost model*). IFRS provides an alternative, the **revaluation model**, that permits long-lived assets to be reported at their fair values, as long as active markets exist for the assets so their fair value can be reliably (and somewhat objectively) estimated. Firms must choose the same treatment for similar assets (e.g., land and buildings) so they cannot revalue only specific assets that are more likely to increase than decrease in value. The revaluation model is rarely used in practice by IFRS reporting firms.

Revaluation under IFRS can result from either an increase or decrease in fair value from one period to the next. An initial revaluation to fair value below historical cost results in a loss that is reported on the income statement, decreasing net income and shareholders' equity. A subsequent upward revaluation to reflect an increase in fair value is reported as a gain in the income statement to the extent that it reverses a previously reported loss from revaluation to fair value. Regardless of prior revaluations, any increase in an asset's value above historical cost is not reported as a gain in the income statement, but is reported as a component of shareholders' equity in an account called **revaluation surplus**. Subsequent declines in an asset's value first reduce this surplus, then result in a loss reported on the income statement to the extent that an asset's fair value decreases below its historical cost.

Revaluing an asset's value upward will result in:

- Greater total assets and greater shareholders' equity.
- Higher depreciation expense, and thus lower profitability, in periods after revaluation.

LOS 30.h: Explain the impairment of property, plant, and equipment, and intangible assets.

CFA® Program Curriculum, Volume 3, page 425

Both IFRS and U.S. GAAP require firms to write down impaired assets by recognizing a loss in the income statement. However, there are differences in applying the standards.

 Professor's Note: The following discussion applies to both tangible and intangible long-lived assets with finite lives that are held for use.

Impairments under IFRS

Under IFRS, the firm must annually assess whether events or circumstances indicate an **impairment** of an asset's value has occurred. For example, there may have been a significant decline in the market value of the asset or a significant change in the asset's physical condition. If so, the asset's value must be tested for impairment.

An asset is impaired when its carrying value (original cost less accumulated depreciation) exceeds the **recoverable amount**. The recoverable amount is the greater of its fair value less any selling costs and its **value in use.** The value in use is the present value of its future cash flow stream from continued use.

If impaired, the asset's value must be written down on the balance sheet to the recoverable amount. An impairment loss, equal to the excess of carrying value over the recoverable amount, is recognized in the income statement.

Under IFRS, the loss can be reversed if the value of the impaired asset recovers in the future. However, the loss reversal is limited to the original impairment loss. Thus, the carrying value of the asset after reversal cannot exceed the carrying value before the impairment loss was recognized.

Impairments under U.S. GAAP

Under U.S. GAAP, an asset is tested for impairment only when events and circumstances indicate the firm may not be able to recover the carrying value through future use.

Determining an impairment and calculating the loss potentially involves two steps. In the first step, the asset is tested for impairment by applying a **recoverability test**. If the asset is impaired, the second step involves measuring the loss.

Recoverability. An asset is considered impaired if the carrying value (original cost less accumulated depreciation) is greater than the asset's future *undiscounted* cash flow stream. Because the recoverability test is based on estimates of future undiscounted cash flows, tests for impairment involve considerable management discretion.

Loss measurement. If impaired, the asset's value is written down to fair value on the balance sheet and a loss, equal to the excess of carrying value over the fair value of the asset (or the *discounted* value of its future cash flows if the fair value is not known), is recognized in the income statement.

Under U.S. GAAP, loss recoveries are not permitted.

Professor's Note: The difference between testing for impairment and measuring the impairment loss can be confusing. In testing for impairment, undiscounted cash flows are used. Once impairment has been detected, the loss is based on fair value or the discounted expected future cash flows. Using undiscounted cash flows to test for impairment keeps PP&E assets from becoming "impaired" by increases in the discount rate when interest rates increase.

Example: Asset impairment

Information related to equipment owned by Brownfield Company follows:

Original cost	$900,000
Accumulated depreciation to date	$100,000
Expected future cash flows	$825,000
Fair value	$790,000
Value in use	$785,000
Selling costs	$30,000

Assuming Brownfield will continue to use the equipment, test the asset for impairment under both IFRS and U.S. GAAP and discuss the results.

Answer:

The carrying value of the equipment is $900,000 original cost – $100,000 accumulated depreciation = $800,000, and the recoverable amount under IFRS is $785,000 (greater of $785,000 value in use and $760,000 fair value less selling costs). Under IFRS, the asset is written down on the balance sheet to the $785,000 recoverable amount, and a $15,000 loss ($800,000 carrying value – $785,000 recoverable amount) is recognized in the income statement.

Under U.S. GAAP, the asset is not impaired because the $825,000 expected future cash flows exceed the $800,000 carrying value.

Intangible Assets with Indefinite Lives

Intangible assets with indefinite lives are not amortized; rather, they are tested for impairment at least annually. An impairment loss is recognized when the carrying amount exceeds fair value.

Professor's Note: The details of impairment for indefinite-lived intangibles, such as goodwill, are covered at Level II.

Long-Lived Assets Held for Sale

If a firm reclassifies a long-lived asset from *held for use* to *held for sale* because management intends to sell it, the asset is tested for impairment. At this point, the asset is no longer depreciated or amortized. The held-for-sale asset is impaired if its carrying value exceeds its net realizable value (fair value less selling costs). If impaired, the asset is written down to net realizable value and the loss is recognized in the income statement.

For long-lived assets held for sale, the loss can be reversed under IFRS and U.S. GAAP if the value of the asset recovers in the future. However, the loss reversal is limited to the original impairment loss. Thus, the carrying value of the asset after reversal cannot exceed the carrying value before the impairment was recognized.

LOS 30.i: Explain the derecognition of property, plant, and equipment, and intangible assets.

CFA® Program Curriculum, Volume 3, page 427

Eventually, long-lived assets are removed from the balance sheet. **Derecognition** occurs when assets are sold, exchanged, or abandoned.

When a long-lived asset is sold, the asset is removed from the balance sheet and the difference between the sale proceeds and the carrying value of the asset is reported as a gain or loss in the income statement. The carrying value is equal to original cost minus accumulated depreciation and any impairment charges.

The gain or loss is usually reported in the income statement as a part of other gains and losses, or reported separately if material. Also, if the firm presents its cash flow statement using the indirect method, the gain or loss is removed from net income to compute cash flow from operations because the proceeds from selling a long-lived asset are an investing cash inflow.

If a long-lived asset is abandoned, the treatment is similar to a sale, except there are no proceeds. In this case, the carrying value of the asset is removed from the balance sheet and a loss of that amount is recognized in the income statement.

If a long-lived asset is exchanged for another asset, a gain or loss is computed by comparing the carrying value of the old asset with fair value of the old asset (or the fair value of the new asset if that value is clearly more evident). The carrying value of the old asset is removed from the balance sheet and the new asset is recorded at its fair value.

LOS 30.j: Describe the financial statement presentation of and disclosures relating to property, plant, and equipment, and intangible assets.

CFA® Program Curriculum, Volume 3, page 429

IFRS Disclosures

Under IFRS, the firm must disclose the following for each class of property, plant, and equipment (PP&E):

- Basis for measurement (usually historical cost).
- Useful lives or depreciation rate.
- Gross carrying value and accumulated depreciation.
- Reconciliation of carrying amounts from the beginning of the period to the end of the period.

The firm must also disclose:

- Title restrictions and assets pledged as collateral.
- Agreements to acquire PP&E in the future.

If the revaluation (fair value) model is used, the firm must disclose:

- The revaluation date.
- How fair value was determined.
- Carrying value using the historical cost model.

Under IFRS, the disclosure requirements for intangible assets are similar to those for PP&E, except that the firm must disclose whether the useful lives are finite or indefinite.

For impaired assets, the firm must disclose:

- Amounts of impairment losses and reversals by asset class.
- Where the losses and loss reversals are recognized in the income statement.
- Circumstances that caused the impairment loss or reversal.

U.S. GAAP Disclosures

Under U.S. GAAP, the PP&E disclosures include:

- Depreciation expense by period.
- Balances of major classes of assets by nature and function, such as land, improvements, buildings, machinery, and furniture.
- Accumulated depreciation by major classes or in total.
- General description of depreciation methods used.

Under U.S. GAAP, the disclosure requirements for intangible assets are similar to those for PP&E. In addition, the firm must provide an estimate of amortization expense for the next five years.

For impaired assets, the firm must disclose:

- A description of the impaired asset.
- Circumstances that caused the impairment.
- How fair value was determined.
- The amount of loss.
- Where the loss is recognized in the income statement.

LOS 30.k: Compare the financial reporting of investment property with that of property, plant, and equipment.

CFA® Program Curriculum, Volume 3, page 435

Under IFRS, property that a firm owns for the purpose of collecting rental income, earning capital appreciation, or both, is classified as **investment property**. U.S. GAAP does not distinguish investment property from other kinds of long-lived assets.

IFRS gives firms the choice of using a cost model or a fair value model when valuing investment property, if a fair value for the property can be established reliably. A firm generally must use the same valuation model (cost or fair value) for all of its investment properties.

The cost model for investment property is the same as the cost model for valuing property, plant, and equipment, but the fair value model is different from the revaluation model we described earlier. Recall that under the revaluation model, any revaluation above historical cost is recognized as revaluation surplus in owners' equity. For investment property, however, revaluation above historical cost is recognized as a gain on the income statement.

Firms are required to disclose which valuation model they use for investment property. Firms that use the fair value model must state how they determine the fair value of investment property and reconcile its beginning and ending values. Firms that use the cost model must disclose the fair value of their investment property, along with the disclosures that are required for other types of long-lived assets (e.g., useful lives, depreciation methods used).

In some cases, a firm may change its use of a property such that it becomes investment property or is no longer classified as investment property. For example, a firm may move its offices out of a building it owns and begin renting the space to others. If the firm uses the fair value model, the financial statement treatment of the asset's value depends on the nature of the change, as summarized in Figure 2. If the firm uses the cost model, the property's carrying amount does not change when it is transferred into or out of investment property.

Figure 2: Transfers To or From Investment Property (Fair Value Model)

Transfer From	Transfer To	Financial Statement Treatment
Owner-occupied	Investment property	Treat as revaluation: recognize gain only if it reverses previously recognized loss
Inventory	Investment property	Recognize gain or loss if fair value is different from carrying amount
Investment property	Owner-occupied or inventory	Fair value of asset at date of transfer will be its cost under new classification

KEY CONCEPTS

LOS 30.a

When a firm makes an expenditure, it can either capitalize the cost as an asset on the balance sheet or expense the cost in the income statement for the current period. Capitalizing results in higher assets, higher equity, and higher operating cash flow compared to expensing. Capitalizing also results in higher earnings in the first year and lower earnings in subsequent years as the asset is depreciated.

Interest incurred during construction of an asset is generally capitalized. The capitalized interest is added to the asset's value and depreciated over the life of the asset. Because the capitalized interest results in a higher interest coverage ratio (lower denominator), some analysts reverse the transaction and add the capitalized interest to interest expense for the period.

LOS 30.b

The cost of a purchased finite-lived intangible asset is amortized over its useful life. Indefinite-lived intangible assets are not amortized, but are tested for impairment at least annually. The cost of internally developed intangible assets is expensed.

Under IFRS, research costs are expensed and development costs are capitalized. Under U.S. GAAP, both research and development costs are expensed as incurred.

LOS 30.c

Depreciation methods:
- Straight-line: Equal amount of expense each period.
- Accelerated (declining balance): Greater depreciation expense in the early years and less depreciation expense in the later years of an asset's life.
- Units-of-production: Expense based on usage rather than time.

In the early years of an asset's life, accelerated depreciation results in higher depreciation expense, lower net income, and lower ROA and ROE compared to straight-line depreciation. Cash flow is the same assuming tax depreciation is unaffected by the choice of method for financial reporting.

Firms can reduce depreciation expense and increase net income by using longer useful lives and higher salvage values.

©2012 Kaplan, Inc.

LOS 30.d

Straight-line method:

$$\text{depreciation expense} = \frac{\text{original cost} - \text{salvage value}}{\text{depreciable life}}$$

Double-declining balance (DDB), an accelerated depreciation method:

DDB depreciation in year $x =$

$$\frac{2}{\text{depreciable life in years}} \times \text{book value at beginning of year } x$$

Units of production method:

$$\frac{\text{original cost} - \text{salvage value}}{\text{life in output units}} \times \text{output units used in the period}$$

IFRS requires component depreciation, in which significant parts of an asset are identified and depreciated separately.

LOS 30.e

Amortization for intangible assets is identical to the depreciation of tangible assets. It is also necessary to estimate useful lives and salvage values for amortization. However, estimating useful lives is complicated by any factors that limit the use of the intangible assets, such as legal, regulatory, contractual, competitive, and economic factors.

LOS 30.f

The same methods used for depreciating tangible assets—straight-line, accelerated, and units-of-production—are used for intangible assets with finite lives.

LOS 30.g

Under IFRS, firms have the option to revalue assets based on fair value under the revaluation model. U.S. GAAP does not permit revaluation.

The impact of revaluation on the income statement depends on whether the initial revaluation resulted in a gain or loss. If the initial revaluation resulted in a loss (decrease in carrying value), the initial loss would be recognized in the income statement and any subsequent gain would be recognized in the income statement only to the extent of the previously reported loss. Revaluation gains beyond the initial loss bypass the income statement and are recognized in shareholders' equity as a revaluation surplus.

If the initial revaluation resulted in a gain (increase in carrying value), the initial gain would bypass the income statement and be reported as a revaluation surplus. Later revaluation losses would first reduce the revaluation surplus.

LOS 30.h

Under IFRS, an asset is impaired when its carrying value exceeds the recoverable amount. The recoverable amount is the greater of fair value less selling costs and the value in use (present value of expected cash flows). If impaired, the asset is written down to the recoverable amount. Loss recoveries are permitted, but not above historical cost.

Under U.S. GAAP, an asset is impaired if its carrying value is greater than the asset's undiscounted future cash flows. If impaired, the asset is written down to fair value. Subsequent recoveries are not allowed for assets held for use.

Asset impairments result in losses in the income statement. Impairments have no impact on cash flow as they have no tax or other cash flow effects until disposal of the asset.

LOS 30.i

When a long-lived asset is *sold*, the difference between the sale proceeds and the carrying (book) value of the asset is reported as a gain or loss in the income statement.

When a long-lived asset is *abandoned*, the carrying value is removed from the balance sheet and a loss is recognized in that amount.

If a long-lived asset is *exchanged* for another asset, a gain or loss is computed by comparing the carrying value of the old asset with fair value of the old asset (or fair value of the new asset if more clearly evident).

LOS 30.j

There are many differences in the disclosure requirements for tangible and intangible assets under IFRS and U.S. GAAP. However, firms are generally required to disclose:
- Carrying values for each class of asset.
- Accumulated depreciation and amortization.
- Title restrictions and assets pledged as collateral.
- For impaired assets, the loss amount and the circumstances that caused the loss.
- For revalued assets (IFRS only), the revaluation date, how fair value was determined, and the carrying value using the historical cost model.

LOS 30.k

Under IFRS (but not U.S. GAAP), investment property is defined as property owned for the purpose of earning rent, capital appreciation, or both. Firms can account for investment property using the cost model or the fair value model. Unlike the revaluation model for property, plant, and equipment, increases in the fair value of investment property above its historical cost are recognized as gains on the income statement if the firm uses the fair value model.

©2012 Kaplan, Inc.

CONCEPT CHECKERS

1. Red Company immediately expenses its development costs while Black
    Company capitalizes its development costs. All else equal, Red Company will:
    A. show smoother reported earnings than Black Company.
    B. report higher operating cash flow than Black Company.
    C. report higher asset turnover than Black Company.

2. Which of the following statements about indefinite-lived intangible assets is *most
    accurate*?
    A. They are amortized on a straight-line basis over a period not to exceed 40
        years.
    B. They are reported on the balance sheet indefinitely.
    C. They never appear on the balance sheet unless they are internally developed.

3. In the early years of an asset's life, a firm using the double-declining balance
    method, as compared to a firm using straight-line depreciation, will report
    lower:
    A. depreciation expense.
    B. operating cash flow.
    C. retained earnings.

4. East Company purchased a new truck at the beginning of this year for $30,000.
    The truck has a useful life of eight years or 150,000 miles, and an estimated
    salvage value of $3,000. If the truck is driven 16,500 miles this year, how much
    depreciation will East report under the double-declining balance (DDB) method
    and the units-of-production (UOP) method?

	DDB	UOP
A.	$7,500	$2,970
B.	$7,500	$3,300
C.	$6,750	$2,970

5. Which of the following is *least likely* considered in determining the useful life an
    intangible asset?
    A. Initial cost.
    B. Legal, regulatory, or contractual provisions.
    C. Provisions for renewal or extension.

6. At the beginning of this year, Fairweather Corp. incurred $200,000 of research
    costs and $100,000 of development costs to create a new patent. The patent is
    expected to have a useful life of 40 years with no salvage value. Calculate the
    carrying value of the patent at the end of this year, assuming Fairweather follows
    U.S. GAAP.
    A. $0.
    B. $97,500.
    C. $292,500.

7. Two years ago, Metcalf Corp. purchased machinery for $800,000. At the end of last year, the machinery had a fair value of $720,000. Assuming Metcalf uses the revaluation model, what amount, if any, is recognized in Metcalf's net income this year if the machinery's fair value is $810,000?
    A. $0.
    B. $80,000.
    C. $90,000.

8. According to U.S. GAAP, an asset is impaired when:
    A. the firm cannot fully recover the carrying amount of the asset through operations.
    B. accumulated depreciation plus salvage value exceeds acquisition cost.
    C. the present value of future cash flows from an asset exceeds its carrying value.

9. A firm recently recognized a $15,000 loss on the sale of machinery used in its manufacturing operation. The original cost of the machinery was $100,000 and the accumulated depreciation at the date of sale was $60,000. What amount did the firm receive from the sale?
    A. $25,000.
    B. $45,000.
    C. $85,000.

10. Which of the following disclosures would *least likely* be found in the financial statement footnotes of a firm?
    A. Accumulated depreciation.
    B. Carrying values by asset class.
    C. Average age of assets.

©2012 Kaplan, Inc.

ANSWERS – CONCEPT CHECKERS

1. **C** As compared to a firm that capitalizes its expenditures, a firm that immediately expenses expenditures will report lower assets. Thus, asset turnover (revenue / average assets) will be higher for the expensing firm (lower denominator).

2. **B** Indefinite-lived intangible assets are not amortized; rather, they are reported on the balance sheet indefinitely unless they are impaired.

3. **C** In the early years, accelerated depreciation will result in higher depreciation expense; thus, lower net income. Lower net income will result in lower retained earnings.

4. **A** Double-declining balance = $30,000 book value × (2/8) = $7,500.

   Units-of-production = ($30,000 cost − $3,000 salvage value) / 150,000 miles = $0.18 per mile.

   16,500 miles driven × $0.18 per mile = $2,970.

5. **A** Initial cost has nothing to do with the useful life of an intangible asset.

6. **A** Under U.S. GAAP, research and development costs are expensed as incurred. Thus, the entire $300,000 of R&D is expensed this year. The result is a zero carrying value.

7. **B** Under the revaluation method, Metcalf reports the equipment on the balance sheet at fair value. At the end of last year, an $80,000 loss was recognized (from $800,000 to $720,000) in the income statement. Any recovery is recognized in the income statement to the extent of the loss. Any remainder is recognized in shareholders' equity as revaluation surplus. Thus, at the end of this year, an $80,000 gain is recognized in the income statement, and a $10,000 revaluation surplus is recognized in shareholders' equity.

8. **A** An asset is impaired when the firm cannot recover the carrying value. Under U.S. GAAP, recoverability is tested based on undiscounted future cash flows.

9. **A** Gain or loss is equal to the sale proceeds minus the carrying value (cost minus accumulated depreciation) at the time of sale. Given the loss of $15,000 and carrying value of $40,000 ($100,000 − $60,000), we can solve for the proceeds of $25,000 (−15,000 + 40,000).

10. **C** The average age is not a required disclosure. However, it can be calculated given other disclosures.

The following is a review of the Financial Reporting and Analysis principles designed to address the learning outcome statements set forth by CFA Institute. This topic is also covered in:

INCOME TAXES

EXAM FOCUS

In many countries, financial reporting standards and tax reporting standards differ. Candidates should be aware of the terminology that relates to each set of standards, notably taxes payable, which are the taxes actually due to the government, and income tax expense, which is reported on the income statement and reflects taxes payable plus any deferred income tax expense. The timing of revenue and expense recognition in the income statement and the tax return may lead to the creation of deferred tax liabilities, which the company may have to pay in the future, or deferred tax assets, which may provide benefits in the future. For the exam, you should know that some differences between taxable and pretax income are temporary, while some are permanent and will never reverse. Be prepared to calculate taxes payable, tax expense, deferred tax liabilities and assets, and be able to make the necessary adjustments for analytical purposes.

LOS 31.a: Describe the differences between accounting profit and taxable income, and define key terms, including deferred tax assets, deferred tax liabilities, valuation allowance, taxes payable, and income tax expense.

CFA® Program Curriculum, Volume 3, page 450

Financial accounting standards (IFRS and U.S. GAAP) are often different than income tax laws and regulations. As a result, the amount of income tax expense recognized in the income statement may differ from the actual taxes owed to the taxing authorities.

Tax Return Terminology

- **Taxable income.** Income subject to tax based on the tax return.
- **Taxes payable.** The tax liability on the balance sheet caused by *taxable income*. This is also known as current tax expense, but do not confuse this with *income tax expense* (see below).
- **Income tax paid.** The actual cash flow for income taxes including payments or refunds from other years.
- **Tax loss carryforward.** A current or past loss that can be used to reduce taxable income (thus, taxes payable) in the future. Can result in a deferred tax asset.
- **Tax base.** Net amount of an asset or liability used for tax reporting purposes.

Financial Reporting Terminology

- **Accounting profit.** Pretax financial income based on financial accounting standards. Also known as *income before tax* and *earnings before tax*.

©2012 Kaplan, Inc.

- **Income tax expense.** Expense recognized in the income statement that includes taxes payable and *changes* in deferred tax assets and liabilities (DTA and DTL). The income tax expense equation is:

  income tax expense = taxes payable + ΔDTL – ΔDTA

- **Deferred tax liabilities.** Balance sheet amounts that result from an excess of income tax expense over taxes payable that are expected to result in future cash outflows.
- **Deferred tax assets.** Balance sheet amounts that result from an excess of taxes payable over income tax expense that are expected to be recovered from future operations. Can also result from tax loss carryforwards.
- **Valuation allowance.** Reduction of deferred tax assets based on the likelihood the assets will not be realized.
- **Carrying value.** Net balance sheet value of an asset or liability.
- **Permanent difference.** A difference between taxable income (tax return) and pretax income (income statement) that will not reverse in the future.
- **Temporary difference.** A difference between the tax base and the carrying value of an asset or liability that will result in either taxable amounts or deductible amounts in the future. Several examples of how temporary differences arise are presented later in this review.

LOS 31.b: Explain how deferred tax liabilities and assets are created and the factors that determine how a company's deferred tax liabilities and assets should be treated for the purposes of financial analysis.

CFA® Program Curriculum, Volume 3, page 452

Differences between the treatment of an accounting item for tax reporting and for financial reporting can occur when:

- The timing of revenue and expense recognition in the income statement and the tax return differ.
- Certain revenues and expenses are recognized in the income statement but never on the tax return or vice-versa.
- Assets and/or liabilities have different carrying amounts and tax bases.
- Gain or loss recognition in the income statement differs from the tax return.
- Tax losses from prior periods may offset future taxable income.
- Financial statement adjustments may not affect the tax return or may be recognized in different periods.

Deferred Tax Liabilities

A **deferred tax liability** is created when income tax expense (income statement) is greater than taxes payable (tax return) due to temporary differences. Deferred tax liabilities occur when:

- Revenues (or gains) are recognized in the income statement before they are included on the tax return due to temporary differences.
- Expenses (or losses) are tax deductible before they are recognized in the income statement.

Deferred tax liabilities are expected to reverse (i.e., they are caused by temporary differences) and result in future cash outflows when the taxes are paid.

The most common way that deferred tax liabilities are created is when different depreciation methods are used on the tax return and the income statement.

Deferred Tax Assets

A **deferred tax asset** is created when taxes payable (tax return) are greater than income tax expense (income statement) due to temporary differences. Deferred tax assets occur when:

- Revenues (or gains) are taxable before they are recognized in the income statement.
- Expenses (or losses) are recognized in the income statement before they are tax deductible.
- Tax loss carryforwards are available to reduce future taxable income.

Similar to deferred tax liabilities, deferred tax assets are expected to reverse through future operations. However, deferred tax assets are expected to provide future tax savings, while deferred tax liabilities are expected to result in future cash outflows.

Post-employment benefits, warranty expenses, and *tax loss carryforwards* are typical causes of deferred tax assets.

Treatment for Analytical Purposes

If deferred tax liabilities are expected to reverse in the future, they are best classified by an analyst as liabilities. If, however, they are not expected to reverse in the future, they are best classified as equity (DTL decreased and equity increased by the same amount). The key question is, "When or will the total deferred tax liability be reversed in the future?" In practice, the treatment of deferred taxes for analytical purposes varies. An analyst must decide on the appropriate treatment on a case-by-case basis.

LOS 31.c: Determine the tax base of a company's assets and liabilities.

CFA® Program Curriculum, Volume 3, page 455

Tax Base of Assets

An asset's **tax base** is the amount that will be deducted (expensed) on the tax return in the future as the economic benefits of the asset are realized. The **carrying value** is the value of the asset reported on the financial statements, net of depreciation and amortization.

©2012 Kaplan, Inc.

Following are a few examples of calculating the tax bases of various assets.

Depreciable equipment. The cost of equipment is $100,000. In the income statement, depreciation expense of $10,000 is recognized each year for ten years. On the tax return, the asset is depreciated at $20,000 per year for five years.

At the end of the first year, the tax base is $80,000 ($100,000 cost − $20,000 accumulated tax depreciation) and the carrying value is $90,000 ($100,000 cost − $10,000 accumulated financial depreciation). A deferred tax liability ($10,000 × tax rate) is created to account for the timing difference from different depreciation for tax and for financial reporting.

Sale of the machine for $100,000, for example, would result in a gain of $10,000 on the income statement and a gain of $20,000 on the tax return. This would reverse the deferred tax liability.

Research and development. At the beginning of this year, $75,000 of R&D was expensed in the income statement. On the tax return, the R&D was capitalized and is amortized on a straight-line basis over three years.

At the end of the first year, the tax base is $50,000 ($75,000 cost − $25,000 accumulated tax amortization) and the asset has no carrying value (does not appear on the balance sheet) because the entire cost was expensed. Note that amortization for tax here leads to a deferred tax asset, since earnings before tax are less than taxable income.

Accounts receivable. Gross receivables totaling $20,000 are outstanding at year-end. Because collection is uncertain, the firm recognizes bad debt expense of $1,500 in the income statement. For tax purposes, bad debt expense cannot be deducted until the receivables are deemed worthless.

At the end of the year, the tax base of the receivables is $20,000 since no bad debt expense has been deducted on the tax return. The carrying value is $18,500 ($20,000 − $1,500 bad debt expense). Again, a deferred tax asset is the result.

Tax Base of Liabilities

A liability's tax base is the carrying value of the liability minus any amounts that will be deductible on the tax return in the future. The tax base of revenue received in advance is the carrying value minus the amount of revenue that will *not* be taxed in the future.

Following are a few examples of calculating the tax bases of various liabilities.

Customer advance. At year-end, $10,000 was received from a customer for goods that will be shipped next year. On the tax return, revenue received in advance is taxable when collected.

The carrying value of the liability is $10,000. The carrying value will be reduced when the goods are shipped next year. For revenue received in advance, the tax base is equal to the carrying value minus any amounts that will *not* be taxed in the future. Since the customer advance has already been taxed, $10,000 will not be taxed in the future. Thus, the customer advance liability has a tax base of zero ($10,000 carrying value – $10,000 revenue not taxed in the future). Since the $10,000 has been taxed but not yet reported as revenue on the income statement, a deferred tax asset is created.

Warranty liability. At year-end, a firm estimates that $5,000 of warranty expense will be required on goods already sold. On the tax return, warranty expense is not deductible until the warranty work is actually performed. The warranty work will be performed next year.

The carrying value of the warranty liability is $5,000. The tax base is equal to the carrying value minus the amount deductible in the future. Thus, the warranty liability has a tax base of zero ($5,000 carrying value – $5,000 warranty expense deductible in the future). Delayed recognition of this expense for tax results in a deferred tax asset.

Note payable. The firm has an outstanding promissory note with a principal balance of $30,000. Interest accrues at 10% and is paid at the end of each quarter.

The promissory note is treated the same way on the tax return and in the financial statements. Thus, the carrying value and the tax base are both $30,000. Interest paid is included in both pre-tax income on the income statement and in taxable income on the tax return. With no timing difference, no deferred tax items are created.

LOS 31.d: Calculate income tax expense, income taxes payable, deferred tax assets, and deferred tax liabilities, and calculate and interpret the adjustment to the financial statements related to a change in the income tax rate.

CFA® Program Curriculum, Volume 3, page 455

Professor's Note: The effects of changing tax rates on deferred tax assets and liabilities are explained in the next LOS.

©2012 Kaplan, Inc.

Example: Deferred tax liabilities

Assume the original cost of an asset is $600,000. The asset has a 3-year life and no salvage value is expected. For tax purposes, the asset is depreciated using an accelerated depreciation method with tax return depreciation of $300,000 in year 1, $200,000 in year 2, and $100,000 in year 3. The firm recognizes straight-line (SL) depreciation expense of $200,000 each year in its income statements. Earnings before interest, taxes, depreciation, and amortization (EBITDA) is $500,000 each year. The firm's tax rate is 40%. Calculate the firm's income tax expense, taxes payable, and deferred tax liability for each year of the asset's life.

Answer:

The following tables illustrate the calculation of taxes payable reported on the tax return and income tax expense reported in the income statement.

Tax Return (40% Tax Rate, Accelerated Depreciation)

	Year 1	Year 2	Year 3	Total 1–3
EBITDA	$500,000	$500,000	$500,000	$1,500,000
Depreciation	$300,000	$200,000	$100,000	$600,000
Taxable income	$200,000	$300,000	$400,000	$900,000
Tax rate	× 0.40	× 0.40	× 0.40	× 0.40
Tax payable	$80,000	$120,000	$160,000	$360,000

Income Statement (40% Tax Rate, SL Depreciation)

	Year 1	Year 2	Year 3	Total 1–3
EBITDA	$500,000	$500,000	$500,000	$1,500,000
Depreciation	$200,000	$200,000	$200,000	$600,000
Pre-tax income	$300,000	$300,000	$300,000	$900,000
Tax rate	× 0.40	× 0.40	× 0.40	× 0.40
Income tax expense	$120,000	$120,000	$120,000	$360,000

In year 1, the firm recognizes $120,000 of income tax expense on the income statement but taxes payable (tax return) are only $80,000. So, income tax expense is *initially* higher than taxes payable. The $40,000 difference is deferred to a future period by using an accelerated depreciation method for tax purposes. The $40,000 is reported on the balance sheet by creating a DTL.

The tax base and the carrying value of the asset are used to calculate the *balance* of the DTL. At the end of year 1, the carrying value of the asset is $400,000 and the tax base of the asset is $300,000. By multiplying the $100,000 difference by the 40% tax rate, we get the *balance* of the DTL of $40,000.

We can reconcile income tax expense and taxes payable with the *change* in the DTL. In this example, the DTL increased $40,000 (from zero to $40,000) during year 1. Thus, income tax expense in year 1 is $120,000 ($80,000 taxes payable + $40,000 *change* in the DTL).

In year 2, depreciation expense is the same on the tax return and the income statement. Thus, taxable income is equal to pretax income and there is no change in the DTL. Income tax expense in year 2 is $120,000 ($120,000 taxes payable + zero *change* in the DTL).

In year 3, the firm recognizes income tax expense of $120,000 on the income statement but $160,000 in taxes payable (tax return). The $40,000 deferred tax liability recognized at the end of year 1 has reversed as a result of lower depreciation expense using the accelerated method on the tax return. In year 3, income tax expense is $120,000 [$160,000 taxes payable + (–$40,000 *change* in DTL)].

Note that over the useful life of the asset, total depreciation, total taxable (and pretax) income, and total taxes payable (and income tax expense) are the same on the financial statements and the tax return. Also, at the end of year 3, both the tax base and the carrying value of the asset are equal to zero. By using accelerated depreciation for tax purposes, the firm *deferred* $40,000 of taxes from year 1 to year 3.

Example: Deferred tax assets

Consider warranty guarantees and associated expenses. Pretax income (financial reporting) includes an accrual for warranty expense, but warranty cost is not deductible for taxable income until the firm has made actual expenditures to meet warranty claims. Suppose:

- A firm has sales of $5,000 for each of two years.
- The firm estimates that warranty expense will be 2% of annual sales ($100).
- The actual expenditure of $200 to meet all warranty claims was not made until the second year.
- Assume a tax rate of 40%.

Calculate the firm's income tax expense, taxes payable, and deferred tax assets for year 1 and year 2.

©2012 Kaplan, Inc.

Answer:

For tax reporting, taxable income and taxes payable for two years are:

Tax Reporting—Warranty Expense

	Year 1	Year 2
Revenue	$5,000	$5,000
Warranty expense	0	200
Taxable income	$5,000	$4,800
Taxes payable	2,000	1,920
Net income	$3,000	$2,880

For financial reporting, pretax income and tax expense are:

Financial Reporting—Warranty Expense

	Year 1	Year 2
Revenue	$5,000	$5,000
Warranty expense	100	100
Pretax income	$4,900	$4,900
Tax expense	1,960	1,960
Net income	$2,940	$2,940

In year 1, the firm reports $1,960 of tax expense in the income statement, but $2,000 of taxes payable are reported on the tax return. In this example, taxes payable are *initially* higher than tax expense and the $40 difference is reported on the balance sheet by creating a DTA.

The tax base and the carrying value of the warranty liability are used to calculate the *balance* of the DTA. At the end of year 1, the carrying value of the warranty liability is $100 (the warranty expense has been recognized in the income statement but it has not been paid), and the tax base of the liability is zero (the warranty expense has not been recognized on the tax return). By multiplying the $100 difference by the 40% tax rate, we get the *balance* of the DTA of $40 [($100 carrying value – zero tax base) × 40%].

We can reconcile income tax expense and taxes payable with the *change* in the DTA. In this example, the DTA increased $40 (from zero to $40) during year 1. Thus, income tax expense in year 1 is $1,960 ($2,000 taxes payable – $40 increase in the DTA).

In year 2, the firm recognizes $1,960 of tax expense in the income statement but only $1,920 is reported on the tax return (taxes payable). The $40 deferred tax asset recognized at the end of year 1 has reversed as a result of the warranty expense recognition on the tax return. So, in year 2, income tax expense is $1,960 ($1,920 taxes payable + $40 decrease in DTA).

Professor's Note: To summarize, if taxable income (on the tax return) is less than pretax income (on the income statement) and the difference is expected to reverse in future years, a deferred tax liability is created. If taxable income is greater than pretax income and the difference is expected to reverse in future years, a deferred tax asset is created.

LOS 31.e: Evaluate the impact of tax rate changes on a company's financial statements and ratios.

CFA® Program Curriculum, Volume 3, page 460

When the income tax rate changes, deferred tax assets and liabilities are adjusted to reflect the new rate. The adjustment can also affect income tax expense.

An increase in the tax rate will increase both deferred tax liabilities and deferred tax assets. A decrease in the tax rate will decrease both deferred tax liabilities and deferred tax assets.

DTL and DTA values on the balance sheet must be changed because the new tax rate is the rate expected to be in force when the associated reversals occur. If there is an increase (decrease) in the tax rate, when previously deferred income is recognized for tax, the tax due will be higher (lower), and when expense items previously reported in the financial statements are recognized for tax, the benefit will be greater (less).

Changes in the balance sheet values of DTLs and DTAs to account for a change in the tax rate will affect income tax expense in the current period.

income tax expense = taxes payable + ΔDTL – ΔDTA

If tax rates increase, the increase in the DTL is added to taxes payable and the increase in the DTA is subtracted from taxes payable to arrive at income tax expense.

If tax rates decrease, the decrease in the DTL would result in lower income tax expense and the decrease in the DTA would result in higher income tax expense. In the case of the DTL we are adding a negative change, and in the case of the DTA we are subtracting a negative change.

The following example illustrates the effects of a change in the tax rate.

©2012 Kaplan, Inc.

Example: Accounting effects of a change in a firm's tax rate

A firm owns equipment with a carrying value of $200,000 and a tax base of $160,000 at year-end. The tax rate is 40%. In this case, the firm will report a DTL of $16,000 [($200,000 carrying value – $160,000 tax base) × 40%]. The firm also has a DTA of $10,000 that was created by bad debt that was recognized as an expense in the income statement but has not yet been deducted on the tax return. The bad debt expense created a DTA of $4,000 [($10,000 tax base – zero carrying value) × 40%]. Calculate the effect on the firm's income tax expense if the tax rate decreases to 30%.

Answer:

As a result of the decrease in tax rate, the balance of the DTL is reduced to $12,000 [($200,000 carrying value – $160,000 tax base) × 30%]. Thus, due to the lower tax rate, the change in the DTL is –$4,000 ($16,000 reported DTL – $12,000 adjusted DTL).

The balance of the DTA is reduced to $3,000 [($10,000 tax base – zero carrying value) × 30%]. Thus, due to the lower tax rate, the DTA decreases by $1,000 ($4,000 reported DTA – $3,000 adjusted DTA).

Using the income tax equation, we can see that income tax expense decreases by $3,000 (income tax expense = taxes payable + ΔDTL – ΔDTA).

LOS 31.f: Distinguish between temporary and permanent differences in pre-tax accounting income and taxable income.

CFA® Program Curriculum, Volume 3, page 460

A **permanent difference** is a difference between taxable income and pretax income that will not reverse in the future. Permanent differences do not create deferred tax assets or deferred tax liabilities. Permanent differences can be caused by revenue that is not taxable, expenses that are not deductible, or tax credits that result in a direct reduction of taxes.

Permanent differences will cause the firm's **effective tax rate** to differ from the **statutory tax rate**. The statutory rate is the tax rate of the jurisdiction where the firm operates. The effective tax rate is derived from the income statement.

$$\text{effective tax rate} = \frac{\text{income tax expense}}{\text{pretax income}}$$

The statutory rate and effective rate may also differ if the firm is operating in more than one tax jurisdiction.

A **temporary difference** refers to a difference between the tax base and the carrying value of an asset or liability that will result in taxable amounts or deductible amounts in the future. If the temporary difference is expected to reverse in the future and the balance sheet item is expected to provide future economic benefits, a DTA or DTL is created.

Temporary differences can be **taxable temporary differences** that result in expected future taxable income or **deductible temporary differences** that result in expected future tax deductions.

Example: Temporary and permanent differences between taxes payable and income tax expense

Using the following table and the examples of determining the tax base of assets and liabilities presented earlier, identify the type of difference (taxable temporary, deductible temporary, or permanent), and determine if the difference creates a DTA or a DTL.

	Tax Base	Carrying Value	Type of Difference	Result
Assets				
Depreciable equipment	$80,000	$90,000		
Research and development	50,000	0		
Accounts receivable	20,000	18,500		
Municipal bond interest	5,000	5,000		
Liabilities				
Customer advance	$0	$10,000		
Warranty liability	0	5,000		
Officers' life insurance	0	0		
Note payable	30,000	30,000		
Interest paid	0	0		

Answer:

Depreciable equipment. Accelerating depreciation expense on the tax return will result in a taxable temporary difference. Taxable income will be higher in the future because accelerated depreciation will be lower when the reversal occurs. Since the carrying value of the asset is greater than the tax base, a DTL is created.

Research and development. Capitalized R&D for tax purposes will result in a deductible temporary difference as taxable income will be lower in the future when the reversal occurs. Since the tax base of the asset is greater than the carrying value, a DTA is created.

Accounts receivable. Delaying bad debt expense for tax purposes will result in a deductible temporary difference as taxable income will be lower in the future when the reversal occurs. Since the tax base of the asset is greater than the carrying value, a DTA is created.

Municipal bond interest. Since municipal bond interest is typically not taxable, it results in a permanent difference. No deferred taxes are recognized.

©2012 Kaplan, Inc.

Customer advance. Recognizing the customer advance on the tax return will result in a deductible temporary difference as COGS is included in taxable income in the future when the goods are delivered. Since the carrying value of the liability is greater than the tax base, a DTA is created.

Warranty liability. Delaying warranty expense for tax purposes will result in a deductible temporary difference as taxable income will be lower in the future when the reversal occurs. Since the carrying value of the liability is greater than the tax base, a DTA is created.

Officers' life insurance. Since officers' life insurance is not tax deductible, it results in a permanent difference. No deferred taxes are recognized.

Note payable and interest paid. No temporary differences result from the note payable or the interest paid on the note. No deferred taxes are recognized.

Temporary differences leading to DTLs can arise from an investment in another firm (e.g., subsidiaries, affiliates, branches, and joint ventures) when the parent company recognizes earnings from the investment before dividends are received. However, if the parent company can control the timing of the future reversal and it is probable the temporary difference will not reverse, no DTL is reported.

A temporary difference from an investment will result in a DTA only if the temporary difference is expected to reverse in the future, and sufficient taxable profits are expected to exist when the reversal occurs.

LOS 31.g: Describe the valuation allowance for deferred tax assets—when it is required and what impact it has on financial statements.

CFA® Program Curriculum, Volume 3, page 465

Although deferred taxes are created from temporary differences that are expected to reverse in the future, neither deferred tax assets nor deferred tax liabilities are carried on the balance sheet at their discounted present value. However, deferred tax assets are assessed at each balance sheet date to determine the likelihood of sufficient future taxable income to recover the tax assets. Without future taxable income, a DTA is worthless.

According to U.S. GAAP, if it is more likely than not (greater than a 50% probability) that some or all of a DTA will not be realized (insufficient future taxable income to recover the tax asset), then the DTA must be reduced by a **valuation allowance**. The valuation allowance is a contra account that reduces the net balance sheet value of the DTA. Increasing the valuation allowance will decrease the net balance sheet DTA, increasing income tax expense and decreasing net income.

If circumstances change, the net DTA can be increased by decreasing the valuation allowance. This would result in higher earnings.

It is up to management to defend the recognition of all deferred tax assets. If a company has order backlogs or existing contracts which are expected to generate future taxable income, a valuation allowance might not be necessary. However, if a company has cumulative losses over the past few years or a history of inability to use tax loss carryforwards, then the company would need to use a valuation allowance to reflect the likelihood that a deferred tax asset will never be realized.

Because an increase (decrease) in the valuation allowance will decrease (increase) earnings, management can manipulate earnings by changing the valuation allowance.

Whenever a company reports substantial deferred tax assets, an analyst should review the company's financial performance to determine the likelihood that those assets will be realized. Analysts should also scrutinize changes in the valuation allowance to determine whether those changes are economically justified.

 Professor's Note: A valuation allowance account is only used for deferred tax assets. Under U.S. GAAP, deferred tax assets and deferred tax liabilities appear separately on the balance sheet, and they are not typically netted.

LOS 31.h: Compare a company's deferred tax items.

CFA® Program Curriculum, Volume 3, page 469

Companies are required to disclose details on the source of the temporary differences that cause the deferred tax assets and liabilities reported on the balance sheet. Changes in those balance sheet accounts are reflected in income tax expense on the income statement. Here are some common examples of temporary differences you may encounter:

- A deferred tax liability results from using accelerated *depreciation* for tax purposes and straight-line depreciation for the financial statements. The analyst should consider the firm's growth rate and capital spending levels when determining whether the difference will actually reverse.
- *Impairments* generally result in a deferred tax asset since the writedown is recognized immediately in the income statement, but the deduction on the tax return is generally not allowed until the asset is sold or disposed of.
- *Restructuring* generates a deferred tax asset because the costs are recognized for financial reporting purposes when the restructuring is announced, but not deducted for tax purposes until actually paid. Note that restructuring usually results in significant cash outflows (net of the tax savings) in the years after the restructuring costs are reported.
- In the United States, firms that use LIFO for their financial statements are required to use LIFO for tax purposes, so no temporary differences result. However, in countries where this is not a requirement, temporary differences can result from the *choice of inventory cost-flow method*.
- *Post-employment benefits* and *deferred compensation* are both recognized for financial reporting when earned by the employee but not deducted for tax purposes until actually paid. These can result in a deferred tax asset that will be reversed when the benefits or compensation are paid.
- A deferred tax adjustment is made to stockholders' equity to reflect the future tax impact of unrealized gains or losses on *available-for-sale marketable securities* that are taken directly to equity. No DTL is added to the balance sheet for the future tax liability when gains/losses are realized.

©2012 Kaplan, Inc.

Example: Analyzing deferred tax item disclosures

WCCO, Inc.'s income tax expense has consistently been larger than taxes payable over the last three years. WCCO disclosed in the footnotes to its 20X5 financial statements the major items recorded as deferred tax assets and liabilities (in millions of dollars), as shown in the following table.

Deferred Tax Disclosures in Footnotes to WCCO, Inc., Financial Statements

	20X5	20X4	20X3
Employee benefits	$278	$310	$290
International tax loss carryforwards	101	93	115
Subtotal	379	403	405
Valuation allowance	(24)	(57)	(64)
Deferred tax asset	355	346	341
Property, plant, and equipment	452	361	320
Unrealized gains on available-for-sale securities	67	44	23
Deferred tax liability	519	405	343
Deferred income taxes	$164	$59	$2

Use the table above to explain why income tax expense has exceeded taxes payable over the last three years. Also explain the effect of the change in the valuation allowance on WCCO's earnings for 20X5.

Answer:

The company's deferred tax asset balance results from international tax loss carryforwards and employee benefits (most likely pension and other post-retirement benefits), offset by a valuation allowance. The company's deferred tax liability balance results from property, plant, and equipment (most likely from using accelerated depreciation methods for tax purposes and straight-line on the financial statements) and unrealized gains on securities classified as available-for-sale (because the unrealized gain is not taxable until realized).

Income tax expense is equal to taxes payable plus deferred income tax expense. Because deferred tax liabilities have been growing faster than deferred tax assets, deferred income tax expense has been positive, resulting in income tax expense being higher than taxes payable.

Management decreased the valuation allowance by $33 million in 20X5. This resulted in a reduction in deferred income tax expense and an increase in reported earnings for 20X5.

LOS 31.i: Analyze disclosures relating to deferred tax items and the effective tax rate reconciliation, and explain how information included in these disclosures affects a company's financial statements and financial ratios.

CFA® Program Curriculum, Volume 3, page 469

Typically, the following deferred tax information is disclosed:

- Deferred tax liabilities, deferred tax assets, any valuation allowance, and the net change in the valuation allowance over the period.
- Any unrecognized deferred tax liability for undistributed earnings of subsidiaries and joint ventures.
- Current-year tax effect of each type of temporary difference.
- Components of income tax expense.
- Reconciliation of reported income tax expense and the tax expense based on the statutory rate.
- Tax loss carryforwards and credits.

Analyzing the Effective Tax Rate Reconciliation

Some firms' reported income tax expense differs from the amount based on the statutory income tax rate. Recall that the statutory rate is the tax rate of the jurisdiction where the firm operates. The differences are generally the result of:

- Different tax rates in different tax jurisdictions (countries).
- Permanent tax differences: tax credits, tax-exempt income, nondeductible expenses, and tax differences between capital gains and operating income.
- Changes in tax rates and legislation.
- Deferred taxes provided on the reinvested earnings of foreign and unconsolidated domestic affiliates.
- Tax holidays in some countries (watch for special conditions such as termination dates for the holiday or a requirement to pay the accumulated taxes at some point in the future).

Understanding the differences between reported income tax expense and the amount based on the statutory income tax rate will enable the analyst to better estimate future earnings and cash flow.

When estimating future earnings and cash flows, the analyst should understand each element of the reconciliation, including its relative impact, how it has changed with time, and how it is likely to change in the future.

In analyzing trends in tax rates, it is important to only include reconciliation items that are continuous in nature rather than those that are sporadic. Items including different rates in different countries, tax-exempt income, and non-deductible expenses tend to be continuous. Other items are almost always sporadic, such as the occurrence of large asset sales and tax holiday savings. The disclosures of each financial statement should be reviewed based on the footnotes and management discussion and analysis.

©2012 Kaplan, Inc.

Example: Analyzing the tax rate reconciliation

Novelty Distribution Company (NDC) does business in the United States and abroad. The company's reconciliation between effective and statutory tax rates for three years is provided in the following figure. Analyze the trend in effective tax rates over the three years shown.

Statutory U.S. Federal Income Tax Rate Reconciliation

	20X3	20X4	20X5
Statutory U.S. federal income tax rate	35.0%	35.0%	35.0%
State income taxes, net of related federal income tax benefit	2.1%	2.2%	2.3%
Benefits and taxes related to foreign operations	(6.5%)	(6.3%)	(2.7%)
Tax rate changes	0.0%	0.0%	(2.0%)
Capital gains on sale of assets	0.0%	(3.0%)	0.0%
Special items	(1.6%)	8.7%	2.5%
Other, net	0.8%	0.7%	(1.4%)
Effective income tax rates	29.8%	37.3%	33.7%

	20X3	20X4	20X5
Taxable income	$2,330.00	$1,660.00	$2,350.00
Statutory U.S. federal income tax	815.50	581.00	822.50
State income taxes, net of related federal income tax benefit	48.93	36.52	54.05
Benefits and taxes related to foreign operations	(151.45)	(104.58)	(63.45)
Tax rate changes	–	–	(47.00)
Capital gains on sale of assets	–	(49.80)	–
Special items	(37.28)	144.42	58.75
Other, net	18.64	11.62	(32.90)
Effective income taxes	$694.34	$619.18	$791.95

Answer:

For some trend analysis, the analyst may want to convert the reconciliation from percentages to absolute numbers. However, for this example, the trends can be analyzed simply by using the percentages.

The effective tax rate is upward trending over the 3-year period. Contributing to the upward trend is an increase in the state income tax rate and the loss of benefits related to taxes on foreign income. In 20X4, a loss related to the sale of assets partially offset an increase in taxes created by special items. In 20X3 and 20X5, the special items and the other items also offset each other. The fact that the special items and other items are so volatile over the 3-year period suggests that it will be difficult for an analyst to forecast the effective tax rate for NDC for the foreseeable future without additional information. This volatility also reduces comparability with other firms.

LOS 31.j: Identify the key provisions of and differences between income tax accounting under IFRS and U.S. GAAP.

CFA® Program Curriculum, Volume 3, page 474

Accounting for income taxes under U.S. GAAP and IFRS is similar in most respects. However, there are some differences. Many differences relate to the different tax laws and regulations of the different countries. Figure 1 is a summary of a few of the more important differences.

©2012 Kaplan, Inc.

Figure 1: Tax Accounting Differences, IFRS vs. U.S. GAAP

	U.S. GAAP	IFRS
Revaluation of fixed assets and intangible assets	Not applicable, no revaluation allowed.	Deferred taxes are recognized in equity.
Undistributed profit from an investment in a subsidiary	No deferred taxes for foreign subsidiaries that meet the indefinite reversal criterion. No deferred taxes for domestic subsidiaries if the amounts are tax free.	Deferred taxes are recognized unless the parent is able to control the distribution of profit and it is probable the temporary difference will not reverse in the future.
Undistributed profit from an investment in a joint venture (JV)	No deferred taxes for foreign corporate JVs that meet the indefinite reversal criterion.	Deferred taxes are recognized unless the venturer is able to control the sharing of profit and it is probable the temporary difference will not reverse in the future.
Undistributed profit from an investment in an associate firm.	Deferred taxes are recognized from temporary differences.	Deferred taxes are recognized unless the investor is able to control the sharing of profit and it is probable the temporary difference will not reverse in the future.
Deferred tax asset recognition	Recognized in full and then reduced if "more likely than not" that some or all of the tax asset will not be realized.	Recognized if "probable" that sufficient taxable profit will be available to recover the tax asset.
Tax rate used to measure deferred taxes	Enacted tax rate only.	Enacted or substantively enacted tax rate.
Presentation of deferred taxes on the balance sheet	Classified as current or noncurrent based on the classification of the underlying asset or liability.	Netted and classified as noncurrent.

KEY CONCEPTS

LOS 31.a

Deferred tax terminology:

- **Taxable income.** Income subject to tax based on the tax return.
- **Accounting profit.** Pretax income from the income statement based on financial accounting standards.
- **Deferred tax assets.** Balance sheet asset value that results when taxes payable (tax return) are greater than income tax expense (income statement) and the difference is expected to reverse in future periods.
- **Deferred tax liabilities.** Balance sheet liability value that results when income tax expense (income statement) is greater than taxes payable (tax return) and the difference is expected to reverse in future periods.
- **Valuation allowance.** Reduction of deferred tax assets (contra account) based on the likelihood that the future tax benefit will not be realized.
- **Taxes payable.** The tax liability from the tax return. Note that this term also refers to a liability that appears on the balance sheet for taxes due but not yet paid.
- **Income tax expense.** Expense recognized in the income statement that includes taxes payable and changes in deferred tax assets and liabilities.

LOS 31.b

A *deferred tax liability* is created when income tax expense (income statement) is higher than taxes payable (tax return). Deferred tax liabilities occur when revenues (or gains) are recognized in the income statement before they are taxable on the tax return, or expenses (or losses) are tax deductible before they are recognized in the income statement.

A *deferred tax asset* is created when taxes payable (tax return) are higher than income tax expense (income statement). Deferred tax assets are recorded when revenues (or gains) are taxable before they are recognized in the income statement, when expenses (or losses) are recognized in the income statement before they are tax deductible, or when tax loss carryforwards are available to reduce future taxable income.

Deferred tax liabilities that are not expected to reverse, typically because of expected continued growth in capital expenditures, should be treated for analytical purposes as equity. If deferred tax liabilities are expected to reverse, they should be treated for analytical purposes as liabilities.

LOS 31.c

An asset's tax base is its value for tax purposes. The tax base for a depreciable fixed asset is its cost minus any depreciation or amortization previously taken on the tax return. When an asset is sold, the taxable gain or loss on the sale is equal to the sale price minus the asset's tax base.

A liability's tax base is its value for tax purposes. When there is a difference between the book value of a liability on a firm's financial statements and its tax base that will result in future taxable gains or losses when the liability is settled, the firm will recognize a deferred tax asset or liability to reflect this future tax or tax benefit.

©2012 Kaplan, Inc.

LOS 31.d

If taxable income is less than pretax income and the cause of the difference is expected to reverse in future years, a DTL is created. If taxable income is greater than pretax income and the difference is expected to reverse in future years, a DTA is created.

The balance of the DTA or DTL is equal to the difference between the tax base and the carrying value of the asset or liability, multiplied by the tax rate.

Income tax expense and taxes payable are related through the change in the DTA and the change in the DTL: income tax expense = taxes payable + ΔDTL – ΔDTA.

LOS 31.e

When a firm's income tax rate increases (decreases), deferred tax assets and deferred tax liabilities are both increased (decreased) to reflect the new rate. Changes in these values will also affect income tax expense.

An increase in the tax rate will increase both a firm's DTL and its income tax expense. A decrease in the tax rate will decrease both a firm's DTL and its income tax expense.

An increase in the tax rate will increase a firm's DTA and decrease its income tax expense. A decrease in the tax rate will decrease a firm's DTA and increase its income tax expense.

LOS 31.f

A temporary difference is a difference between the tax base and the carrying value of an asset or liability that will result in taxable amounts or deductible amounts in the future.

A permanent difference is a difference between taxable income and pretax income that will not reverse in the future. Permanent differences do not create DTAs or DTLs.

LOS 31.g

If it is more likely than not that some or all of a DTA will not be realized (because of insufficient future taxable income to recover the tax asset), then the DTA must be reduced by a valuation allowance. The valuation allowance is a contra account that reduces the DTA value on the balance sheet. Increasing the valuation allowance will increase income tax expense and reduce earnings. If circumstances change, the DTA can be revalued upward by decreasing the valuation allowance, which would increase earnings.

LOS 31.h

Temporary differences between earnings before taxes (financial statements) and taxable income (tax return) result in the creation of deferred tax assets or deferred tax liabilities. Such differences can result from differences in depreciation methods or inventory costing methods (IFRS), impairment charges, restructuring costs, or post-employment benefits.

LOS 31.i

Firms are required to reconcile their effective income tax rate with the applicable statutory rate in the country where the business is domiciled. Analyzing trends in individual reconciliation items can aid in understanding past earnings trends and in predicting future effective tax rates. Where adequate data is provided, they can also be helpful in predicting future earnings and cash flows or for adjusting financial ratios.

LOS 31.j
The accounting treatment of income taxes under U.S. GAAP and their treatment under IFRS are similar in most respects. One major difference relates to the revaluation of fixed assets and intangible assets. U.S. GAAP prohibits upward revaluations, but they are permitted under IFRS and any resulting effects on deferred tax are recognized in equity.

©2012 Kaplan, Inc.

CONCEPT CHECKERS

1. Which of the following statements is *most accurate*? The difference between taxes payable for the period and the tax expense recognized on the financial statements results from differences:
   A. in management control.
   B. between basic and diluted earnings.
   C. between financial and tax accounting.

2. Which of the following tax definitions is *least accurate*?
   A. Taxable income is income based on the rules of the tax authorities.
   B. Taxes payable are the amount due to the government.
   C. Pretax income is income tax expense divided by one minus the statutory tax rate.

Use the following data to answer Questions 3 through 9.
- A firm acquires an asset for $120,000 with a 4-year useful life and no salvage value.
- The asset will generate $50,000 of cash flow for all four years.
- The tax rate is 40% each year.
- The firm will depreciate the asset over three years on a straight-line (SL) basis for tax purposes and over four years on a SL basis for financial reporting purposes.

3. Taxable income in year 1 is:
   A. $6,000.
   B. $10,000.
   C. $20,000.

4. Taxes payable in year 1 are:
   A. $4,000.
   B. $6,000.
   C. $8,000.

5. Pretax income in year 4 is:
   A. $6,000.
   B. $10,000.
   C. $20,000.

6. Income tax expense in year 4 is:
   A. $4,000.
   B. $6,000.
   C. $8,000.

7. Taxes payable in year 4 are:
   A. $4,000.
   B. $6,000.
   C. $20,000.

8.   At the end of year 2, the firm's balance sheet will report a deferred tax:
      A. asset of $4,000.
      B. asset of $8,000.
      C. liability of $8,000.

9.   Suppose tax rates rise during year 2 to 50%. At the end of year 2, the firm's balance sheet will show a deferred tax liability of:
      A. $5,000.
      B. $6,000.
      C. $10,000.

10.   An increase in the tax rate causes the balance sheet value of a deferred tax asset to:
      A. decrease.
      B. increase.
      C. remain unchanged.

11.   In its first year of operations, a firm produces taxable income of –$10,000. The prevailing tax rate is 40%. The firm's balance sheet will report a deferred tax:
      A. asset of $4,000.
      B. asset of $10,000.
      C. liability of $4,000.

12.   An analyst is comparing a firm to its competitors. The firm has a deferred tax liability that results from accelerated depreciation for tax purposes. The firm is expected to continue to grow in the foreseeable future. How should the liability be treated for analysis purposes?
      A. It should be treated as equity at its full value.
      B. It should be treated as a liability at its full value.
      C. The present value should be treated as a liability with the remainder being treated as equity.

13.   Which one of the following statements is *most accurate*? Under the liability method of accounting for deferred taxes, a decrease in the tax rate at the beginning of the accounting period will:
      A. increase taxable income in the current period.
      B. increase a deferred tax asset.
      C. reduce a deferred tax liability.

14.   While reviewing a company, an analyst identifies a permanent difference between taxable income and pretax income. Which of the following statements *most accurately* identifies the appropriate financial statement adjustment?
      A. The amount of the tax implications of the difference should be added to the deferred tax liabilities.
      B. The present value of the amount of the tax implications of the difference should be added to the deferred tax liabilities.
      C. The effective tax rate for calculating tax expense should be adjusted.

©2012 Kaplan, Inc.

15. An analyst is reviewing a company with a large deferred tax asset on its balance sheet. She has determined that the firm has had cumulative losses for the last three years and has a large amount of inventory that can only be sold at sharply reduced prices. Which of the following adjustments should the analyst make to account for the deferred tax assets?
   A. Record a deferred tax liability to offset the effect of the deferred tax asset on the firm's balance sheet.
   B. Recognize a valuation allowance to reflect the fact that the deferred tax asset is unlikely to be realized.
   C. Do nothing. The difference between taxable and pretax income that caused the deferred tax asset is likely to reverse in the future.

16. If the tax base of an asset exceeds the asset's carrying value and a reversal is expected in the future:
   A. a deferred tax asset is created.
   B. a deferred tax liability is created.
   C. neither a deferred tax asset nor a deferred tax liability is created.

17. The author of a new textbook received a $100,000 advance from the publisher this year. $40,000 of income taxes were paid on the advance when received. The textbook will not be finished until next year. Determine the tax basis of the advance at the end of this year.
   A. $0.
   B. $40,000.
   C. $100,000.

18. According to IFRS, the deferred tax consequences of revaluing held-for-use equipment upward is reported on the balance sheet:
   A. as an asset.
   B. as a liability.
   C. in stockholders' equity.

19. KLH Company reported the following:
   - Gross DTA at the beginning of the year $10,500
   - Gross DTA at the end of the year $11,250
   - Valuation allowance at the beginning of the year $2,700
   - Valuation allowance at the end of the year $3,900

   Which of the following statements *best* describes the expected earnings of the firm? Earnings are expected to:
   A. increase.
   B. decrease.
   C. remain relatively stable.

ANSWERS – CONCEPT CHECKERS

1. **C** The difference between taxes payable for the period and the tax expense recognized on the financial statements results from differences between financial and tax accounting.

2. **C** Pretax income and income tax expense are not always linked because of temporary and permanent differences.

3. **B** Annual depreciation expense for tax purposes is ($120,000 cost – $0 salvage value) / 3 years = $40,000. Taxable income is $50,000 – $40,000 = $10,000.

4. **A** Taxes payable is taxable income × tax rate = $10,000 × 40% = $4,000. (The $10,000 was calculated in question #3.)

5. **C** Annual depreciation expense for financial purposes is ($120,000 cost – $0 salvage value) / 4 years = $30,000. Pretax income is $50,000 – $30,000 = $20,000.

6. **C** Because there has been no change in the tax rate, income tax expense is pretax income × tax rate = $20,000 × 40% = $8,000. (The $20,000 was calculated in question #5.)

7. **C** Note that the asset was fully depreciated for tax purposes after year 3, so taxable income is $50,000. Taxes payable for year 4 = taxable income × tax rate = $50,000 × 40% = $20,000.

8. **C** At the end of year 2, the tax base is $40,000 ($120,000 cost – $80,000 accumulated tax depreciation) and the carrying value is $60,000 ($120,000 cost – $60,000 accumulated financial depreciation). Since the carrying value exceeds the tax base, a DTL of $8,000 [($60,000 carrying value – $40,000 tax base) × 40%] is reported.

9. **C** The deferred tax liability is now $10,000 [($60,000 carrying value – $40,000 tax base) × 50%].

10. **B** If tax rates increase, the balance sheet value of a deferred tax asset will also increase.

11. **A** The tax loss carryforward results in a deferred tax asset equal to the loss multiplied by the tax rate.

12. **A** The DTL is not expected to reverse in the foreseeable future. The liability should be treated as equity at its full value.

13. **C** If the tax rate decreases, balance sheet DTL and DTA are both reduced. Taxable income is unaffected.

14. **C** If a permanent difference between taxable income and pretax income is identifiable, the effective tax rate for calculating tax expense should be adjusted.

15. **B** A valuation allowance is used to offset deferred tax assets if it is unlikely that those assets will be realized. Because the company has a history of losses and inventory that is unlikely to generate future profits, it is unlikely the company will realize its deferred tax assets in full.

16. **A** If the tax base of an asset exceeds the carrying value, a deferred tax asset is created. Taxable income will be lower in the future when the reversal occurs.

©2012 Kaplan, Inc.

17. **A** For revenue received in advance, the tax base is equal to the carrying value minus any amounts that will *not* be taxed in the future. Since the advance has already been taxed, $100,000 will *not* be taxed in the future. Thus, the textbook advance liability has a tax base of $0 ($100,000 carrying value – $100,000 revenue not taxed in the future).

18. **C** The deferred tax consequences of revaluing an asset upward under IFRS are reported in stockholders' equity.

19. **B** The valuation allowance account increased from $2,700 to $3,900. The most likely explanation is the future earnings are expected to decrease, thereby reducing the value of the DTA.

NON-CURRENT (LONG-TERM) LIABILITIES

Study Session 9

EXAM FOCUS

Candidates must understand the financial statement effects of issuing a bond at par, at a discount, or at a premium. You must be able to calculate the book value of the bond and interest expense at any point in time using the effective interest rate method. Also, be able to calculate the gain or loss from retiring a bond before its maturity date. You must thoroughly understand how the classification of a lease as either an operating or finance lease affects the balance sheet, income statement, and cash flow statement from both the lessee and lessor perspectives. Be able to distinguish between the two types of pension plans and identify the financial statement reporting of a defined benefit plan. Finally, be able to evaluate a firm's solvency using the various leverage and coverage ratios.

FINANCING LIABILITIES

A **bond** is a contractual promise between a borrower (the bond issuer) and a lender (the bondholder) that obligates the bond issuer to make payments to the bondholder over the term of the bond. Typically, two types of payments are involved: (1) periodic interest payments, and (2) repayment of principal at maturity.

Bond Terminology

- The **face value**, also known as the **maturity value** or **par value**, is the amount of principal that will be paid to the bondholder at maturity. The face value is used to calculate the coupon payments.
- The **coupon rate** is the interest rate stated in the bond that is used to calculate the coupon payments.
- The **coupon payments** are the periodic interest payments to the bondholders and are calculated by multiplying the face value by the coupon rate.
- The **effective rate of interest** is the interest rate that equates the present value of the future cash flows of the bond and the issue price. The effective rate is the market rate of interest required by bondholders and depends on the bond's risks (e.g., default risk, liquidity risk), as well as the overall structure of interest rates and the timing of the bond's cash flows. *Do not confuse the market rate of interest with the coupon rate.* The coupon rate is typically fixed for the term of the bond. The market rate of interest on a firm's bonds, however, will likely change over the bond's life, which changes the bond's market value as well.
- The **balance sheet liability** of a bond is equal to the present value of its remaining cash flows (coupon payments and face value), discounted at the market rate of interest *at issuance*. At maturity, the liability will equal the face value of the bond. The balance sheet liability is also known as the book value or carrying value of the bond.

©2012 Kaplan, Inc.

- The **interest expense** reported in the income statement is calculated by multiplying the book value of the bond liability at the beginning of the period by the market rate of interest of the bond when it was issued.

At the date of issuance, the market rate of interest may be equal to, less than, or greater than the coupon rate.

- When the market rate is equal to the coupon rate, the bond is a par bond (priced at face value).
- When the market rate is greater than the coupon rate, the bond is a discount bond (priced below par).
- When the market rate is less than the coupon rate, the bond is a premium bond (priced above par).

LOS 32.a: Determine the initial recognition, initial measurement and subsequent measurement of bonds.

CFA® Program Curriculum, Volume 3, page 488

Bonds Issued at Par

When a bond is issued at par, the bond's yield at issuance is equal to the coupon rate. In this case, the present value of the coupon payments plus the present value of the face amount is equal to the par value. The effects on the financial statements are straightforward:

- On the balance sheet, assets and liabilities increase by the bond proceeds (face value). The book value of the bond liability will not change over the term of the bond.
- On the income statement, interest expense for the period is equal to the coupon payment because the yield at issuance and the coupon rate are the same.
- On the cash flow statement, the issue proceeds are reported as a cash inflow from financing activities and the coupon payments are reported as cash outflows from operating activities (under U.S. GAAP; they may be reported as CFO or CFF outflows under IFRS). At maturity, repayment of the face value is reported as a cash outflow from financing activities.

Bonds Issued at a Discount or Premium

When the bond's yield at issuance is not equal to the coupon rate, the proceeds received (the present value of the coupon payments plus the present value of the face value) are not equal to par value. In this case, the bond is issued at a *premium* or a *discount*. The premium or discount at the issue date is usually relatively small for coupon bonds.

If the coupon rate is less than the bond's yield, the proceeds received will be less than the face value. The difference is known as a discount. The coupon rate is lower than the coupon rate that would make the market price of the bond equal to its par value. Investors will pay less than face value because of the lower coupon rate. Such bonds are known as **discount bonds**.

If the coupon rate is greater than the bond's yield, the bond price and the proceeds received will be greater than face value. We refer to such bonds as **premium bonds**. In this case, investors will pay more for the above-market coupon payments.

Balance Sheet Measurement

When a company issues a bond, assets and liabilities both initially increase by the bond proceeds. At any point in time, the book value of the bond liability will equal the present value of the remaining future cash flows (coupon payments and face value) discounted at the bond's yield at issuance.

 Professor's Note: Interest expense and the book value of a bond liability are calculated using the bond's yield at the time it was issued, not its yield today. This is a critical point.

A premium bond is reported on the balance sheet at more than its face value. As the premium is amortized (reduced), the book value of the bond liability will decrease until it reaches the face value of the bond at maturity.

A discount bond is reported on the balance sheet at less than its face value. As the discount is amortized, the book value of the bond liability will increase until it reaches face value at maturity.

LOS 32.b: Discuss the effective interest method and calculate interest expense, amortisation of bond discounts/premiums, and interest payments.

CFA® Program Curriculum, Volume 3, page 492

For a bond issued at a premium or discount, interest expense and coupon interest payments are not equal. Interest expense includes amortization of any discount or premium. Using the **effective interest rate method**, interest expense is equal to the book value of the bond liability at the beginning of the period, multiplied by the bond's yield at issuance.

- For a premium bond, interest expense is less than the coupon payment (yield < coupon rate). The difference between interest expense and the coupon payment is the amortization of the premium. The premium amortization is subtracted each period from the bond liability on the balance sheet. Thus, interest expense will decrease over time as the bond liability decreases.
- For a discount bond, interest expense is greater than the coupon payment (yield > coupon rate). The difference between interest expense and the coupon payment is the amortization of the discount. The amortization of the discount each period is added to the bond liability on the balance sheet. Therefore, interest expense will increase over time as the bond liability increases.

©2012 Kaplan, Inc.

Professor's Note: In the case of a discount bond, the coupon is too low relative to the required rate of return of the market. The purposes of amortizing the discount are to (1) increase the book value of the bond liability over time, and (2) increase interest expense so that the coupon payment plus discount amortization is approximately equal to the interest expense that would have prevailed had the bond been issued at par. Conversely, amortizing a premium decreases the book value of the bond liability over time and decreases interest expense.

The effective interest rate method of amortizing a discount or premium is required under IFRS. Under U.S. GAAP, the effective interest rate method is preferred, but the straight-line method is allowed if the results are not materially different. The straight-line method is similar to straight-line depreciation in that the total discount or premium at issuance is amortized by equal amounts each period over the life of the bond.

While coupon interest is paid in cash, amortization is a noncash item. When presenting the cash flow statement using the indirect method, net income must be adjusted to remove the effects of any amortization of a discount or premium in order to calculate cash flow from operations.

Firms that follow U.S. GAAP must report cash interest paid in the cash flow statement as an operating cash flow. Firms that follow IFRS can report cash interest paid as either an operating or financing cash flow. Therefore, it may be necessary to reclassify interest paid when comparing firms that follow different standards.

Professor's Note: Some analysts believe classifying interest expense as an operating activity is inconsistent with treating the bond proceeds as a financing activity. In addition, treating interest expense as an operating activity incorrectly describes the economics of a bond issued at a premium or discount. For bonds issued at a discount, cash flow from operations is overstated. This is because the coupon payment is reported as an operating cash flow, while the discount, when paid (as part of a bond's maturity payment), is reported as a financing cash flow. Stated differently, had the firm issued the bond at par, the coupon payment would have been higher to match the market rate of interest. Reclassifying interest as a financing activity in the cash flow statement corrects this inconsistent treatment.

Example: Book values and cash flows

On December 31, 20X2, a company issued a 3-year, 10% annual coupon bond with a face value of $100,000. Calculate the book value of the bond at year-end 20X2, 20X3, and 20X4, and the interest expense for 20X3, 20X4, and 20X5, assuming the bond was issued at a market rate of interest of (a) 10%, (b) 9%, and (c) 11%.

Answer:

(a) Bond issued at par. If the market rate of interest at issuance is 10%, the book value of the bonds will always be $100,000, and the interest expense will always be $10,000, which is equal to the coupon payment of 0.10 × $100,000. There is no discount or premium to amortize.

(b) Premium bond. If the market rate of interest is 9%, the present value of the cash payments (a 3-year annuity of $10,000 and a payment in three years of $100,000) is $102,531:

N = 3; PMT = 10,000; FV = 100,000; I/Y = 9; CPT → PV = $102,531

 Professor's Note: The present value computed in this manner will have a minus sign.

The following table shows the interest expense and book value at the end of each year.

Interest Expense and Book Value for a Premium Bond

Year	(1) Beginning Book Value	(2) Interest Expense (1) × 9%	(3) Coupon	(4) Ending Book Value (1) + (2) – (3)
20X3	$102,531	$9,228	$10,000	$101,759
20X4	101,759	9,158	10,000	100,917
20X5	100,917	9,083	10,000	100,000

The premium amortization for 20X3 is 10,000 – 9,228 = $772. For 20X4, the amortization is 10,000 – 9,158 = $842. Finally, for 20X5, premium amortization is $917. Note that the premium has been fully amortized upon maturity so that the book value of the bond equals par value.

(c) Discount bond. If the market rate of interest is 11%, the present value of the cash payments (a 3-year annuity of $10,000 and a payment in three years of $100,000) is $97,556.

N = 3; PMT = 10,000; FV = 100,000; I/Y = 11; CPT → PV = $97,556

©2012 Kaplan, Inc.

The following table shows the interest expense and book value at the end of each year.

Interest Expense and Book Value for a Discount Bond

Year	(1) Beginning Book Value	(2) Interest Expense (1) × 11%	(3) Coupon	(4) Ending Book Value (1) + (2) – (3)
20X3	$97,556	$10,731	$10,000	$98,287
20X4	98,287	10,812	10,000	99,099
20X5	99,099	10,901	10,000	100,000

Again, the pattern of discount amortization is such that the discount is fully amortized upon maturity, when the book value of the bond equals par value.

Zero-coupon bonds make no periodic interest payments. A zero-coupon bond, also known as a *pure-discount bond*, is issued at a discount from its par value and its annual interest expense is implied, but not explicitly paid. The actual interest payment is included in the face value that is paid at maturity. The effects of zero-coupon bonds on the financial statements are qualitatively the same as any discount bond, but the impact is larger because the discount is larger.

Issuance Costs

Issuing a bond involves legal and accounting fees, printing costs, sales commissions, and other fees. Under U.S. GAAP, issuance costs are capitalized as an asset (deferred charge) and allocated to the income statement as an expense over the term of the bond.

Under IFRS, the initial bond liability on the balance sheet is reduced by the amount of issuance costs, increasing the bond's effective interest rate. In effect, issuance costs are treated as unamortized discount.

Consider a $1 million bond issued for $980,000 with issuance costs of $5,000. Under U.S. GAAP, the firm would increase assets by $980,000 ($975,000 cash and $5,000 deferred charge) and increase liabilities by $980,000. Under IFRS, the bond's issuance costs reduce the bond liability reported on the balance sheet. Thus, the firm will increase assets and liabilities by $975,000.

Under both U.S. GAAP and IFRS, bond issuance costs are usually netted against the bond proceeds and reported on the cash flow statement as a financing cash flow.

Fair Value Reporting Option

Recall that the book value of a bond liability is based on its market yield *at issuance*. So, as long as the bond's yield does not change, the bond liability represents fair (market) value. However, if the yield changes, the balance sheet liability is no longer equal to fair value.

An *increase* in the bond's yield will result in a *decrease* in the fair value of the bond liability. Conversely, a *decrease* in the bond's yield *increases* its fair value. Changes in yield result in a divergence between the book value of the bond liability and the fair value of the bond. The fair value of the bond is the economic liability at a point in time.

IFRS and U.S. GAAP give firms the irrevocable option to report debt at fair value. Under this option, gains (decreases in bond liability) and losses (increases in bond liability) that result from changes in bonds' market yields are reported in the income statement.

For analysis, the market value of a firm's debt may be more appropriate than its book value. For example, a firm that issued a bond when interest rates were low is relatively better off when interest rates increase. This is because the firm could repurchase the bond at its now-lower market value. Decreasing the bond liability on the balance sheet to market value increases equity and decreases the debt-to-assets and debt-to-equity ratios. If interest rates have decreased since issuance, adjusting debt to its market value will have the opposite effects.

Summary of Financial Statement Effects of Issuing a Bond

Figure 1: Cash Flow Impact of Issuing a Bond

	Cash Flow from Financing	*Cash Flow from Operations*
Issuance of debt	Increased by cash received (Present value of the bond at the market interest rate)	No effect
Periodic interest payments	No effect	Decreased by interest paid [(coupon rate) × (face or par value)]
Payment at maturity	Decreased by face (par) value	No effect

Figure 2: Income Statement Impact of Issuing a Bond

$$\text{interest expense} = \left(\begin{array}{c} \text{market rate} \\ \text{at issue} \end{array} \right) \times \left(\begin{array}{c} \text{balance sheet value of} \\ \text{liability at beginning of period} \end{array} \right)$$

Issued at Par	*Issued at a Premium*	*Issued at a Discount*
Market rate = coupon rate	Market rate < coupon rate	Market rate > coupon rate
Interest expense = coupon rate × face value = cash paid	Interest expense = cash paid − amortization of premium	Interest expense = cash paid + amortization of discount
Interest expense is constant	Interest expense decreases over time	Interest expense increases over time

©2012 Kaplan, Inc.

Figure 3: Balance Sheet Impact of Issuing a Bond

> Long-term debt is carried at the present value of the remaining cash payments discounted at the market rate prevailing when the debt was issued.

Issued at Par	Issued at a Premium	Issued at a Discount
Carried at face value	Carried at face value plus premium	Carried at face value less discount
	The liability decreases as the premium is amortized to interest expense	The liability increases as the discount is amortized to interest expense

LOS 32.c: Discuss the derecognition of debt.

CFA® Program Curriculum, Volume 3, page 498

When bonds mature, no gain or loss is recognized by the issuer. At maturity, any original discount or premium has been fully amortized; thus, the book value of a bond liability and its face value are the same. The cash outflow to repay a bond is reported in the cash flow statement as a financing cash flow.

A firm may choose to **redeem** bonds before maturity because interest rates have fallen, because the firm has generated surplus cash through operations, or because funds from the issuance of equity make it possible (and desirable).

When bonds are redeemed before maturity, a gain or loss is recognized by subtracting the redemption price from the book value of the bond liability at the reacquisition date. For example, consider a firm that reacquires $1 million face amount of bonds at 102% of par when the carrying value of the bond liability is $995,000. The firm will recognize a loss of $25,000 ($995,000 carrying value – $1,020,000 redemption price). Had the carrying value been greater than the redemption price, the firm would have recognized a gain.

Under U.S. GAAP, any remaining unamortized bond issuance costs must be written off and included in the gain or loss calculation. Writing off the cost of issuing the bond will reduce a gain or increase a loss. No write-off is necessary under IFRS because the issuance costs are already accounted for in the book value of the bond liability.

Any gain or loss from redeeming debt is reported in the income statement, usually as a part of continuing operations, and additional information is disclosed separately. Redeeming debt is usually not a part of the firm's day-to-day operations; thus, analysts often eliminate the gain or loss from the income statement for analysis and forecasting.

When presenting the cash flow statement using the indirect method, any gain (loss) is subtracted from (added to) net income in calculating cash flow from operations. The redemption price is reported as an outflow from financing activities.

LOS 32.d: Explain the role of debt covenants in protecting creditors.

CFA® Program Curriculum, Volume 3, page 500

Debt covenants are restrictions imposed by the lender on the borrower to protect the lender's position. Debt covenants can reduce default risk and thus reduce borrowing costs. The restrictions can be in the form of affirmative covenants or negative covenants.

With **affirmative covenants**, the borrower promises to do certain things, such as:

- Make timely payments of principal and interest.
- Maintain certain ratios (such as the current, debt-to-equity, and interest coverage ratios) in accordance with specified levels.
- Maintain collateral, if any, in working order.

With **negative covenants**, the borrower promises to refrain from certain activities that might adversely affect its ability to repay the outstanding debt, such as:

- Increasing dividends or repurchasing shares.
- Issuing more debt.
- Engaging in mergers and acquisitions.

The bondholders can demand immediate repayment of principal if the firm violates a covenant (referred to as **technical default**). Analyzing the covenants is a necessary component of the credit analysis of a bond. Bond covenants are typically discussed in the financial statement footnotes.

Covenants protect bondholders from actions the firm may take that would harm the value of the bondholders' claims to the firm's assets and earnings (i.e., decrease credit quality). To the extent that covenants restrict, for example, the firm's ability to invest, take on additional debt, or pay dividends, analysis of covenants can be important when valuing the firm's equity (especially involving its growth prospects) as well as when analyzing and valuing its debt securities.

 Professor's Note: Debt covenants are described further in the Study Session on fixed income investments.

LOS 32.e: Discuss the financial statement presentation of and disclosures relating to debt.

CFA® Program Curriculum, Volume 3, page 501

Firms will often report all of their outstanding long-term debt on a single line on the balance sheet. The portion that is due within the next year is reported as a current liability. The firm separately discloses more detail about its long-term debt in the footnotes. These disclosures are useful in determining the timing and amounts of future cash outflows. The footnote disclosure usually includes a discussion of:

- The nature of the liabilities.

- Maturity dates.
- Stated and effective interest rates.
- Call provisions and conversion privileges.
- Restrictions imposed by creditors.
- Assets pledged as security.
- The amount of debt maturing in each of the next five years.

A discussion of the firm's long-term debt is also found in the Management Discussion and Analysis section. This discussion is both quantitative, such as identifying obligations and commitments that are due in the future, and qualitative, such as discussing capital resource trends and material changes in the mix and cost of debt.

LOS 32.f: Discuss the motivations for leasing assets instead of purchasing them.

CFA® Program Curriculum, Volume 3, page 504

A **lease** is a contractual arrangement whereby the **lessor**, the owner of the asset, allows the **lessee** to use the asset for a specified period of time in return for periodic payments.

Leases are classified as either finance leases or operating leases. In the United States, a finance lease is known as a *capital lease*.

A **finance lease** is, in substance, a purchase of an asset that is financed with debt. Accordingly, at the inception of the lease, the lessee will add equal amounts to both assets and liabilities on the balance sheet. Over the term of the lease, the lessee will recognize depreciation expense on the asset and interest expense on the liability.

An **operating lease** is essentially a rental arrangement. No asset or liability is reported by the lessee and the periodic lease payments are simply recognized as rental expense in the income statement.

Leasing can have certain benefits:

- *Less costly financing.* Typically, a lease requires no initial down payment. Thus, the lessee conserves cash.
- *Reduced risk of obsolescence.* At the end of the lease, the asset can be returned to the lessor.
- *Less restrictive provisions.* Leases can provide more flexibility than other forms of financing because the lease agreement can be negotiated to better suit the needs of each party.
- *Off-balance-sheet financing.* Entering into an operating lease does not result in a balance sheet liability, so reported leverage ratios are lower compared to borrowing the funds to purchase assets.
- *Tax reporting advantages.* In the United States, firms can create a **synthetic lease** whereby the lease is treated as an ownership position for tax reporting. This allows the lessee to deduct depreciation expense and interest expense for tax purposes. For financial reporting, the lease is treated as a rental agreement and the lessee does not report the lease liability on the balance sheet.

LOS 32.g: Distinguish between a finance lease and an operating lease from the perspectives of the lessor and the lessee.

CFA® Program Curriculum, Volume 3, page 505

Lessee's Perspective

Under IFRS, the classification of a lease is determined by the economic substance of the transaction. If substantially all the rights and risks of ownership are transferred to the lessee, the lease is treated as a finance lease. Circumstances that require a lease to be treated as a finance lease include:

- Title to the leased asset is transferred to the lessee at the end of the lease.
- The lessee can purchase the leased asset for a price that is significantly lower than the fair value of the asset at some future date.
- The lease term covers a major portion of the asset's economic life.
- The present value of the lease payments is substantially equal to the fair value of the leased asset.
- The leased asset is so specialized that only the lessee can use the asset without significant modifications.

Under U.S. GAAP, the criteria are conceptually similar, but are more specific than under IFRS. A lessee must treat a lease as a capital (finance) lease if *any* of the following criteria are met:

- Title to the leased asset is transferred to the lessee at the end of the lease period.
- A *bargain purchase option* permits the lessee to purchase the leased asset for a price that is significantly lower than the fair market value of the asset at some future date.
- The lease period is 75% or more of the asset's economic life.
- The present value of the lease payments is 90% or more of the fair value of the leased asset.

A lease not meeting any of these criteria is classified as an operating lease. Lessees often prefer operating leases because no liability is reported. Recall that with a finance lease, the lessee reports both an asset and a liability on the balance sheet.

Lessor's Perspective

From the lessor's perspective, the lease is also classified as either an operating lease or a finance (capital) lease.

Under IFRS, classification by the lessor is the same as the lessee's; that is, if substantially all the rights and risks of ownership are transferred to the lessee, the lease is treated as a finance lease. Otherwise, the lease is treated as an operating lease.

Under U.S. GAAP, if any one of the capital (finance) lease criteria for lessees is met, and the collectability of lease payments is reasonably certain, and the lessor has substantially completed performance, the lessor must treat the lease as a capital (finance) lease. Otherwise, the lessor will treat the lease as an operating lease.

©2012 Kaplan, Inc.

With an operating lease, the lessor recognizes rental income and continues to report and depreciate the leased asset on its balance sheet. With a capital (finance) lease, the lessor removes the leased asset from the balance sheet and replaces it with a lease investment account (lease receivable).

LOS 32.h: Determine the initial recognition, initial measurement, and subsequent measurement of finance leases.

CFA® Program Curriculum, Volume 3, page 506

Reporting by the Lessee

The treatment of a lease as either an operating lease or finance lease determines whether the lease is reported on the balance sheet, how the lease expense is recognized in the income statement, and the classification of the lease payments on the cash flow statement.

Operating lease. At the inception of the lease, the balance sheet is unaffected. No asset or liability is reported by the lessee. During the term of the lease, *rent expense* equal to the lease payment is recognized in the lessee's income statement. In the cash flow statement, the lease payment is reported as an outflow from operating activities.

Finance lease. At the inception of the lease, the lower of the present value of future minimum lease payments or the fair value of the leased asset is recognized as both an asset and as a liability on the lessee's balance sheet. Over the term of the lease, the asset is depreciated in the income statement and interest expense is recognized. Interest expense is equal to the lease liability at the beginning of the period multiplied by the lease interest rate.

 Professor's Note: In a finance lease, the interest rate used by the lessee is the lower of the lessee's incremental borrowing rate and the lessor's implicit rate.

In the cash flow statement, the lease payment is separated into its interest and principal components. Just as with any amortizing loan, the principal portion of the lease payment is equal to the total payment minus the interest portion. Under U.S. GAAP, interest paid is reported in the cash flow statement as an outflow from operating activities and the principal payment is reported as an outflow from financing activities.

 Professor's Note: Under IFRS, firms can choose to report interest paid in the cash flow statement as an operating or financing cash flow.

Example: Accounting for a finance lease

Affordable Leasing Company leases a machine for its own use for four years with annual payments of $10,000. At the end of the lease, the machine is returned to the lessor, who will sell it for its scrap value. The appropriate interest rate is 6%.

Calculate the impact of the lease on Affordable Leasing's balance sheet and income statement for each of the four years, including the immediate impact. Affordable Leasing depreciates all assets on a straight-line basis. Assume the lease payments are made at the end of the year.

Answer:

The lease is classified as a finance lease because the asset is being leased for 75% or more of its useful life (we know this because at the end of the lease term, the asset will be sold for scrap). The present value of the lease payments at 6% is $34,651.

$$N = 4; \ I/Y = 6; \ PMT = -10,000; \ FV = 0; \ CPT \rightarrow PV = \$34,651$$

This amount is immediately recorded as both an asset and a liability on the lessee's balance sheet.

> *Professor's Note: Here we are assuming the payments are made at the end of the year. Watch out on the exam. If the lease had called for beginning of the year payments, it would have been necessary to change the payment mode on your calculator in order to compute the present value.*

Over the next four years, depreciation will be $34,651 / 4 = $8,663 per year. The book value of the asset will decline each year by the depreciation expense.

The interest expense and liability values are shown in the following table. Note that the *principal repayment amount each period is* equal to the lease payment minus the interest expense for the period (6% times the liability at the beginning of the period).

Affordable Leasing Example: Finance Lease Calculations

Year	*(1)* Beginning Leasehold Value	*(2)* Interest Expense *(1) × 6%*	*(3)* Lease Payment	*(4)* Lease Liability *(1) + (2) – (3)*	*(5)* Book Value of the Asset
0				$34,651	$34,651
1	$34,651	$2,079	10,000	26,730	25,988
2	26,730	1,604	10,000	18,334	17,326
3	18,334	1,100	10,000	9,434	8,663
4	9,434	566	10,000	0	0

©2012 Kaplan, Inc.

Column 5 shows the ending book value of the leased asset each year. Note that, initially, depreciation is greater than the amortization (principal repayment) of the loan, so the asset's book value declines more rapidly than the lease liability. In the later years of the lease term, annual interest expense is less and the amortization of the lease liability is greater. The book value of the leased asset and the lease liability are again equal (both are zero) at the end of the lease term.

Financial Statement and Ratio Effects of Operating and Finance Leases

Balance sheet. A finance lease results in a reported asset and a liability. Consequently, turnover ratios that use total or fixed assets in their denominators will be lower when a lease is treated as a finance lease as compared to an operating lease. For the same reason, return on assets will also be lower for finance leases. Most importantly, leverage ratios, such as the debt-to-assets ratio and the debt-to-equity ratio, will be higher with finance leases than with operating leases because of the reported liability. The principal payment due within the next year is reported as a current liability on the lessee's balance sheet. This reduces the lessee's current ratio and working capital (current assets minus current liabilities).

Because the liability for an operating lease does not appear on the lessee's balance sheet, operating leases are sometimes referred to as *off-balance-sheet financing activities*.

Income statement. Operating income (EBIT) will be higher for companies that use finance leases relative to companies that use operating leases. With an operating lease, the entire lease payment is an operating expense, while for a finance lease, only the depreciation of the leased asset (not the interest portion of the lease payment) is treated as an operating expense.

In the previous example, assume Affordable Leasing can treat the lease as either an operating lease or a finance lease. Figure 4 compares the income statement effects.

Figure 4: Affordable Leasing: Impact of Lease Accounting Method on the Income Statement

Year	Operating Lease	Finance Lease		
	Rent Expense	Depreciation	Interest	Finance Lease Expense
1	$10,000	$8,663	$2,079	$10,742
2	10,000	8,663	1,604	10,267
3	10,000	8,663	1,100	9,763
4	10,000	8,663	566	9,229
	$40,000			$40,000

Total expense over the life of a lease will be the same whether it is accounted for as an operating lease or a finance (capital) lease because the sum of depreciation expense and interest expense will equal the total of the lease payments. In the early years of a finance lease, however, the interest expense is higher, so the sum of depreciation and interest expense is greater than the lease payment. Consequently, net income will be lower for a finance lease in its early years and higher in its later years, compared to an operating lease.

Cash flow statement. Total cash flow is unaffected by the accounting treatment of a lease. In our example, the total cash outflow is $10,000 per year. If the lease is treated as an operating lease (rent expense = $10,000), then the total cash payment reduces cash flow from operations. If the lease is treated as a finance lease, then only the portion of the lease payment that is considered interest expense reduces cash flow from operations. The part of the lease payment considered repayment of principal reduces cash flow from financing activities. Figure 5 illustrates that for a finance lease, cash flow from operations (CFO) is higher, and cash flow from financing (CFF) is lower, compared to an operating lease.

Figure 5: Affordable Leasing: Impact on Cash Flow

	Finance Lease		Operating Lease
Year	*CF Operations*	*CF Financing*	*CF Operations*
1	–$2,079	–$7,921	–$10,000
2	–1,604	–8,396	–10,000
3	–1,100	–8,900	–10,000
4	–566	–9,434	–10,000

If Affordable Leasing treats the lease as a finance lease, operating cash outflow is $2,079 in Year 1, and if it treats the lease as an operating lease, operating cash outflow is $10,000. Companies with finance leases will show higher CFO relative to firms that use operating leases (all else the same).

Figure 6 and Figure 7 summarize the differences between the effects of finance leases and operating leases on the financial statements and ratios of the lessee.

Figure 6: Financial Statement Impact of Lease Accounting

	Finance Lease	*Operating Lease*
Assets	Higher	Lower
Liabilities (current and long-term)	Higher	Lower
Net income (in the early years)	Lower	Higher
Net income (later years)	Higher	Lower
Total net income	Same	Same
EBIT (operating income)	Higher	Lower
Cash flow from operations	Higher	Lower
Cash flow from financing	Lower	Higher
Total cash flow	Same	Same

©2012 Kaplan, Inc.

Figure 7: Ratio Impact of Lease Accounting

	Finance Lease	Operating Lease
Current ratio (CA / CL)	Lower	Higher
Working capital (CA – CL)	Lower	Higher
Asset turnover (Revenue / TA)	Lower	Higher
Return on assets* (NI / TA)	Lower	Higher
Return on equity* (NI / SE)	Lower	Higher
Debt / Assets	Higher	Lower
Debt / Equity	Higher	Lower

* In the early years of the lease.

In sum, all the ratios in Figure 7 are worse when the lease is capitalized. The only improvements from a finance lease are higher EBIT (because interest is not subtracted in calculating EBIT), higher CFO (because principal repayment is CFF), and higher net income in the later years of the lease (because interest plus depreciation is less than the lease payment in the later years).

> *Professor's Note: There are two points that candidates often find confusing. First, interest payments are an operating cash flow but are not considered an operating expenditure. That is, they are not subtracted in calculating operating income (EBIT). Second, adding equal amounts to assets and liabilities will typically increase the debt-to-assets ratio. Because assets are typically larger than debt (liabilities), the numerator of the debt-to-assets ratio increases by a greater proportion than the denominator when equal amounts are added to each, so the ratio increases. With respect to the current ratio and working capital, the current year principal amortization for a finance lease is added to current liabilities, but there is no increase in current assets because the asset is long-lived.*

Reporting by the Lessor

From the lessor's perspective, a capital lease under U.S. GAAP is treated as either a *sales-type* lease or a *direct financing* lease. If the present value of the lease payments exceeds the carrying value of the asset, the lease is treated as a sales-type lease. If the present value of the lease payments is equal to the carrying value, the lease is treated as a direct financing lease.

IFRS does not distinguish between a sales-type lease and a direct financing lease. However, similar treatment to a sales-type lease is allowed under IFRS for finance leases originated by manufacturers or dealers. In this case, the present value of the lease payments likely exceeds the carrying value of the asset.

Sales-Type Lease

A **sales-type lease** is treated as if the lessor sold the asset for the present value of the lease payments and provided a loan to the buyer in the same amount. Sales-type leases are typical when the lessor is a manufacturer or dealer because the cost (balance sheet value) of the leased asset is usually less than its fair value.

At the inception of the lease, the lessor recognizes a sale equal to the present value of the lease payments, and cost of goods sold equal to the carrying value of the asset. Just as with a normal sales transaction, the difference between the sales price and cost of goods sold is gross profit. The asset is removed from the balance sheet and a **lease receivable** is created, equal to the present value of the lease payments. As the lease payments are received, the principal portion of the payment reduces the lease receivable and the interest portion of the lease payment is recognized as interest income. The interest portion of each lease payment is equal to the lease receivable at the beginning of the period multiplied by the lease interest rate.

In the cash flow statement, the interest portion of the lease payment is reported as an inflow from operating activities, and the principal reduction is reported as an inflow from investing activities, just as with an amortizing loan.

Direct Financing Lease

In a **direct financing lease**, no gross profit is recognized by the lessor at the inception of the lease. Because the present value of the lease payments is equal to the carrying value of the leased asset, the lessor is simply providing a financing function to the lessee. In this case, the lessor is not usually a manufacturer or dealer, but has purchased the asset from a third party.

At the inception of the lease, the lessor removes the asset from its balance sheet and creates a lease receivable in the same amount. As the lease payments are received, the principal portion of each payment reduces the lease receivable.

In the income statement, the lessor recognizes interest income over the term of the lease. The interest portion of each lease payment is equal to the lease receivable at the beginning of the period multiplied by the interest rate.

In the cash flow statement, the interest portion of the lease payment is reported as an inflow from operating activities and the principal reduction is reported as an inflow from investing activities.

©2012 Kaplan, Inc.

Example: Direct financing lease

Assume Johnson Company purchases an asset for $69,302 to lease to Carver, Inc. for four years with an annual lease payment of $20,000 at the end of each year. At the end of the lease, Carver will own the asset for no additional payment. The implied interest rate in the lease is 6% (N = 4, PV = −69,302, PMT = 20,000, FV = 0, CPT I/Y → 6). Determine how Johnson should account for the lease payments from Carver.

Answer:

Since the present value of lease payments of $69,302 is equal to the carrying value of the asset, Johnson treats the lease as a direct financing lease. Johnson removes the leased asset from the balance sheet and records a lease receivable of $69,302. The lease payments are recorded as follows:

Year	(1) Beginning Lease Receivable	(2) Interest Income (1) × 6%	(3) Lease Payment	(4) Ending Lease Receivable (1) + (2) − (3)
0				$69,302
1	$69,302	$4,158	$20,000	$53,460
2	53,460	3,208	20,000	36,668
3	36,668	2,200	20,000	18,868
4	18,868	1,132	20,000	0

Interest income received each year will increase earnings. In the cash flow statement, the interest income is reported as an inflow from operating activities. The principal reduction (column 3 – column 2) reduces the lease receivable and is treated in the cash flow statement as an inflow from investing activities.

If Johnson had manufactured the equipment with a cost of goods of $60,000, it would have recorded a gross profit of $69,302 – $60,000 = $9,302 at lease inception, put a lease receivable of $69,302 on its balance sheet, and then accounted for the interest income portion of the lease payments just as in the table above.

Operating Lease

If the lease is treated as an operating lease, the lessor simply recognizes the lease payment as rental income. In addition, the lessor will keep the leased asset on its balance sheet and depreciate it over its useful life.

Returning to our example, if Johnson treats the lease as an operating lease, $20,000 of rental income is recognized each year. In addition, depreciation expense of $17,325.50 ($69,302 / 4 years) is also recognized. Figure 8 compares the income from a direct financing lease and an operating lease.

Figure 8: Income Comparison of a Direct Financing Lease and Operating Lease

	Direct Financing Lease	Operating Lease		
Year	Interest Income	Rental Income	Depreciation Expense	Operating Lease Income
1	$4,158	$20,000	$17,325	$2,675
2	3,208	20,000	17,326	2,674
3	2,200	20,000	17,325	2,675
4	1,132	20,000	17,326	2,674
	$10,698			$10,698

Total income over the life of the lease is the same for an operating lease and a direct financing lease. However, in the early years of the lease, the income reported from the direct financing lease is higher than the income reported from the operating lease. Just as with an amortizing loan, the interest is higher in the early years. This situation reverses in the later years of the lease.

In the cash flow statement, the lease classifications result in significant differences in cash flow from operations, as shown in Figure 9.

Figure 9: Cash Flow Comparison to the Lessor of a Direct Financing Lease and an Operating Lease

	Direct Financing Lease		Operating Lease
Year	CF Operations	CF Investing	CF Operations
1	$4,158	$15,842	$20,000
2	3,208	16,792	20,000
3	2,200	17,800	20,000
4	1,132	18,868	20,000

Total cash flow is the same for an operating lease and a direct financing lease. However, cash flow from operations is higher with the operating lease. With a direct financing lease, the lease payment is separated into the interest portion (CFO) and principal portion (CFI).

> *Professor's Note: From the lessee's perspective, principal is a financing outflow. From the lessor's perspective, principal is a return of capital invested in the lease. Thus, the principal is reported as an investing inflow.*

©2012 Kaplan, Inc.

LOS 32.i: Compare the disclosures relating to finance and operating leases.

CFA® Program Curriculum, Volume 3, page 509

Both lessees and lessors are required to disclose useful information about finance leases and operating leases in the financial statements or in the footnotes, including:

*   General description of the leasing arrangement.
*   The nature, timing, and amount of payments to be paid or received in each of the next five years. Lease payments after five years can be aggregated.
*   Amount of lease revenue and expense reported in the income statement for each period presented.
*   Amounts receivable and unearned revenues from lease arrangements.
*   Restrictions imposed by lease agreements.

For lessees, analysts often use the disclosures to estimate the off-balance-sheet liabilities of operating leases.

> *Professor's Note: Unfortunately, the interest rate used in the lease calculations is not always disclosed. Thus, it may be necessary for an analyst to derive the interest rate in order to make adjustments for analytical purposes. Deriving the interest rate and carrying out the lease adjustments are covered at Level II.*

LOS 32.j: Describe defined contribution and defined benefit pension plans.

CFA® Program Curriculum, Volume 3, page 520

A **pension** is a form of deferred compensation earned over time through employee service. The most common pension arrangements are defined contribution plans and defined benefit plans.

A **defined contribution plan** is a retirement plan in which the firm contributes a sum each period to the employee's retirement account. The firm's contribution can be based on any number of factors, including years of service, the employee's age, compensation, profitability, or even a percentage of the employee's contribution. In any event, the firm makes no promise to the employee regarding the future value of the plan assets. The investment decisions are left to the employee, who assumes all of the investment risk.

In a **defined benefit plan**, the firm promises to make periodic payments to employees after retirement. The benefit is usually based on the employee's years of service and the employee's compensation at, or near, retirement. For example, an employee might earn a retirement benefit of 2% of her final salary for each year of service. Consequently, an employee with 20 years of service and a final salary of $100,000, would receive $40,000 ($100,000 final salary × 2% × 20 years of service) each year upon retirement until death. Because the employee's future benefit is defined, the employer assumes the investment risk.

A company that offers defined pension benefits typically funds the plan by contributing assets to a separate legal entity, usually a trust. The plan assets are managed to generate the income and principal growth necessary to pay the pension benefits as they come due.

LOS 32.k: Compare the presentation and disclosure of defined contribution and defined benefit pension plans.

CFA® Program Curriculum, Volume 3, page 520

The financial reporting requirements for defined contribution plans are straightforward. Pension expense is simply equal to the employer's contribution. There is no future obligation to report on the balance sheet as a liability.

Financial reporting for a defined benefit plan is much more complicated than for a defined contribution plan because the employer must estimate the value of the future obligation to its employees. The obligation involves forecasting a number of variables, such as future compensation levels, employee turnover, average retirement age, mortality rates, and an appropriate discount rate.

For a defined benefit plan, the **net pension asset** or **net pension liability** is a key element for analysis. If the fair value of the plan's assets is greater than the estimated pension obligation, the plan is said to be *overfunded* and the sponsoring firm records a net pension asset on its balance sheet. If the fair value of the plan's assets is less than the estimated pension obligation, the plan is *underfunded* and the firm records a net pension liability.

The change in the net pension asset or liability is recognized on the firm's financial statements each year. Some components are included in net income while others are recorded as other comprehensive income. Figure 10 illustrates the treatments under IFRS and U.S. GAAP.

©2012 Kaplan, Inc.

Figure 10: Components of the Change in a Net Pension Asset or Liability

(a) IFRS Reporting

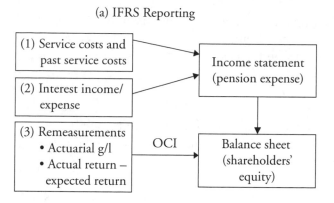

(b) U.S. GAAP Reporting

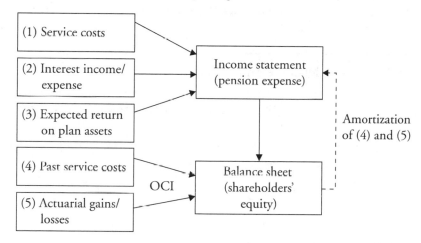

Treatment under IFRS

Under IFRS, three components make up the change in net pension asset or liability: service costs, net interest expense or income, and remeasurements. Pension expense on the income statement is the sum of service costs and the net interest expense or income. Remeasurements are recognized as other comprehensive income.

Service cost is the present value of additional benefits earned by an employee over the year. Net interest expense (income) is the beginning value of net pension liability (asset) multiplied by the discount rate assumed when determining the present value of plan assets. This discount rate is chosen by management but should reflect the yield of a highly rated corporate bond.

Remeasurements are the third component. These include actuarial gains or losses and the difference between the actual return on plan assets and the return included in net interest expense or income. Under IFRS, remeasurements are not amortized to the income statement over time.

Treatment under U.S. GAAP

Five components make up the change in net pension asset or liability under U.S. GAAP. Pension expense in the current period has three components: service costs, net interest expense or income, and the expected return on plan assets (a positive expected return decreases pension expense).

Two components are recognized in other comprehensive income: past service costs (retroactive benefits awarded to employees when a plan is initiated or amended) and actuarial gains or losses. These are amortized to pension expense, which allows companies to smooth their effects on pension expenses over time.

For manufacturing companies, under either IFRS or U.S. GAAP, pension expense is allocated to inventory and cost of goods sold for employees who provide direct labor to production and to salary or administrative expense for other employees. As a result, pension expense does not appear separately on the income statement for manufacturing companies. An analyst must examine the financial statement notes to find the details of these companies' pension expense.

LOS 32.l: Calculate and interpret leverage and coverage ratios.

CFA® Program Curriculum, Volume 3, page 523

Analysts use solvency ratios to measure a firm's ability to satisfy its long-term obligations. In evaluating solvency, analysts look at leverage ratios and coverage ratios.

Leverage Ratios

Leverage ratios focus on the balance sheet by measuring the amount of debt in a firm's capital structure. For calculating these ratios, "debt" refers to interest-bearing obligations. Non-interest bearing liabilities, such as accounts payable, accrued liabilities, and deferred taxes, are not considered debt.

- *Debt-to-assets ratio* = total debt / total assets.

  Measures the percentage of total assets financed with debt.

- *Debt-to-capital ratio* = total debt / (total debt + total equity).

  Measures the percentage of total capital financed with debt. Debt-to-capital is similar to the debt-to-assets ratio, except that total capital excludes non-interest bearing liabilities. Recall the balance sheet equation A = L + E. Thus, total assets and total capital differ by the firm's non-interest bearing liabilities.

- *Debt-to-equity ratio* = total debt / total equity.

  Measures the amount of debt financing relative to the firm's equity base. A firm whose debt-to-equity ratio is 1.0 has equal amounts of debt and equity. Stated differently, its debt-to-capital ratio is 50%.

©2012 Kaplan, Inc.

- *Financial leverage ratio* = average total assets / average total equity.

  Measure of leverage used in the DuPont formula.

All of these leverage ratios are interpreted similarly; that is, the higher the ratio, the higher the leverage. When comparing firms, analysts must remember that in some countries, debt financing is more popular than equity financing. Firms in these countries will have higher leverage.

Coverage Ratios

Coverage ratios focus on the income statement by measuring the sufficiency of earnings to repay interest and other fixed charges when due. Two popular coverage ratios are the interest coverage ratio and the fixed charge coverage ratio.

- *Interest coverage* = EBIT / interest payments.

  A firm with lower interest coverage will have more difficulty meeting its interest payments.

- *Fixed charge coverage* = (EBIT + lease payments) / (interest payments + lease payments).

  Similar to interest coverage ratio but more inclusive because operating lease payments are added to the numerator and denominator. Significant operating lease payments will reduce this ratio as compared to interest coverage. Fixed charge coverage is more meaningful for firms that engage in significant operating leases.

Example: Leverage and coverage ratios

Westcliff Corporation is a hardware wholesaler. The following table shows selected information from Westcliff's most recent financial statements.

Liabilities and Equity	20X9	20X8
Accounts payable	$360,000	$310,000
Notes payable	385,200	321,100
Current maturities of long-term debt	60,000	60,000
Accrued liabilities	90,800	117,600
Total current liabilities	$896,000	$808,700
Long-term debt	740,000	800,000
Shareholders' equity	727,600	588,700
Total liabilities and equity	$2,363,600	$2,197,400

Partial Income Statement	20X9	20X8
Gross profit	$610,500	$580,800
Administrative expense	187,000	177,200
Lease expense	24,000	22,800
Earnings before interest and taxes	$399,500	$380,800
Interest expense	$168,000	$116,100

Discuss Westcliff's solvency using the appropriate leverage and coverage ratios.

Answer:

When evaluating solvency, accounts payable and accrued liabilities are not considered debt. Debt only includes interest bearing obligations:

	20X9	20X8
Notes payable	$385,200	$321,100
Current maturities of long-term debt	60,000	60,000
Long-term debt	740,000	800,000
Total debt	$1,185,200	$1,181,100

©2012 Kaplan, Inc.

Westcliff's leverage and coverage ratios are calculated as follows:

Debt-to-assets 2009: 1,185,200 debt / 2,363,600 assets = 50.1%
Debt-to-assets 2008: 1,181,100 debt / 2,197,400 assets = 53.7%

Debt-to-equity 2009: 1,185,200 debt / 727,600 equity = 1.6
Debt-to-equity 2008: 1,181,100 debt / 588,700 equity = 2.0

Debt-to-total capital 2009: 1,185,200 debt / 1,912,800 total capital = 62.0%
Debt-to-total capital 2008: 1,181,100 debt / 1,769,800 total capital = 66.7%

(Note: Total capital = total debt + shareholders' equity.)

Interest coverage 2009: 399,500 EBIT / 168,000 interest expense = 2.4
Interest coverage 2008: 380,800 EBIT / 116,100 interest expense = 3.3

Fixed charge coverage 2009:

(399,500 EBIT + 24,000 lease payments) / (168,000 interest expense + 24,000 lease payments) = 2.2

Fixed charge coverage 2008:

(380,800 EBIT + 22,800 lease payments) / (116,100 interest expense + 22,800 lease payments) = 2.9

Leverage declined in 20X9 using all three measures, mainly as a result of an increase in shareholders' equity. On the other hand, both coverage ratios declined in 20X9 as a result of higher interest expense. One possible explanation for the increase in interest expense, given lower leverage, is that interest rates are increasing.

KEY CONCEPTS

LOS 32.a

When a bond is issued, assets and liabilities both initially increase by the bond proceeds. At any point in time, the book value of the bond liability is equal to the present value of the remaining future cash flows (coupon payments and maturity value) discounted at the market rate of interest at issuance. The proceeds are reported in the cash flow statement as an inflow from financing activities.

A premium bond (coupon rate > market yield at issuance) is reported on the balance sheet at a value greater than its face value. As the premium is amortized (reduced), the book value of the bond liability will decrease until it reaches its face value at maturity.

A discount bond (market yield at issuance > coupon rate) is reported on the balance sheet at less than its face value. As the discount is amortized, the book value of the bond liability will increase until it reaches its face value at maturity.

LOS 32.b

Interest expense includes amortization of any discount or premium at issuance. Using the effective interest rate method, interest expense is equal to the book value of the bond liability at the beginning of the period multiplied by the bond's yield at issuance.

For a premium bond, interest expense is less than the coupon payment (yield < coupon rate). The difference between interest expense and the coupon payment is subtracted from the bond liability on the balance sheet.

For a discount bond, interest expense is greater than the coupon payment (yield > coupon rate). The difference between interest expense and the coupon payment is added to the bond liability on the balance sheet.

LOS 32.c

When bonds are redeemed before maturity, a gain or loss is recognized equal to the difference between the redemption price and the carrying (book) value of the bond liability at the reacquisition date. Under U.S. GAAP, any remaining unamortized bond issuance costs must also be written off and included in the gain or loss calculation. Writing off the unamortized issuance costs will reduce a gain or increase a loss. No write-off is necessary under IFRS because issuance costs are already included in book value of the bond liability.

LOS 32.d

Debt covenants are restrictions on the borrower that protect the bondholders' interests, thereby reducing both default risk and borrowing costs. Covenants can include restrictions on dividend payments and share repurchases; mergers and acquisitions; sale, leaseback, and disposal of certain assets; and issuance of new debt in the future. Other covenants require the firm to maintain ratios or financial statement items at specific levels.

©2012 Kaplan, Inc.

LOS 32.e

The firm separately discloses details about its long-term debt in the footnotes. These disclosures are useful for determining the timing and amount of future cash outflows. The disclosures usually include a discussion of the nature of the liabilities, maturity dates, stated and effective interest rates, call provisions and conversion privileges, restrictions imposed by creditors, assets pledged as security, and the amount of debt maturing in each of the next five years.

LOS 32.f

Compared to purchasing an asset, leasing may provide the lessee with less costly financing, reduce the risk of obsolescence, and include less restrictive provisions than a typical loan. Synthetic leases provide tax advantages and keep the lease liability off the balance sheet.

LOS 32.g

Under IFRS, if substantially all the rights and risks of ownership are transferred to the lessee, the lease is treated as a finance lease by both the lessee and lessor. Otherwise, the lease is an operating lease.

Under U.S. GAAP, the lessee must treat a lease as a capital (finance) lease if any one of the following criteria is met:
- Title to the leased asset is transferred to the lessee at the end of the lease period.
- A bargain purchase option exists.
- The lease period is 75% or more of the asset's economic life.
- The present value of the lease payments is 90% or more of the fair value of the leased asset.

Under U.S. GAAP, the lessor capitalizes the lease if any one of the finance lease criteria for lessees is met, collectability of lease payments is reasonably certain, and the lessor has substantially completed performance.

LOS 32.h

A finance lease is, in substance, a purchase of an asset that is financed with debt. At any point in time, the lease liability is equal to the present value of the remaining lease payments.

From the lessee's perspective, finance lease expense consists of depreciation of the asset and interest on the loan. The finance lease payment consists of an operating outflow of cash (interest expense) and a financing outflow of cash (principal reduction).

An operating lease is simply a rental arrangement; no asset or liability is reported by the lessee. The rental payment is reported as an expense and as an operating outflow of cash.

From the lessor's perspective, a finance lease is either a sales-type lease or a direct financing lease. In either case, a lease receivable is created at the inception of the lease, equal to the present value of the lease payments. The lease payments are treated as part interest income (CFO) and part principal reduction (CFI).

With a sales-type lease, the lessor recognizes gross profit at the inception of the lease and interest income over the life of the lease. With a direct financing lease, the lessor recognizes interest income only.

LOS 32.i

Both lessees and lessors are required to disclose useful information about finance leases and operating leases in the financial statements or in the footnotes, including:

- General description of the leasing arrangement.
- The nature, timing, and amount of payments to be paid or received in each of the next five years. Lease payments after five years can be aggregated.
- Amount of lease revenue and expense reported in the income statement for each period presented.
- Amounts receivable and unearned revenues from lease arrangements.
- Restrictions imposed by lease agreements.

LOS 32.j

In a defined contribution plan, the employer contributes a certain sum each period to the employee's retirement account. The employer makes no promise regarding the future value of the plan assets; thus, the employee assumes all of the investment risk.

In a defined benefit plan, the employer promises to make periodic payments to the employee after retirement. Because the employee's future benefit is defined, the employer assumes the investment risk. Accounting is complicated because many assumptions are involved.

LOS 32.k

A firm reports a net pension liability on its balance sheet if the fair value of a defined benefit plan's assets is less than the estimated pension obligation, or a net pension asset if the fair value of the plan's assets is greater than the estimated pension obligation. The change in the net pension asset or liability is reflected in a firm's comprehensive income each year.

Under IFRS, service costs (including past service costs) and interest income or expense on the beginning plan balance are included in pension expense on the income statement. Remeasurements are recorded in other comprehensive income. These include actuarial gains or losses and the difference between the actual return and the expected return on plan assets.

Under U.S. GAAP, service costs, interest income or expense, and the expected return on plan assets are included in pension expense. Past service costs and actuarial gains or losses are recorded in other comprehensive income and amortized over time to the income statement.

Pension expense for a defined contribution pension plan is equal to the employer's contributions.

LOS 32.1

Analysts use solvency ratios to measure a firm's ability to satisfy its long-term obligations. In evaluating solvency, analysts look at leverage ratios and coverage ratios.

Leverage ratios, such as debt-to-assets, debt-to-capital, debt-to-equity, and the financial leverage ratio, focus on the balance sheet.

Debt-to-assets ratio = total debt / total assets

Debt-to-capital ratio = total debt / (total debt + total equity)

Debt-to-equity ratio = total debt / total equity

Financial leverage ratio = average total assets / average total equity

Coverage ratios, such as interest coverage and fixed charge coverage, focus on the income statement.

Interest coverage = EBIT / interest payments

Fixed charge coverage = (EBIT + lease payments) / (interest payments + lease payments)

CONCEPT CHECKERS

Use the following data to answer Questions 1 through 8.

A firm issues a $10 million bond with a 6% coupon rate, 4-year maturity, and annual interest payments when market interest rates are 7%.

1. The bond can be classified as a:
    A. discount bond.
    B. par bond.
    C. premium bond.

2. The annual coupon payments will each be:
    A. $600,000.
    B. $676,290.
    C. $700,000.

3. Total of all cash payments to the bondholders is:
    A. $12,400,000.
    B. $12,738,721.
    C. $12,800,000.

4. The initial book value of the bonds is:
    A. $9,400,000.
    B. $9,661,279.
    C. $10,000,000.

5. For the first period the interest expense is:
    A. $600,000.
    B. $676,290.
    C. $700,000.

6. If the market rate changes to 8% and the bonds are carried at amortized cost, the book value of the bonds at the end of the first year will be:
    A. $9,484,581.
    B. $9,661,279.
    C. $9,737,568.

7. The total interest expense reported by the issuer over the life of the bond will be:
    A. $2,400,000.
    B. $2,738,721.
    C. $2,800,000.

8. For analytical purposes, what is the impact on the debt-to-equity ratio if the market rate of interest increases after the bond is issued?
    A. An increase.
    B. A decrease.
    C. No change.

©2012 Kaplan, Inc.

9. Using the effective interest rate method, the reported interest expense of a bond issued at a premium will:
    A. decrease over the term of the bond.
    B. increase over the term of the bond.
    C. remain unchanged over the term of the bond.

10. According to U.S. GAAP, the coupon payment on a bond is:
    A. reported as an operating cash outflow.
    B. reported as a financing cash outflow.
    C. reported as part operating cash outflow and part financing cash outflow.

11. At the beginning of 20X6, Cougar Corporation enters a finance lease requiring five annual payments of $10,000 each beginning on the first day of the lease. Assuming the lease interest rate is 8%, the amount of interest expense recognized by Cougar in 20X6 is *closest* to:
    A. $2,650.
    B. $3,194.
    C. $3,450.

12. Which of the following is *least likely* to be disclosed in the financial statements of a bond issuer?
    A. The amount of debt that matures in each of the next five years.
    B. Collateral pledged as security in the event of default.
    C. The market rate of interest on the balance sheet date.

13. As compared to purchasing an asset, which of the following is *least likely* an incentive to structure a transaction as a finance lease?
    A. At the end of the lease, the asset is returned to the lessor.
    B. The terms of the lease terms can be negotiated to better meet each party's needs.
    C. The lease enhances the balance sheet by the lease liability.

14. In a defined benefit pension plan:
    A. pension expense and the amount funded each period must be the same.
    B. no promise is made concerning the ultimate benefits to be paid to the employees.
    C. the employer assumes the majority of the investment risk.

15. A net pension asset or net pension liability is equal to the difference between the fair value of plan assets and the expected pension obligation under:
    A. IFRS only.
    B. U.S. GAAP only.
    C. Both IFRS and U.S. GAAP.

16.   At the end of last year, Maui Corporation's assets and liabilities were as follows:

Total assets	$98,500
Accrued liabilities	$5,000
Short-term debt	$12,000
Bonds payable	$39,000

Maui's debt-to-equity ratio is *closest* to:

A. 1.2.

B. 1.3.

C. 1.4.

©2012 Kaplan, Inc.

ANSWERS – CONCEPT CHECKERS

1. **A**   This bond is issued at a discount since the coupon rate < market rate.

2. **A**   Coupon payment = (coupon rate × face value of bond) = 6% × $10,000,000 = $600,000.

3. **A**   Four coupon payments and the face value = ($600,000 × 4) + $10,000,000 = $12,400,000.

4. **B**   The present value of a 4-year annuity of $600,000 plus a 4-year lump sum of $10 million, all valued at a discount rate of 7%, equals $9,661,279. Choice C can be eliminated because the bond was issued at a discount.

5. **B**   Market interest rate × book value = 7% × $9,661,279 = $676,290.

6. **C**   The new book value = beginning book value + interest expense – coupon payment = $9,661,279 + $676,290 – $600,000 = $9,737,569. The interest expense was calculated in question 5. Alternatively, changing N from 4 to 3 and calculating the PV will yield the same result. The change in market rates will not affect amortized costs.

7. **B**   Coupon payments + discount interest = coupon payments + (face value – issue value) = $2,400,000 + ($10,000,000 – $9,661,279) = $2,738,721.

8. **B**   An increase in the market rate will decrease the price of a bond. For analytical purposes, adjusting the bond liability to its economic value will result in a lower debt-to-equity ratio (lower numerator and higher denominator).

9. **A**   Interest expense is based on the book value of the bond. As the premium is amortized, the book value of the bond decreases until it reaches face value.

10. **A**   The actual coupon payment on a bond is reported as operating cash outflow under U.S. GAAP.

11. **A**   At the inception of the lease, the present value of the lease payments is $43,121 (BGN mode: N = 5, I = 8, PMT = 10,000, FV = 0, solve for PV). After the first payment is made, the balance of the lease liability is $43,121 – 10,000 principal payment = $33,121. Interest expense for the first year is $33,121 × 8% = $2,650.

12. **C**   The market rate on the balance sheet date is not typically disclosed. The amount of debt principal scheduled to be repaid over the next five years and collateral pledged (if any) are generally included in the footnotes to the financial statements.

13. **C**   Operating leases enhance the balance sheet by excluding any lease liability. With a finance lease, an asset and a liability are reported on the balance sheet as with purchase made with debt.

14. **C**   In a defined benefit plan, the employer is, in effect, guaranteeing benefits to the employees when they retire. Thus, the employer bears the investment risk.

15. **C**   Under both IFRS and U.S. GAAP, a net pension asset or net pension liability reflects the difference between the fair value of plan assets and the expected pension obligation. The remaining differences between IFRS and U.S. GAAP reporting of defined benefit pensions concern which components of the change in a net pension asset or liability are reported in net income versus other comprehensive income.

16. **A**   Because A – L = E, shareholders' equity is 98,500 assets – 5,000 accrued liabilities – 12,000 short-term debt – 39,000 bonds payable = $42,500. Thus, debt-to-equity is (12,000 short-term debt + 39,000 bonds payable) / 42,500 equity = 1.2. Only interest-bearing liabilities are considered debt. Accrued liabilities are not interest bearing.

©2012 Kaplan, Inc.

The following is a review of the Financial Reporting and Analysis principles designed to address the learning outcome statements set forth by CFA Institute. This topic is also covered in:

FINANCIAL REPORTING QUALITY: RED FLAGS AND ACCOUNTING WARNING SIGNS

Study Session 10

EXAM FOCUS

This review covers a broad array of methods to manipulate earnings through the choice of accounting methods and estimates. There are some long lists that you cannot be expected to replicate. You should, however, understand every point on every list, how income or balance sheet items are affected, and why the indicated warning sign suggests accounting manipulation. With this in mind, focus strongly on the warning signs of various accounting irregularities. Remember, firms may manipulate earnings to decrease or increase them. Firms may artificially decrease earnings in periods of good earnings growth in such a way that they can be "stored," only to reappear in a future period when results would have otherwise fallen short of expectations.

LOS 33.a: Describe incentives that might induce a company's management to overreport or underreport earnings.

CFA® Program Curriculum, Volume 3, page 538

Firms are motivated to **manage earnings** because of the potential benefits.

Management may be motivated to *overstate net income* to:

- Meet earnings expectations.
- Remain in compliance with lending covenants.
- Receive higher incentive compensation.

Managing earnings can also involve *understating net income*. Management may be motivated to underreport earnings to:

- Obtain trade relief in the form of quotas or protective tariffs.
- Negotiate favorable terms from creditors.
- Negotiate favorable labor union contracts.

Firms may also be motivated to *manage the balance sheet*. For example, by overstating assets or understating liabilities, the firm appears more solvent. Conversely, a firm might understate assets or overstate liabilities to appear less solvent in order to negotiate concessions with creditors and other interested parties. A firm may also manage its balance sheet in order to enhance performance ratios. For example, lower assets will result in a higher return on assets ratio and a higher asset turnover ratio.

LOS 33.b: Describe activities that will result in a low quality of earnings.

CFA® Program Curriculum, Volume 3, page 539

Generally accepted accounting principles (GAAP) can be exploited by a firm to achieve a specific outcome while meeting the letter, but not the spirit, of the accounting standards; however, earnings quality will usually deteriorate. Low quality earnings are the result of:

- *Selecting acceptable accounting principles that misrepresent the economics of a transaction.* For example, a firm might choose the units-of-production method of depreciation in periods when the consumption of the asset is better measured by the straight-line or accelerated methods. If the units-of-production method results in lower depreciation than the straight-line method early in the asset's life, earnings will be accelerated to the early years of the asset's life.
- *Structuring transactions to achieve a desired outcome.* For example, a firm might structure the terms of a lease to avoid capital lease recognition, resulting in lower liabilities, lower leverage ratios, and lower fixed assets.
- *Using aggressive or unrealistic estimates and assumptions.* For example, lengthening the lives of depreciable assets or increasing the salvage value will result in lower depreciation expense and higher earnings.
- *Exploiting the intent of an accounting principle.* For example, some firms have applied a narrow rule regarding unconsolidated special purposes entities (SPE) to a broad range of transactions, because leverage is lower if the firm does not consolidate the SPE.

LOS 33.c: Describe the three conditions that are generally present when fraud occurs, including the risk factors related to these conditions.

CFA® Program Curriculum, Volume 3, page 539

Users of financial information should become familiar with the risk factors and warning signs of fraud. Statement on Auditing Standards No. 99, *Consideration of Fraud in a Financial Statement Audit* (SAS No. 99), issued by the American Institute of Certified Public Accountants (AICPA), identifies three conditions that are usually present when fraud occurs. These conditions, known as the **fraud triangle**, are illustrated in Figure 1. Note that not all of these conditions need to be present for fraud to occur.

Figure 1: "Fraud Triangle"

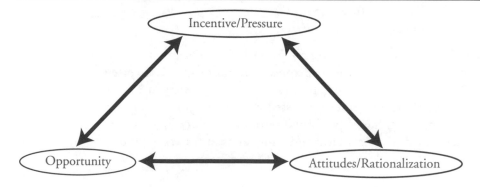

©2012 Kaplan, Inc.

Study Session 10

Cross-Reference to CFA Institute Assigned Reading #33 – Financial Reporting Quality: Red Flags and Accounting Warning Signs

- **Incentive or pressure** is the motive that exists to commit fraud. For example, management may want to meet earnings expectations because their compensation depends the firm's stock price.
- **Opportunity** exists when there is a weakness in internal controls.
- **Attitudes or rationalization** is a mindset that fraudulent behavior is justified.

Incentives and Pressures

SAS No. 99 identified four risk factors related to the incentives or pressures (motive) that may lead to fraudulent reporting.

1. *Threats to financial stability or profitability* as a result of economic, industry, or firm conditions such as:

   - Intense competition or market saturation, along with declining margins.
   - Vulnerability to rapid changes in technology, rates of product obsolescence, or interest rates.
   - Declining customer demand or increasing business failures.
   - Operating losses that may result in bankruptcy, foreclosure, or a hostile takeover.
   - Recurring negative operating cash flow or inability to generate positive cash flow while reporting earnings or earnings growth.
   - Rapid growth or unusual profitability.
   - New accounting standards, laws, or regulatory requirements.

2. *Excessive third-party pressures* on management from:

   - Aggressive or unrealistic profitability or trend expectations.
   - Debt or equity financing requirements in order to stay competitive.
   - Stock exchange listing requirements.
   - Debt covenants and repayment requirements.
   - Impact of real or perceived effects of poor financial performance on a pending transaction, such as a business acquisition.

3. *Personal net worth of management or the board of directors is threatened* because of:

   - A significant financial interest in the firm.
   - A significant amount of contingent compensation based on achieving aggressive targets for stock price, operating profit, or cash flow.
   - Personal guarantees of the firm's debt.

4. *Excessive pressure on management or operating personnel to meet internal financial goals*, including sales and profitability targets.

Opportunities for Fraud

SAS No. 99 identified four risk factors related to the opportunities to commit fraud in financial reporting.

1. The *nature of the firm's industry or operations* might involve:
   - Significant related-party transactions, particularly when those parties are unaudited, or audited by another firm.
   - Ability to dictate terms and conditions to suppliers and customers that may result in transactions that are not at arm's length.

- Significant estimates and judgments in accounting for assets, liabilities, revenues, and expenses.
- Unusual or complex transactions, especially near year-end, such as transactions that present "substance over form" issues.
- Operations that exist or transactions that occur internationally where cultures and business practices may differ.
- Bank accounts or operations located in tax-havens without clear business justification.

2. *Ineffective management monitoring* as a result of:

- Management being dominated by a single person or small group.
- Ineffective oversight by the board of directors or audit committee.

3. *A complex or unstable organizational structure* as evidenced by:

- Difficulty in determining who is in control.
- Organizational structure that involves unusual legal entities or unusual lines of authority.
- High turnover among management, legal counsel, or board members.

4. *Deficient internal controls* that can result from:

- Inadequate monitoring controls.
- High turnover rates of accounting and information technology personnel.
- Ineffective accounting and information systems.

> *Professor's Note: The last three factors relate to corporate governance. In firms with more effective corporate governance systems, the opportunities to commit fraud are limited. See the topic review of corporate governance in the Study Session on corporate finance for more details.*

Attitudes and Rationalizations

SAS No. 99 identified the following risk factors related to attitudes and rationalization to justify fraudulent behavior:

1. *Inappropriate ethical standards* or failure to effectively communicate or support a firm's ethical standards.

2. *Excessive participation by nonfinancial management in the selection of accounting standards* and the determination of estimates.

3. Known history or allegations of *violations of laws and regulations by management or board members.*

4. *A management obsession with maintaining or increasing the firm's stock price or earnings trend.*

5. *Making commitments to third parties to achieve aggressive results.*

6. *Failing to correct known reportable conditions* in a timely manner.

©2012 Kaplan, Inc.

7. *Inappropriately minimizing earnings for tax purposes.*

8. Management's continued *use of materiality as a basis to justify inappropriate or questionable accounting methods.*

9. *A strained relationship between management and the current or previous auditor* as evidenced by any of the following:

   • Frequent disputes on accounting, auditing, and reporting issues.
   • Unreasonable demands on the auditor, such as unreasonable time constraints.
   • Restricting the auditor's access to people and information.
   • Limiting the auditor's ability to effectively communicate with the board of directors and audit committee.
   • Domineering management behavior toward the auditor.

LOS 33.d: Describe common accounting warning signs and methods for detecting each.

CFA® Program Curriculum, Volume 3, page 539

Aggressive revenue recognition. The most common earnings manipulation technique is recognizing revenue *too soon*. Recall that revenue is recognized in the income statement when it is earned and payment is reasonably assured. Usually revenue is recognized at delivery but, in some cases, revenue can be recognized before delivery takes place. Firms are required to report their revenue recognition policies in the financial statement footnotes. It is important to understand when revenue recognition takes place.

Some examples of aggressive recognition include:

• Bill-and-hold arrangements whereby revenue is recognized before the goods are shipped.
• Sales-type leases whereby the lessor recognizes a sale, and profit, at the inception of the lease, especially when the lessee does not capitalize the lease.
• Recognizing revenue before fulfilling all of the terms and conditions of sale.
• Recognizing revenue from swaps and barter transactions with third parties.

Different growth rates of operating cash flow and earnings. Over time, there should be a fairly stable relationship between the growth of operating cash flow and earnings. If not, earnings manipulation may be occurring. A firm that is reporting growing earnings, but negative or declining operating cash flow, may be recognizing revenue too soon and/or delaying the recognition of expense.

The relationship of operating cash flow and earnings can be measured with the **cash flow earnings index** (operating cash flow/net income). An index that is consistently less than one or that is declining over time is suspect.

Abnormal sales growth as compared to the economy, industry, or peers. Abnormal growth may be the result of superior management or products, but may also indicate accounting irregularities. Receivables that are growing faster than sales, as indicated by an increasing average collection period, may be evidence of aggressive revenue recognition.

Abnormal inventory growth as compared to sales growth. Increasing inventory may be an indication of obsolete products or poor inventory management, but it could also result from overstating inventory, decreasing the cost of goods sold and thereby increasing gross profit and net profit.

 Professor's Note: Recall that ending inventory is equal to beginning inventory plus purchases minus cost of goods sold (COGS). If ending inventory is too high, COGS will be too low, all else equal.

Boosting revenue with nonoperating income and nonrecurring gains. Some firms try to reclassify nonoperating income and nonrecurring gains as revenue, in effect, moving these items "up" the income statement. Net income is the same but revenue growth is higher.

Delaying expense recognition. By capitalizing operating expenditures, the firm delays expense recognition to future periods. Watch for an increase in assets with unusual sounding names such as "deferred marketing charges" or "deferred customer acquisition costs."

Abnormal use of operating leases by lessees. Operating leases are common in most firms. However, some firms use this off-balance-sheet financing technique to improve ratios and reduce perceived leverage. Analysts should compare the firm's use of leasing, as a financing source, to its industry peers. For analytical purposes, consider treating operating leases as capital leases.

Hiding expenses by classifying them as extraordinary or nonrecurring. The result is to move expenses "down" the income statement and boost income from continuing operations.

LIFO liquidations. When a LIFO firm sells more inventory than it purchases or produces during a period of rising prices, it reduces the cost of goods sold and increases profit, although taxes are higher as well. Such profits are not sustainable because the firm will eventually run out of inventory. A declining **LIFO reserve** (the difference between LIFO inventory and what it would be under FIFO, which must be disclosed by firms that use LIFO) is an indication of a LIFO liquidation. Firms should disclose the effects of a LIFO liquidation in the financial statement footnotes.

Abnormal gross margin and operating margin as compared to industry peers. Abnormal margins may be the result of superior management or cost controls; however, they may be an indication of accounting irregularities. Determine the firm's conservatism by comparing the firm's accounting principles, as disclosed in the footnotes, to those of its industry peers.

Extending the useful lives of long-term assets. Depreciating or amortizing the cost of an asset over more periods results in higher reported earnings. Compare the useful lives of the firm's assets with those of its industry peers.

©2012 Kaplan, Inc.

Aggressive pension assumptions. Aggressive assumptions such as a high discount rate, low compensation growth rate, or high expected rate of return on pension assets will result in lower pension expense and higher reported earnings. Compare these assumptions with those of its industry peers.

Year-end surprises. Higher earnings in the fourth quarter that cannot be explained by seasonality may be an indication of manipulation.

Equity method investments and off-balance-sheet special purpose entities. Equity method investments are not consolidated. However, the pro-rata share of the investee's earnings are included in net income. Watch for frequent use of nonconsolidated special purpose entities.

Other off-balance-sheet financing arrangements including debt guarantees. Firms must disclose these arrangements in the financial statement footnotes. For analytical purposes, consider increasing balance sheet liabilities for these arrangements.

 Professor's Note: Keep in mind that these are warning signs of low quality earnings. They are not necessarily indications that fraud has occurred or will occur.

KEY CONCEPTS

LOS 33.a
Management may be motivated to overstate earnings to meet analyst expectations, remain in compliance with debt covenants, or because higher reported earnings will increase their compensation. Management may be motivated to understate earnings to obtain trade relief, renegotiate advantageous repayment terms with existing creditors, negotiate more advantageous union labor contracts, or "save" earnings to report in a future period.

LOS 33.b
Low earnings quality can result from selecting accounting principles that misrepresent the economics of transactions, structuring transactions primarily to achieve a desired effect on reported earnings, using aggressive or unrealistic estimates and assumptions, or exploiting the intent of an accounting standard.

LOS 33.c
The "fraud triangle" consists of:
- *Incentives and pressures*—the motive to commit fraud.
- *Opportunities*—the firm has a weak internal control system.
- *Attitudes and rationalizations*—the mindset that fraud is justified.

Risk factors related to incentives and pressures for fraud include:
- Threats to the firm's financial stability or profitability.
- Excessive third-party pressures on management.
- Threats to the personal net worth of management or board members.
- Excessive pressure on management and employees to meet internal targets.

Risk factors related to opportunities for fraud include:
- The nature of the industry or operations.
- Ineffective monitoring of management.
- Complex or unstable organizational structure.
- Deficient internal controls.

Risk factors related to attitudes and rationalizations for fraud include:
- Inappropriate or inadequately supported ethical standards.
- Excessive participation by nonfinancial management in selecting accounting methods.
- A history of legal and regulatory violations by management or board members.
- Obsessive attention to the stock price or earnings trend.
- Aggressive commitments to third parties.
- Failure to correct known compliance problems.
- Minimizing earnings inappropriately for tax reporting.
- Continued use of materiality to justify inappropriate accounting.
- A strained relationship with the current or previous auditor.

©2012 Kaplan, Inc.

LOS 33.d

Common warning signs of earnings manipulation include:

- Aggressive revenue recognition.
- Different growth rates of operating cash flow and earnings.
- Abnormal comparative sales growth.
- Abnormal inventory growth as compared to sales.
- Moving nonoperating income and nonrecurring gains up the income statement to boost revenue.
- Delaying expense recognition.
- Excessive use of off-balance-sheet financing arrangements including leases.
- Classifying expenses as extraordinary or nonrecurring and moving them down the income statement to boost income from continuing operations.
- LIFO liquidations.
- Abnormal comparative margin ratios.
- Aggressive assumptions and estimates.
- Year-end surprises.
- Equity method investments with little or no cash flow.

CONCEPT CHECKERS

1. Which of the following is *least likely* to be a motivation to overreport net income?
    A. Meet earnings expectations.
    B. Negotiate labor union contracts.
    C. Remain in compliance with bond covenants.

2. Which of the following is *most likely* an example of accounting fraud?
    A. Using aggressive pension assumptions.
    B. Booking revenue from a fictitious customer.
    C. Selecting an acceptable depreciation method that misrepresents the economics of the transaction.

3. The "fraud triangle" consists of:
    A. incentive or pressure, opportunity, and attitudes or rationalization.
    B. ineffective management, unstable organizational structure, and deficient internal controls.
    C. inappropriate ethical standards, violations of laws or regulations, and failing to correct known reportable conditions.

4. Competitive threats to the profitability or financial stability of a firm are *best* categorized as an accounting fraud risk factor related to:
    A. opportunities.
    B. incentives and pressures.
    C. attitudes and rationalizations.

5. According to Statement on Auditing Standards No. 99, Consideration of Fraud in a Financial Statement Audit, which of the following is *least likely* to be a risk factor related to opportunities to commit fraudulent accounting?
    A. Significant related-party transactions.
    B. High turnover among accounting and information systems personnel.
    C. Aggressive or unrealistic profitability expectations from third parties.

6. Accounting fraud risk factors related to attitudes and rationalizations are *least likely* to include:
    A. management has a strained relationship with the current or previous auditor.
    B. the firm does not effectively communicate an appropriate set of ethical standards.
    C. a high proportion of management's compensation depends on the firm exceeding targets for earnings or the stock price.

7. Which of the following actions is *least likely* to immediately increase earnings?
    A. Selling more inventory than is purchased or produced.
    B. Lowering the salvage value of depreciable assets.
    C. Recognizing revenue before fulfilling all the terms of a sale.

©2012 Kaplan, Inc.

ANSWERS – CONCEPT CHECKERS

1. **B** Negotiating labor union contracts would be a reason to underreport, not overreport, earnings. The other choices are motivations to overreport earnings.

2. **B** Booking revenue from a fictitious customer is fraud.

3. **A** The three components of the fraud triangle are incentive or pressure, opportunity, and attitudes or rationalization.

4. **B** Risk factors related to incentives and pressures include threats to the firm's financial stability or profitability from economic, industry, or firm-specific operating conditions.

5. **C** Unrealistic profitability expectations from third parties is a risk factor related to incentives and pressures. The other choices are risk factors related to management's opportunities to commit fraud.

6. **C** Significant threats to the personal wealth of managers and board members due to the firm not meeting its financial targets are a risk factor related to incentives and pressures. The other choices are risk factors related to attitudes and rationalizations.

7. **B** Lowering the salvage value will result in higher depreciation expense, and thus, lower earnings. The other choices will immediately increase earnings. Selling more inventory than is purchased or produced will increase revenue without increasing cost of goods sold, which will increase earnings. Recognizing revenue before fulfilling all terms of a sale is an aggressive revenue recognition method that will boost earnings.

The following is a review of the Financial Reporting and Analysis principles designed to address the learning outcome statements set forth by CFA Institute. This topic is also covered in:

ACCOUNTING SHENANIGANS ON THE CASH FLOW STATEMENT

Study Session 10

EXAM FOCUS

Management has several ways to manipulate operating cash flow, including deciding how to allocate cash flow between categories and changing the timing of receipt of cash flows. Lengthening the terms of accounts payable, financing accounts payable, securitizing accounts receivable, and repurchasing stock options to offset dilution can affect the categorization and timing of cash flows. Not all increases in operating cash flow are sustainable.

CASH FLOW MANIPULATION

Accrual accounting is easily manipulated because of the many estimates and judgments involved. Operating cash flow is usually unaffected by estimates and judgments. However, firms can still create the perception that sustainable operating cash flow is greater than it actually is.

One technique is to misrepresent a firm's cash generating ability by classifying financing activities as operating activities and vice-versa. Additionally, management has discretion over the timing of cash flows. An analyst should take care to investigate the quality of a company's cash flows and determine whether increases in operating cash flow are sustainable. Management also has discretion over where to report cash flows, and the analyst should be aware that the difference in treatment among companies may make comparisons of cash flow less useful, particularly for valuation.

LOS 34.a: Analyze and describe the following ways to manipulate the cash flow statement: stretching out payables; financing of payables; securitization of receivables; and using stock buybacks to offset dilution of earnings.

CFA® Program Curriculum, Volume 3, page 558

Stretching Accounts Payable

Transactions with suppliers are usually reported as operating activities in the cash flow statement. A firm can temporarily increase operating cash flow by simply stretching accounts payable; that is, delaying payments to its suppliers. By delaying payment, the firm effectively receives no-cost financing. However, stretching payables is not a sustainable source of increased cash flows, since the firm's suppliers may eventually refuse to extend credit because of the slower payments.

©2012 Kaplan, Inc.

One way to determine whether a firm is stretching its payables is to examine the number of days in accounts payable. **Days' sales in payables** is calculated by dividing accounts payable by COGS and multiplying the result by the number of days in the period.

$$\text{days' sales in accounts payable} = \left(\frac{\text{accounts payable}}{\text{COGS}} \right) \times \text{number of days}$$

 Professor's Note: Earlier, we calculated the number of days of payables by dividing 365 by accounts payable turnover. Recall that accounts payable turnover is equal to purchases divided by average accounts payable.

Example: Calculating days' sales in accounts payable

At year-end, Silver Creek Company reported cost of goods sold of $250 million. Ending accounts payable is $50 million. Assuming there are 365 days in a year, calculate the number of days on average it takes Silver Creek to pay its suppliers.

Answer:

$$\text{days' sales in accounts payable} = \left(\frac{\$50}{\$250} \right) \times 365 = 73 \text{ days}$$

Financing Accounts Payable

Delaying the cash flows associated with payables can also be accomplished by entering into a financing arrangement with a third party, usually a financial institution. Such an arrangement allows the firm to manage the timing of the reported operating cash flows.

Consider a manufacturing firm's credit purchases of raw materials. In an indirect cash flow statement, the increase in inventory decreases operating cash flow and the increase in accounts payable increases operating cash flow. Total operating cash flow does not change.

When the account payable is due, a financial institution makes payment to the supplier on behalf of the firm, and the firm reclassifies the account payable to short-term debt. The decrease in accounts payable decreases operating cash flow, and the increase in short-term debt increases financing cash flow. At this point, operating cash flow is lower and financing cash flow is higher, but total cash flow is still unaffected. The firm might time the arrangement so that the lower operating cash flow is offset by higher operating cash flows from other sources, such as seasonal cash flows or cash flows from receivable sales or securitizations. In effect, the firm times the operating cash outflow to occur when other operating cash inflows are higher.

Finally, when the firm repays the financial institution, the firm reports the outflow of cash as a financing activity and not an operating activity. Ultimately, the firm has delayed the outflow of cash. Of course, the financial institution will charge a fee (interest) to handle the arrangement.

Securitizing Accounts Receivable

Firms can immediately convert accounts receivable to cash by borrowing against the receivables or by selling or securitizing the receivables. When a firm borrows with its receivables as collateral, the inflow of cash is reported as a financing activity in the cash flow statement.

When receivables are securitized, they are usually transferred to a bankruptcy remote structure known as a special purpose entity (SPE). The SPE pools the receivables together and sells securities representing an interest in the pool. A securitization is treated just like a collection; that is, the inflow of cash is reported as an operating activity in the cash flow statement because the transaction is reported as a sale. So, by securitizing its accounts receivable, rather than waiting to collect from the customer, a firm can accelerate operating cash flow into the current period.

Accelerating operating cash flow by securitizing receivables is not sustainable because the firm only has a limited amount of accounts receivable.

Securitizing accounts receivable may also affect earnings. When the receivables are securitized, the firm can recognize a gain in some cases. This gain is the result of differences between the book value and fair value of the receivables at the time of securitization. The gain can be affected by a number of estimates, including the expected default rate, the expected prepayment rate, and the discount rate used.

GAAP is silent on where the gains from securitizations should be reported in the income statement. Some firms take a more aggressive approach and include the gains as revenue. Other firms reduce operating expenses by the amount of the gains. Some firms report the gains as a part of nonoperating income.

Repurchasing Stock to Offset Dilution

When a firm's stock options are exercised, shares must be issued. The higher the stock price relative to the exercise price, the more shares that must be issued by the firm. As the shares are issued, earnings per share are diluted (reduced).

Firms often repurchase stock to offset the dilutive effects of stock option exercise. The cash received from the exercise of the option and the outflow of cash from the share repurchase are both reported as financing activities in the cash flow statement. Because there is a tax benefit when options are exercised, exercise increases operating cash flow.

For analytical purposes, the net cash outflow for share repurchases to avoid dilution should be reclassified from financing activities to operating activities to better reflect the substance of the transaction. Since employee stock options are part of compensation, an analyst should subtract the cash outflow from operating cash flow to recognize the true cash cost of options-based compensation.

©2012 Kaplan, Inc.

KEY CONCEPTS

LOS 34.a

Stretching accounts payable by delaying payment is not a sustainable source of operating cash flow. Suppliers may refuse to extend additional credit because of the slower payments. Stretching accounts payable can be identified by increases in the number of days in payables.

Arranging for a third party to finance (pay) a firm's payables in one period, so that the firm can account for repayment as a financing (rather than operating) cash flow in a later period, is a method to decrease operating cash flows in a period of seasonally high CFO and increase them in a subsequent period.

Securitizing accounts receivable accelerates operating cash flow into the current period, but this source of cash is not sustainable and artificially increases receivables turnover. Securitizing receivables may also allow the firm to immediately recognize gains in the income statement.

Some firms repurchase stock to offset the dilutive effect of the exercise of employee stock options. The analyst must determine whether the increase in operating cash flow resulting from the income tax benefits of the exercise of employee stock options is sustainable. For analysis, the net cash outflow to repurchase stock should be considered an operating activity instead of a financing activity, since it is essentially a compensation expense.

CONCEPT CHECKERS

1. Decreasing accounts payable turnover by delaying payments to suppliers is *most likely* to cause cash flow from financing activities to:
   A. increase.
   B. decrease.
   C. remain unchanged.

2. As part of its working capital management program, Rotan Corporation has an accounts payable financing arrangement with the First National Bank. The bank pays Rotan's vendors within 30 days of the invoice date. Rotan reimburses the bank 90 days after the invoice is due. Ignoring interest, what is the *most likely* effect on Rotan's operating cash flow and financing cash flow when the bank is repaid?
   A. Both will decrease.
   B. Neither will decrease.
   C. Only one will decrease.

3. In order to generate cash, Company L securitized its accounts receivable through a special purpose entity. Company M pledged its accounts receivable to a local bank in order to secure a short-term loan. Assuming Company L and Company M are identical in all other respects, which company has higher operating cash flow and which company has higher financing cash flow?

	Higher operating cash flow	Higher financing cash flow
A.	Company L	Company L
B.	Company L	Company M
C.	Company M	Company L

4. Over the past two years, a firm reported higher operating cash flow as a result of securitizing its accounts receivable and from increasing income tax benefits from employee stock options. The tax benefits are solely the result of higher tax rates. What should an analyst conclude about the sustainability of these two sources of operating cash flow?
   A. Both sources are sustainable.
   B. Neither source is sustainable.
   C. Only one of these sources is sustainable.

ANSWERS – CONCEPT CHECKERS

1. **C** Decreasing accounts payable turnover by delaying payments to suppliers is a source of operating cash, not a source of financing cash. Decreasing accounts payable turnover is not a sustainable source of cash flow because suppliers may eventually refuse to extend credit because of the slower payments.

2. **C** When the bank is repaid, the cash outflow is reported as a financing activity. Operating cash flow is not affected when payment is made.

3. **B** The cash received from securitizing receivables is reported as an operating activity. The cash received from borrowing against accounts receivable is reported as a financing activity.

4. **B** Accelerating operating cash flow by securitizing receivables is not sustainable because the firm only has a limited amount of accounts receivable. An increase in tax benefits as a result of higher tax rates is not sustainable. Tax rates could also decrease in the future.

The following is a review of the Financial Reporting and Analysis principles designed to address the learning outcome statements set forth by CFA Institute. This topic is also covered in:

FINANCIAL STATEMENT ANALYSIS: APPLICATIONS

EXAM FOCUS

In this topic review, we will apply the analytic methods detailed in the topic review of Financial Analysis Techniques. Pay special attention to the method outlined for forecasting cash flows. Memorize the four types of items important in the determination of credit quality. Lastly, analyst adjustments to financial statements are covered one more time. Understand the reasons for all the adjustments covered and how the adjustments will affect financial ratios used for valuation and credit analysis.

LOS 35.a: Evaluate a company's past financial performance and explain how a company's strategy is reflected in past financial performance.

CFA® Program Curriculum, Volume 3, page 568

In the review of Financial Analysis Techniques, we introduced a number of financial ratios that can be used to assess a company's profitability, leverage, solvency, and operational efficiency. The analyst can evaluate trends in these ratios, as well as their levels, to evaluate how the company has performed in these areas.

Trends in financial ratios and differences between a firm's financial ratios and those of its competitors or industry averages can indicate important aspects of a firm's business strategy. Consider two firms in the personal computer business. One builds relatively high-end computers with cutting-edge features, and one competes primarily on price and produces computers with various configurations using readily available technology. What differences in their financial statements would we expect to find?

Premium products are usually sold at higher gross margins than less differentiated commodity-like products, so we should expect cost of goods sold to be a higher proportion of sales for the latter. We might also expect the company with cutting-edge features and high quality to spend a higher proportion of sales on research and development, which may be quite minimal for a firm purchasing improved components from suppliers rather than developing new features and capabilities in-house. The ratio of gross profits to operating profits will be larger for a firm that spends highly on research and development or on advertising.

In general, it is important for an analyst to understand a subject firm's business strategy. If the firm claims it is going to improve earnings per share by cutting costs, examination of operating ratios and gross margins over time will reveal whether the firm has actually been able to implement such a strategy and whether sales have suffered as a result.

©2012 Kaplan, Inc.

LOS 35.b: Prepare a basic projection of a company's future net income and cash flow.

CFA® Program Curriculum, Volume 3, page 576

A forecast of future net income and cash flow often begins with a forecast of future sales. Over shorter horizons, the "top down" approach to forecasting sales is used. The analyst begins with a forecast of GDP growth, often supplied by outside research or an in-house economics group. Historical relationships can be used to estimate the relationship between GDP growth and the growth of industry sales. If the subject firm's market share is expected to remain the same, the growth of firm sales will be the same as the growth in industry sales. If the analyst has reason to believe the firm's market share will increase or decrease next period, the market share can be adjusted for this change and then multiplied by estimated industry sales for the next period to get the forecast of firm sales for the period.

In a simple forecasting model, some historical average or trend-adjusted measure of profitability (operating margin, EBT margin, or net margin) can be used to forecast earnings. In complex forecasting models, each item on an income statement and balance sheet can be estimated based on separate assumptions about its growth in relation to revenue growth. For multi-period forecasts, the analyst typically employs a single estimate of sales growth at some point that is expected to continue indefinitely.

To estimate cash flows, the analyst must make assumptions about future sources and uses of cash. The most important of these will be increases in working capital, capital expenditures on new fixed assets, issuance or repayments of debt, and issuance or repurchase of stock. A typical assumption is that noncash working capital as a percentage of sales remains constant. A first-pass model might indicate a need for cash in future periods, and these cash requirements can then be met by projecting necessary borrowing in future periods. For consistency, interest expense in future periods must also be adjusted for any increase in debt.

Figure 1 illustrates this method. This projection assumes the company's sales increase 5% per year, its cost of goods sold is 35% of sales, and operating expenses are 55% of sales. It also assumes noncash working capital stays constant at 85% of sales, and fixed capital requirements will be 5% of sales in each year. Net income is projected to increase over the forecast period, but the analysis reveals that cash is expected to decrease, suggesting a need for financing.

Figure 1: Income and Cash Flow Projection

	20X0	20X1	20X2	20X3	20X4
Sales @ +5% per year	86,145	90,452	94,975	99,724	104,710
Cost of goods sold @ 35% of sales	30,151	31,658	33,241	34,903	36,648
Operating expenses @ 55% of sales	47,380	49,749	52,236	54,848	57,590
Pretax income	8,614	9,045	9,497	9,972	10,471
Taxes @ 35%	3,015	3,166	3,324	3,490	3,665
Net income	5,599	5,879	6,173	6,482	6,806
Cash (Borrowing)	8,615	6,311	3,891	1,350	(1,318)
Noncash working capital @ 85% of sales	73,223	76,884	80,729	84,765	89,003
Current assets	81,838	83,195	84,620	86,116	87,685
Net income	5,599	5,879	6,173	6,482	6,806
– Investment in working capital	3,478	3,661	3,844	4,036	4,238
– Investment in fixed capital @ 5% of sales	4,307	4,523	4,749	4,986	5,235
Change in cash	(2,186)	(2,304)	(2,420)	(2,541)	(2,668)
Beginning cash	10,801	8,615	6,311	3,891	1,350
Ending cash	8,615	6,311	3,891	1,350	(1,318)

LOS 35.c: Describe the role of financial statement analysis in assessing the credit quality of a potential debt investment.

CFA® Program Curriculum, Volume 3, page 585

Traditionally, credit analysts have spoken of the "three Cs," "four Cs," or even the "five Cs" of credit analysis. One version of the three Cs includes: Character, Collateral, and Capacity to repay. Character refers to the firm management's professional reputation and the firm's history of debt repayment. The ability to pledge specific collateral reduces lender risk. It is the third C, the capacity to repay, that requires close examination of a firm's financial statements and ratios. Since some debt is for periods of 30 years or longer, the credit analyst must take a very long-term view of the firm's prospects.

Credit rating agencies such as Moody's and Standard and Poor's employ formulas that are essentially weighted averages of several specific accounting ratios and business characteristics. The specific items used in the formula and their weights vary from industry to industry, but the types of items considered can be separated into four general categories:

1. *Scale and diversification.* Larger companies and those with a wider variety of product lines and greater geographic diversification are better credit risks.

2. *Operational efficiency.* Such items as operating ROA, operating margins, and EBITDA margins fall into this category. Along with greater vertical diversification, high operating efficiency is associated with better debt ratings.

©2012 Kaplan, Inc.

3. *Margin stability.* Stability of the relevant profitability margins indicates a higher probability of repayment (leads to a better debt rating and a lower interest rate). Highly variable operating results make lenders nervous.

4. *Leverage.* Ratios of operating earnings, EBITDA, or some measure of free cash flow to interest expense or total debt make up the most important part of the credit rating formula. Firms with greater earnings in relation to their debt and in relation to their interest expense are better credit risks.

 Professor's Note: We discuss the analysis of credit quality in more detail in our topic review of "Fundamentals of Credit Analysis" in the Study Session on fixed income valuation.

LOS 35.d: Describe the use of financial statement analysis in screening for potential equity investments.

CFA® Program Curriculum, Volume 3, page 589

In many cases, an analyst must select portfolio stocks from the large universe of potential equity investments. Whether the object is to select growth stocks, income stocks, or value stocks, accounting items and ratios can be used to identify a manageable subset of available stocks for further analysis.

Some investment strategies even have financial ratios in their names, such as low price/earnings and low price/sales investing. Multiple criteria are used because a screen based on a single factor can include firms with other undesirable characteristics. For example, a company with a low price/earnings ratio may also have operating losses, declining sales prospects, or very high leverage.

Analysts should be aware that their equity screens will likely include and exclude many or all of the firms in particular industries. A screen to identify firms with low P/E ratios will likely exclude growth companies from the sample. A low price-to-book or high dividend screen will likely include an inordinate proportion of financial services companies.

Backtesting refers to using a specific set of criteria to screen historical data to determine how portfolios based on those criteria would have performed. There is, of course, no guarantee that screening criteria that have identified stocks that outperformed in the past will continue to do so. Analysts must also pay special attention to the potential effects of survivorship bias, data-mining bias, and look-ahead bias (see the topic review of Sampling and Estimation) when evaluating the results of backtesting.

LOS 35.e: Determine and justify appropriate analyst adjustments to a company's financial statements to facilitate comparison with another company.

CFA® Program Curriculum, Volume 3, page 592

Because different companies choose different accounting methods, an analyst must be prepared to adjust the financial statements of one company to make them comparable to those of another company or group of companies. Differences in accounting methods chosen by firms subject to the same standards, as well as differences in accounting methods due to differences in local accounting standards, can make comparisons between companies problematic.

Consider two companies in the same industry that have different depreciation schedules. One company has selected straight-line depreciation even though physical assets in its industry tend to lose most of their productive value early in their economic lives. The analyst would need to adjust the depreciation of that firm so that the net income figures for the firms are comparable. A change in a firm's financial statement depreciation would lead to changes in gross profit, operating profit, and so on, down to net profit and earnings per share.

Differences between U.S. GAAP and IFRS require an analyst to adjust the financial statements of firms from different countries before comparing their financial results. Important differences between the two include their treatments of the effect of exchange rate changes, certain securities held by the firm, and inventory cost flows.

Several adjustments to improve the comparability of firms' financial statements and ratios are as follows.

Investments in Securities

Because the classification of a firm's investment securities affects how changes in their values are recorded, it can significantly affect reported earnings and assets. Recall that unrealized gains and losses on held-for-trading securities are recorded in income, while those on available-for-sale or held-to-maturity securities are not. Additionally, while unrealized gains and losses on held-for-trading and available-for-sale securities are reflected in balance sheet asset values, for held-to-maturity securities they are not.

When these differences in classifications lead to significant differences in reported net income or balance sheet asset values for otherwise comparable companies, an analyst can use disclosures to adjust net income and assets of one firm to what they would have been had their classifications been the same.

One difference between IFRS and U.S. GAAP accounting for investment securities is that under IFRS, unrealized gains and losses on available-for-sale debt securities that result from exchange rate fluctuations are recorded on the income statement. Because they are not recorded as income under U.S. GAAP, an analyst should subtract (add) this component of unrealized gains (losses) from the net income of the IFRS firm to improve comparability.

Inventory Accounting Differences

As we covered in the topic review on inventory accounting, a firm using LIFO (permitted only under U.S. GAAP) will report higher cost of goods sold, lower income, and lower inventory compared to FIFO inventory accounting when costs are rising. The **LIFO reserve**, which all LIFO firms must report, can be used to adjust LIFO cost of goods and inventory to their FIFO-equivalent values.

©2012 Kaplan, Inc.

Example: Adjusting for inventory accounting differences

Albart Industries reports the following using the LIFO inventory costing method at the end of 20X2:

Current assets	$10 million
Current liabilities	$5 million
20X1 LIFO reserve	$500,000
20X2 LIFO reserve	$700,000

A. What is the current ratio at the end of 20X2 before and after the appropriate adjustment for comparability to a similar firm that reports using the FIFO inventory valuation method?

B. What is the appropriate adjustment to the firm's 20X2 COGS to make the firm's income statement comparable to that of a firm that reports under the FIFO method?

Answer:

A. Before adjustment, current ratio = CA / CL = 10 / 5 = 2 at year-end 20X2.

Adding the LIFO reserve to current assets increases the current ratio:

adjusted current ratio = 10.7 / 5 = 2.14

B. The appropriate adjustment is to subtract the *increase in the LIFO reserve* from COGS. COGS should be reduced by $700,000 – $500,000 = $200,000. This will increase gross profit, operating profit, and net income compared to LIFO reporting.

Differences in Depreciation Methods and Estimates

Disclosures related to depreciation are not specific enough to permit adjustments to ensure comparability. However, some qualitative information for comparing companies' methods can be obtained.

Over an asset's life, differences between depreciation methods, estimates of useful lives, and estimates of salvage values used by otherwise comparable firms can lead to significant differences in reported income and balance sheet asset values. A firm that is aggressive in using higher estimates of useful asset lives or asset salvage values will report lower annual depreciation expense and higher net income, compared to a more conservative firm that uses lower estimates of useful lives or salvage values. If the analyst concludes that a firm's aggressive assumptions regarding asset lives, for example, are increasing balance sheet net asset values and reported net income, an adjustment to net income and fixed asset carrying values may be appropriate.

Note as well that upward revaluation of fixed asset values is permitted under IFRS but not under U.S. GAAP. Such a revaluation will increase assets and equity, and in a case where the upward revaluation reverses a previous downward revaluation, the increase in value is also reported on the income statement.

An analyst can estimate the number of years' worth of depreciation a firm has recognized by dividing accumulated depreciation from the balance sheet by depreciation expense from the income statement. The result can be interpreted as the **average age** of the firm's assets. Similarly, an analyst can estimate the **average useful life** of a firm's assets (gross property, plant, and equipment divided by depreciation expense) and their **average remaining useful life** (net property, plant, and equipment divided by depreciation expense). Comparing average ages and useful lives of assets within an industry may reveal differences in firms' future capital spending needs.

Off-Balance-Sheet Financing

Debt ratios should include liabilities for both capital (finance) leases and operating leases. Firms include the estimated present value of future capital lease payments with their financials, so that part is straightforward. Although firms must report payments due under operating leases (each year for five years, and total beyond five years), the present value of these is not a required item. To estimate the present value of operating lease liabilities, an analyst can use the ratio of the present value of capital lease obligations to the sum of these future payments, or make some assumption about the timing of operating lease payments beyond five years and calculate a discount rate to use when calculating the present value of operating lease payments. We illustrate both methods in the following example.

©2012 Kaplan, Inc.

Example: Present value of operating lease obligation

Abration Corp. reported the following for 20X1:

Total assets	$30 million
Total debt	$10 million
Capital lease liability	$3 million

	Capital Lease Payments	*Operating Lease Payments*
20X2	$1 million	$500,000
20X3	$1 million	$500,000
20X4	$1 million	$500,000
20X5	$1 million	$500,000
20X6	$1 million	$500,000
Beyond 20X6	$7 million	$3 million

Present value of capital leases: $6.184 million

Estimate the present value of Abration's operating leases.

Answer:

Method 1: Assume operating leases have the same ratio of PV to payments as the firm's capital leases.

A total of $12 million in capital lease payments and $5.5 million in operating lease payments are due in the future. The ratio of the PV of Abration's capital leases to its total future lease payments is $6.184 million / $12 million = 0.5153. Using this ratio, we can estimate the PV of their operating leases as 0.5153 × $5.5 million = $2.834 million.

Method 2: Estimate discount rate for capital leases and apply it to operating leases.

To calculate a single discount rate that would produce the reported PV of capital leases, we must make an assumption about the timing of capital lease payments beyond 20X6. The annual payments, together with the reported PV, can be used to estimate a discount rate to use when calculating the PV of the operating lease payments.

Some alternatives are as follows: all paid at the end of Year 6, spread evenly over some specific number of years, or payments at the average of the prior five years until the obligation for future payments beyond 20X6 is met.

$7 million in Year 6:
$CF_0 = -6.184$; $C01 = 1$; $F01 = 5$; $C02 = 7$; CPT IRR = 15.8%.

$1.4 million in Years 6 to 10:
$CF_0 = -6.184$; $C01 = 1$; $F01 = 5$; $C02 = 1.4$; $F02 = 5$; CPT IRR = 13.0%.

$1 million in Years 6 to 12:
$CF_0 = -6.184$; $C01 = 1$; $F01 = 12$; CPT IRR = 12.0%.

Note that the further in the future we assume the payments are made, the lower their discount rate given the PV.

If we choose to assume that capital lease payments beyond 20X6 are spread evenly over five years ($1.4 million per year), we will use the discount rate 13%. Making the same assumption about lease payments beyond 20X6 for the operating leases ($600,000 per year for five years), we can calculate the PV of these payments, and, thus, the operating lease liability:

$I/Y = 13$; $CF_0 = 0$; $C01 = 500$; $F01 = 5$; $C02 = 600$; $F02 = 5$; CPT NPV = 2,904

This amount, $2.904 million, should be added to the firm's liabilities and assets (equity need not be adjusted) to better reflect the use of off-balance-sheet financing and to calculate solvency ratios such as debt-to-equity and debt-to-assets.

Goodwill

Two companies with identical assets, but where one has grown through acquisition of some business units while the other has grown internally by creating such business units, will show different balance sheet values for the same assets. For the company that has grown through acquisition:

- Tangible assets of the acquired units will be recorded at fair value as of the acquisition date, rather than at historical cost net of accumulated depreciation.
- Identifiable intangible assets of the acquired units will be valued at their acquisition cost, rather than not being included in balance sheet assets.
- Goodwill, the excess of acquisition price over the fair value of acquired net assets, will be shown on the balance sheet.

Two adjustments are typically made to goodwill to improve comparability in such a case. First, goodwill should be subtracted from assets when calculating financial ratios. Second, any income statement expense from impairment of goodwill in the current period should be reversed, increasing reported net income.

In calculating price to book value of equity per share, an analyst can remove goodwill from assets and recalculate a lower adjusted book value, resulting in a price to adjusted book value ratio that is greater.

©2012 Kaplan, Inc.

Other Intangible Assets

Additional adjustment may be required for IFRS firms that revalue intangible assets upward, which is not permitted under U.S. GAAP. As revaluations that do not reverse previously reported impairment are taken directly to equity, an analyst can improve comparability of financial ratios by reducing intangible asset values (and thereby equity) by the cumulative amount of any such upward revaluations.

An alternative ratio, **price to tangible book value**, removes both goodwill and intangible assets from equity to get tangible book value. This adjustment will reduce assets and equity and produce a ratio that is not affected by differences in intangible asset values resulting from differences in how the assets were acquired.

Analysts should also note that a firm's pre- and post-acquisition financial statements may lack comparability when the acquisition method is used. The acquisition method combines fair value estimates of identifiable assets with historical asset costs on the balance sheet and adds the earnings of the purchased firm with no restatement of prior results.

KEY CONCEPTS

LOS 35.a

Trends in a company's financial ratios and differences between its financial ratios and those of its competitors or industry average ratios can reveal important aspects of its business strategy.

LOS 35.b

A company's future income and cash flows can be projected by forecasting sales growth and using estimates of profit margins and the increases in working capital and fixed assets necessary to support the forecast sales growth.

LOS 35.c

Credit analysis uses a firm's financial statements to assess its credit quality. Indicators of a firm's creditworthiness include its scale and diversification, operational efficiency, margin stability, and use of financial leverage.

LOS 35.d

Potentially attractive equity investments can be identified by screening a universe of stocks, using minimum or maximum values of one or more ratios. Which (and how many) ratios to use, what minimum or maximum values to use, and how much importance to give each ratio all present challenges to the analyst.

LOS 35.e

When companies use different accounting methods or estimates relating to areas such as inventory accounting, depreciation, capitalization, and off-balance-sheet financing, analysts must adjust the financial statements for comparability.

LIFO ending inventory can be adjusted to a FIFO basis by adding the LIFO reserve. LIFO cost of goods sold can be adjusted to a FIFO basis by subtracting the change in the LIFO reserve.

When calculating solvency ratios, analysts should estimate the present value of operating lease obligations and add it to the firm's liabilities.

©2012 Kaplan, Inc.

CONCEPT CHECKERS

1. The table below shows selected data from a company's financial statements.

	20X6	20X7	20X8	20X9
Sales	8,614	9,217	9,862	10,553
COGS	5,304	5,622	6,072	6,679
Purchases	5,257	5,572	6,018	6,620
Inventory	2,525	2,475	2,421	2,362
Accounts receivable	3,491	3,728	3,928	4,352
Accounts payable	1,913	2,102	2,311	2,539

   Based on these results, what was this company's *most likely* strategy for improving its operating activity during this period?
   A. Improve its inventory management.
   B. Change its credit and collections policies with its customers.
   C. Change the degree to which it uses trade credit from suppliers.

2. An analyst who is projecting a company's net income and cash flows is *least likely* to assume a constant relationship between the company's sales and its:
   A. interest expenses.
   B. cost of goods sold.
   C. noncash working capital.

3. Credit analysts are likely to consider a company's credit quality to be improving if the company reduces its:
   A. scale and diversification.
   B. margin stability.
   C. leverage.

4. Which of the following stock screens is *most likely* to identify stocks with high earnings growth rates?
   A. Dividend payout ratio greater than 30%.
   B. Price to cash flow per share ratio less than 12.
   C. Book value to market value ratio less than 25%.

5. An analyst needs to compare the financial statements of Firm X and Firm Y. Which of the following differences in the two firms' financial reporting is *least likely* to require the analyst to make an adjustment?

Firm X	Firm Y
A. Straight-line depreciation	Accelerated depreciation
B. Direct method cash flows	Indirect method cash flows
C. IFRS financial reporting	U.S. GAAP financial reporting

6.   When comparing a firm that uses LIFO inventory accounting to firms that use FIFO, an analyst should:
A. subtract the LIFO reserve from cost of sales.
B. add the change in the LIFO reserve to inventories.
C. subtract the change in the LIFO reserve from cost of sales.

7.   The ratio of a firm's property, plant, and equipment, net of accumulated depreciation, to its annual depreciation expense is *best* interpreted as an estimate of the:
A. average age of the firm's assets.
B. average useful life of the firm's assets.
C. remaining useful life of the firm's assets.

8.   How should an analyst *most appropriately* adjust the financial statements of a firm that uses operating leases to finance its plant and equipment?
A. Increase liabilities.
B. Decrease long-lived assets.
C. Decrease shareholders' equity.

©2012 Kaplan, Inc.

ANSWERS – CONCEPT CHECKERS

1. **A**   To analyze this company's operating strategy, calculate its activity ratios:

	20X7	20X8	20X9
Inventory turnover	2.25	2.48	2.79
Receivables turnover	2.55	2.58	2.55
Payables turnover	2.78	2.73	2.73
Days of inventory on hand	162	147	131
Days of sales outstanding	143	142	143
Number of days of payables	132	134	134

The ratios that have changed most significantly are the ones related to inventory. Receivables and payables performance has remained steady, suggesting no change in the company's use of supplier credit or extension of customer credit.

2. **A**   Projections of net income and cash flows are typically based on assumptions that cost of goods sold, operating expenses, and noncash working capital remain a constant percentage of sales. The projections then show whether additional borrowing is needed during the forecast period. If so, the analyst will adjust the interest expense to reflect the additional debt.

3. **C**   Lower leverage improves a company's creditworthiness. Larger scale, more diversification, higher operating efficiency, and more stable margins also tend to indicate better credit quality.

4. **C**   Firms with high growth rates will tend to have high market values relative to the book value of their equity. Low price to cash flow ratios would tend to identify value stocks rather than growth stocks. Screening for high dividend payout ratios would tend to identify mature firms with relatively few growth opportunities.

5. **B**   Cash flows are the same under either method. Differences in depreciation methods and IFRS versus U.S. GAAP reporting can require an analyst to adjust financial statements to make them comparable.

6. **C**   To adjust LIFO financial statement data to a FIFO basis, add the LIFO reserve to inventories on the balance sheet and subtract the change in the LIFO reserve from cost of sales on the income statement. Remember that the balance sheet is cumulative (use the full LIFO reserve) while the income statement refers to the most recent period (use the change for the period in the LIFO reserve).

7. **C**   Remaining useful life = net PP&E / depreciation expense.

Average age of assets = accumulated depreciation / depreciation expense.

Average useful life = gross PP&E / depreciation expense.

8. **A**   The appropriate adjustment for operating leases is to treat them as if they were capital leases by estimating the present value of the future lease obligations and adding that value to the firm's liabilities and long-lived assets.

24 questions, 36 minutes

1. The fundamental qualitative characteristics of financial statements as described by the IASB conceptual framework *least likely* include:
    A. relevance.
    B. reliability.
    C. faithful representation.

2. A decrease in a firm's inventory turnover ratio is *most likely* to result from:
    A. a writedown of inventory.
    B. goods in inventory becoming obsolete.
    C. decreasing purchases in a period of stable sales.

3. Two firms are identical except that the first pays higher interest charges and lower dividends, while the second pays higher dividends and lower interest charges. Both prepare their financial statements under U.S. GAAP. Compared to the first, the second will have cash flow from financing (CFF) and earnings per share (EPS) that are:

	CFF	EPS
A.	The same	Higher
B.	Lower	Higher
C.	Lower	The same

4. Which of the following is an analyst *least likely* to be able to find on or calculate from either a common-size income statement or a common-size balance sheet?
    A. Inventory turnover.
    B. Operating profit margin.
    C. Debt to equity ratio.

5. If a firm's inventory turnover and number of days of payables both increase, the effect on a firm's cash conversion cycle is:
    A. to shorten it.
    B. to lengthen it.
    C. uncertain.

6. The following information is summarized from Famous, Inc.'s financial statements for the year ended December 31, 20X0:
    - Sales were $800,000.
    - Net profit margin was 20%.
    - Sales to assets was 50%.
    - Equity multiplier is 1.6.
    - Interest expense was $30,000.
    - Dividends declared were $32,000.

    Famous, Inc.'s sustainable growth rate based on results from this period is *closest* to:
    A. 3.2%.
    B. 8.0%.
    C. 12.8%.

©2012 Kaplan, Inc.

7. On January 1, Orange Computers issued employee stock options for 400,000 shares. Options on 200,000 shares have an exercise price of $18, and options on the other 200,000 shares have an exercise price of $22. The year-end stock price was $24, and the average stock price over the year was $20. The change in the number of shares used to calculate diluted earnings per share for the year due to these options is *closest* to:
   A. 20,000 shares.
   B. 67,000 shares.
   C. 100,000 shares.

8. A snowmobile manufacturer that uses LIFO begins the year with an inventory of 3,000 snowmobiles, at a carrying cost of $4,000 each. In January, the company sells 2,000 snowmobiles at a price of $10,000 each. In July, the company adds 4,000 snowmobiles to inventory at a cost of $5,000 each. Compared to using a perpetual inventory system, using a periodic system for the firm's annual financial statements would:
   A. increase COGS by $2 million.
   B. leave ending inventory unchanged.
   C. decrease gross profit by $4 million.

9. Which of the following transactions is *least likely* to increase reported operating cash flow for the period?
   A. Financing of payables.
   B. Securitization of receivables.
   C. Exercise of employee stock options.

10. Train Company paid $8 million to acquire a franchise at the beginning of 20X5 that was expensed in 20X5. If Train had elected to capitalize the franchise as an intangible asset and amortize the cost of the franchise over eight years, what effect would this decision have on Train's 20X5 cash flow from operations (CFO) and 20X6 debt-to-assets-ratio?
   A. Both would be higher with capitalization.
   B. Both would be lower with capitalization.
   C. One would be higher and one would be lower with capitalization.

11. Graphics, Inc. has a deferred tax asset of $4,000,000 on its books. As of December 31, it is probable that $2,000,000 of the deferred tax asset's value will never be realized because of the uncertainty about future income. Graphics, Inc. should:
   A. reduce the deferred tax asset account by $2,000,000.
   B. establish a valuation allowance of $2,000,000.
   C. establish an offsetting deferred tax liability of $2,000,000.

12. Long-lived assets cease to be depreciated when the firm's management decides to dispose of the assets by:
   A. sale.
   B. abandonment.
   C. exchange for another asset.

13. If Lizard Inc., a lessee, treats a 5-year lease as a finance lease with straight line depreciation rather than as an operating lease:
   A. it will have greater equity at lease inception.
   B. its operating income will be less in the first year of the lease.
   C. its CFO will be greater and CFF will be less in the second year of the lease.

14. In the notes to its financial statements, Gilbert Company discloses a €400,000 reversal of an earlier writedown of inventory values, which increases this inventory's carrying value to €2,000,000. It is *most likely* that:
   A. the reasons for this reversal are also disclosed.
   B. a gain of €400,000 appears on the income statement.
   C. the net realizable value of this inventory is €2,000,000.

15. Taking an impairment charge due to a decrease in the value of a long-lived depreciable asset is *least likely*, in the period the impairment is recognized, to reduce a firm's:
   A. net income.
   B. operating income.
   C. taxes payable.

16. Under U.S. GAAP, firms are required to capitalize:
   A. any asset with a useful economic life of more than one year.
   B. interest paid on loans to finance construction of a long-lived asset.
   C. research and development costs for a drug that will almost certainly provide a revenue stream of five years or more.

17. With regard to the exercise of employee stock options, which of the following is *least likely* a concern to the analyst?
   A. Increased operating cash flow from the tax benefits of exercise of the options.
   B. Effects of exercise on investing cash flows.
   C. Classification of the cash flow to repurchase shares.

18. A firm that purchases a building that it intends to rent out for income would report this asset as investment property using the cost model under:
   A. U.S. GAAP only.
   B. IFRS only.
   C. both U.S. GAAP and IFRS.

19. When a company redeems bonds before they mature, the gain or loss on debt extinguishment is calculated as the bonds' carrying amount minus the:
   A. face or par value of the bonds.
   B. amount required to redeem the bonds.
   C. amortized historical cost of the bonds.

©2012 Kaplan, Inc.

20. Victory Corp. received interest income from federally tax exempt bonds of $40,000 in the year 20X0. Its statutory tax rate is 40%. The effect of this difference between taxable and pre-tax income is *most likely* a(n):
    A. decrease in its effective tax rate to below 40%.
    B. increase in its deferred tax asset of $16,000.
    C. increase in its deferred tax liability of $16,000.

21. Under a defined contribution pension plan, which of the following is recognized as a pension expense?
    A. Actuarial gains and losses.
    B. Periodic contributions to the plan.
    C. Service costs incurred during the period.

22. Princeton Company calls its $1,000,000, 9% bonds for $1,010,000. On the call date, the bonds have a book value of $980,000 and unamortized issue costs of $24,000. Under U.S. GAAP, Princeton should report a:
    A. $54,000 loss.
    B. $30,000 loss.
    C. $10,000 gain.

23. An analyst is comparing two firms, one that reports under IFRS and one that reports under FASB standards. An analyst is *least likely* to do which of the following to facilitate comparison of the companies?
    A. Add the LIFO reserve to inventory for a U.S.-based firm that uses LIFO.
    B. Add the present values of each firm's future minimum operating lease payments to both assets and liabilities.
    C. Adjust the income statement of one of the firms if both have significant unrealized gains or losses from changes in the fair values of trading securities.

24. An analyst wants to compare the cash flows of two U.S. companies, one that reports cash flow using the direct method and one that reports it using the indirect method. The analyst is *most likely* to:
    A. convert the indirect statement to the direct method to compare the firms' cash expenditures.
    B. adjust the reported CFO of the firm that reports under the direct method for depreciation and amortization expense.
    C. increase CFI for any dividends reported as investing cash flows by the firm reporting cash flow by the direct method.

SELF-TEST ANSWERS: FINANCIAL REPORTING AND ANALYSIS

1. **B** The fundamental qualitative characteristics of financial statements according to the IASB are relevance and faithful representation.

2. **B** Obsolescence can cause goods in inventory to remain unsold, which tends to reduce the inventory turnover ratio (COGS / average inventory). Writedowns of inventory increase the inventory turnover ratio by decreasing the denominator. If purchases decrease while sales remain stable, inventory decreases, which increases the inventory turnover ratio.

3. **B** Interest paid is an operating cash flow, and dividends paid are a financing cash flow, so the firm that pays higher dividends will have lower CFF. The firm with lower interest expense will have higher EPS.

4. **A** Inventory turnover involves sales (from the income statement) and average inventory (from the balance sheet) so it cannot be calculated from common-size statements. Debt to equity is debt/assets divided by equity/assets. Operating profits/sales can be read directly from the common-size income statement.

5. **A** Cash conversion cycle = collection period + inventory period – payables period.

   An increase in inventory turnover will decrease the inventory period and shorten the cash conversion cycle. An increase in the payables period will also shorten the cash conversion cycle.

6. **C** Famous, Inc.'s sustainable growth rate = (retention rate)(ROE).

   ROE = 0.20(800,000) / [(800,000/0.5)(1/1.6)] = 160,000/1,000,000 = 16%.

   Alternatively:

   ROE = (0.20)(0.50)(1.6) = 0.16 = 16%

   Retention rate = (1 – dividend payout ratio) = 1 – {32,000/[(0.20)(800,000)]} = 0.80.

   Sustainable growth = 0.80 (16%) = 12.8%.

7. **A** Based on the average stock price, only the options at 18 are in the money (and therefore dilutive). Using the treasury stock method, the average shares outstanding for calculating diluted EPS would increase by [(20 – 18)/20] 200,000 = 20,000 shares.

8. **A** Under a perpetual inventory system, the snowmobiles sold in January are associated with the $4,000 cost of the beginning inventory. Cost of sales is $8 million, gross profit is $12 million, and end-of-year inventory is $24 million. Under a periodic inventory system, the snowmobiles sold in January would be associated with the $5,000 cost of the snowmobiles manufactured in July. Cost of sales would be higher by $2 million, gross profit would be lower by $2 million, and ending inventory would be lower by $2 million.

©2012 Kaplan, Inc.

9. **A** Financing payables actually reduces operating cash flow as payables are reclassified as short-term debt. Companies may decrease operating cash flows reported under the indirect method by using this strategy. Securitization of receivables increases operating cash flows as the funds received are treated as an operating cash inflow. Exercise of employee stock options increases operating cash flows due to tax benefits associated with exercise.

10. **C** If the cost were amortized rather than expensed, the $8 million cost of the franchise would be classified as an investing cash flow rather than an operating cash flow, so CFO would increase (and CFI decrease). The asset created by capitalizing the cost would increase assets, so the debt-to-assets ratio would decrease.

11. **B** If it becomes probable that a portion of a deferred tax asset will not be realized, a valuation allowance should be established. A valuation allowance serves to reduce the value of a deferred tax asset for the probability that it will not be realized (the difference between tax payable and income tax expense will not reverse in future periods).

12. **A** Under both IFRS and U.S. GAAP, long-lived assets that are reclassified as held for sale cease to be depreciated. Long-lived assets that are to be abandoned or exchanged are classified as held for use until disposal and continue to be depreciated.

13. **C** With a finance lease, only the interest portion of the lease payment is classified as CFO, so CFO will be greater than it would be with an equivalent operating lease. CFF will be less for a finance lease because the principal portion of each lease payment is classified as a financing cash outflow. Operating income, EBIT, will be reduced only by the (equal) annual depreciation expense with a finance lease, so operating income will be greater for a finance lease than for an operating lease (for which the entire lease payment will be an operating expense). At inception, a finance lease will increase assets and liabilities by the same amount so there is no effect on equity.

14. **A** Required disclosures related to inventories under IFRS include the amount of any reversal of previous writedowns and the circumstances that led to the reversal. Under IFRS, the reversal of an inventory writedown is not recognized as a gain, but instead as a reduction in the cost of sales for the period. From only the information given, we cannot conclude that the net realizable value of the inventory is €2,000,000. This value may be the original cost of the inventory.

15. **C** Impairment charges reduce operating income and net income in the period of the charge. Taxes are not affected because any loss in asset value will reduce taxes only when the asset is disposed of and the loss is actually realized. The debt to equity ratio increases in the period of the charge because equity is reduced.

16. **B** Interest on loans that specifically fund construction of long-lived assets must be capitalized under U.S. GAAP. Assets of insignificant value (e.g., metal waste basket) are typically expensed even when their useful lives are many years. R&D costs are expensed under U.S. GAAP.

17. **B** There are no effects on investing cash flows from the exercise of employee stock options. Option exercise results in a tax deduction that reduces taxes and increases operating cash flow. Since employee incentive stock options are properly part of compensation expense, cash expenditures to repurchase shares and avoid dilution are properly classified as operating cash flows rather than as financing cash flows (their classification under accounting standards).

18. **B** Under IFRS, a firm may value investment property using either the cost model or the fair value model. U.S. GAAP does not distinguish investment property from other types of long-lived assets.

19. **B** Under IFRS, when a company redeems bonds before they mature, the company records a gain or loss equal to the bonds' carrying amount minus the cash amount required to redeem the bonds.

20. **A** The receipt of the tax-exempt interest income will create a permanent difference between pretax income and taxable income. Since the tax-free interest increases pre-tax income, but not income tax expense, the effective tax rate will be less than 40%. No deferred tax liability is created because the difference between pretax and taxable income will never reverse.

21. **B** Under a defined contribution pension plan, a company's only pension expenses are the predetermined contributions required to be made to the plan for the period.

22. **A** Under U.S. GAAP, unamortized issue costs are reported on the balance sheet as an asset and are not included in the book value of the bond liability. Thus, the remainder of the issue costs must be written off when the bond is called.

    Gain or loss on redemption = book value − reacquisition price − unamortized issue costs = $980,000 − $1,010,000 − $24,000 = $54,000 loss.

23. **C** Unrealized gains and losses on trading securities are reported in the income statement under both U.S. and IFRS standards. Since LIFO is not permitted under IFRS, adjusting the inventory amount for a LIFO firm is a likely adjustment. To account for differences in how companies report leases, adding the present value of future minimum operating lease payments to both the assets and liabilities of a firm will remove the effects of lease reporting methods from solvency and leverage ratios.

24. **A** By converting a cash flow statement to the direct method, an analyst can view cash expenses and receipts by category, which will facilitate a comparison of two firms' cash outlays and receipts. CFO is correct under either method and requires no adjustment. Neither dividends received nor dividends paid are classified as CFI under U.S. GAAP.

©2012 Kaplan, Inc.

FORMULAS

Activity Ratios:

$$\text{receivables turnover} = \frac{\text{annual sales}}{\text{average receivables}}$$

$$\text{days of sales outstanding} = \frac{365}{\text{receivables turnover}}$$

$$\text{inventory turnover} = \frac{\text{cost of goods sold}}{\text{average inventory}}$$

$$\text{days of inventory on hand} = \frac{365}{\text{inventory turnover}}$$

$$\text{payables turnover} = \frac{\text{purchases}}{\text{average trade payables}}$$

$$\text{number of days of payables} = \frac{365}{\text{payables turnover ratio}}$$

$$\text{total asset turnover} = \frac{\text{revenue}}{\text{average total assets}}$$

$$\text{fixed asset turnover} = \frac{\text{revenue}}{\text{average net fixed assets}}$$

$$\text{working capital turnover} = \frac{\text{revenue}}{\text{average working capital}}$$

Liquidity Ratios:

$$\text{current ratio} = \frac{\text{current assets}}{\text{current liabilities}}$$

$$\text{quick ratio} = \frac{\text{cash + marketable securities + receivables}}{\text{current liabilities}}$$

$$\text{cash ratio} = \frac{\text{cash + marketable securities}}{\text{current liabilities}}$$

$$\text{defensive interval} = \frac{\text{cash + marketable securities + receivables}}{\text{average daily expenditures}}$$

$$\text{cash conversion cycle} = \left(\begin{array}{c}\text{days sales}\\\text{outstanding}\end{array}\right) + \left(\begin{array}{c}\text{days of inventory}\\\text{on hand}\end{array}\right) - \left(\begin{array}{c}\text{number of days}\\\text{of payables}\end{array}\right)$$

Solvency Ratios:

$$\text{debt-to-equity} = \frac{\text{total debt}}{\text{total shareholders' equity}}$$

$$\text{debt-to-capital} = \frac{\text{total debt}}{\text{total debt} + \text{total shareholders' equity}}$$

$$\text{debt-to-assets} = \frac{\text{total debt}}{\text{total assets}}$$

$$\text{financial leverage} = \frac{\text{average total assets}}{\text{average total equity}}$$

$$\text{interest coverage} = \frac{\text{earnings before interest and taxes}}{\text{interest payments}}$$

$$\text{fixed charge coverage} = \frac{\text{earnings before interest and taxes} + \text{lease payments}}{\text{interest payments} + \text{lease payments}}$$

Profitability Ratios:

$$\text{net profit margin} = \frac{\text{net income}}{\text{revenue}}$$

$$\text{gross profit margin} = \frac{\text{gross profit}}{\text{revenue}}$$

$$\text{operating profit margin} = \frac{\text{operating income}}{\text{revenue}} \text{ or } \frac{\text{EBIT}}{\text{revenue}}$$

$$\text{pretax margin} = \frac{\text{EBT}}{\text{revenue}}$$

$$\text{return on assets (ROA)} = \frac{\text{net income}}{\text{average total assets}}$$

$$\text{return on assets (ROA)} = \frac{\text{net income} + \text{interest expense}(1 - \text{tax rate})}{\text{average total assets}}$$

$$\text{operating return on assets} = \frac{\text{operating income}}{\text{average total assets}} \text{ or } \frac{\text{EBIT}}{\text{average total assets}}$$

$$\text{return on total capital} = \frac{\text{EBIT}}{\text{average total capital}}$$

$$\text{return on equity} = \frac{\text{net income}}{\text{average total equity}}$$

©2012 Kaplan, Inc.

$$\text{return on common equity} = \frac{\text{net income} - \text{preferred dividends}}{\text{average common equity}}$$

$$= \frac{\text{net income available to common}}{\text{average common equity}}$$

Free Cash Flow to the Firm:

FCFF = net income + noncash charges + [interest expense × (1 – tax rate)] – fixed capital investment – working capital investment

FCFF = cash flow from operations + [interest expense × (1 – tax rate)] – fixed capital investment

Free Cash Flow to Equity:

FCFE = cash flow from operations – fixed capital investment + net borrowing

$$\text{common-size income statement ratios} = \frac{\text{income statement account}}{\text{sales}}$$

$$\text{common-size balance sheet ratios} = \frac{\text{balance sheet account}}{\text{total assets}}$$

$$\text{common-size cash flow ratios} = \frac{\text{cash flow statement account}}{\text{revenues}}$$

original DuPont equation: $\text{ROE} = \left(\frac{\text{net profit}}{\text{margin}}\right)\left(\frac{\text{asset}}{\text{turnover}}\right)\left(\frac{\text{leverage}}{\text{ratio}}\right)$

extended DuPont equation:

$$\text{ROE} = \left(\frac{\text{net income}}{\text{EBT}}\right)\left(\frac{\text{EBT}}{\text{EBIT}}\right)\left(\frac{\text{EBIT}}{\text{revenue}}\right)\left(\frac{\text{revenue}}{\text{total assets}}\right)\left(\frac{\text{total assets}}{\text{total equity}}\right)$$

$$\text{basic EPS} = \frac{\text{net income} - \text{preferred dividends}}{\text{weighted average number of common shares outstanding}}$$

$$\text{diluted EPS} = \frac{\left[\text{net income} - \dfrac{\text{preferred}}{\text{dividends}}\right] + \begin{bmatrix}\text{convertible}\\\text{preferred}\\\text{dividends}\end{bmatrix} + \begin{pmatrix}\text{convertible}\\\text{debt}\\\text{interest}\end{pmatrix}(1-t)}{\begin{pmatrix}\text{weighted}\\\text{average}\\\text{shares}\end{pmatrix} + \begin{pmatrix}\text{shares from}\\\text{conversion of}\\\text{conv. pfd. shares}\end{pmatrix} + \begin{pmatrix}\text{shares from}\\\text{conversion of}\\\text{conv. debt}\end{pmatrix} + \begin{pmatrix}\text{shares}\\\text{issuable from}\\\text{stock options}\end{pmatrix}}$$

Coefficients of Variation:

$$\text{CV sales} = \frac{\text{standard deviation of sales}}{\text{mean sales}}$$

$$\text{CV operating income} = \frac{\text{standard deviation of operating income}}{\text{mean operating income}}$$

$$\text{CV net income} = \frac{\text{standard deviation of net income}}{\text{mean net income}}$$

Inventories:

$$\text{ending inventory = beginning inventory + purchases} - \text{COGS}$$

Long-Lived Assets:

$$\text{straight-line depreciation} = \frac{\text{cost} - \text{salvage value}}{\text{useful life}}$$

$$\text{DDB depreciation} = \left(\frac{2}{\text{useful life}}\right)(\text{cost} - \text{accumulated depreciation})$$

$$\text{units-of-production depreciation} = \frac{\text{original cost} - \text{salvage value}}{\text{life in output units}} \times \text{output units in the period}$$

Deferred Taxes:

$$\text{income tax expense = taxes payable} + \Delta\text{DTL} - \Delta\text{DTA}$$

Debt Liabilities:

$$\text{interest expense} = \left(\begin{array}{c}\text{the market rate}\\\text{at issue}\end{array}\right) \times \left(\begin{array}{c}\text{the balance sheet value}\\\text{of the liability at}\\\text{the beginning of the period}\end{array}\right)$$

                    ©2012 Kaplan, Inc.

Performance Ratios:

$$\text{cash flow-to-revenue} = \frac{\text{CFO}}{\text{net revenue}}$$

$$\text{cash return-on-assets} = \frac{\text{CFO}}{\text{average total assets}}$$

$$\text{cash return-on-equity} = \frac{\text{CFO}}{\text{average total equity}}$$

$$\text{cash-to-income} = \frac{\text{CFO}}{\text{operating income}}$$

$$\text{cash flow per share} = \frac{\text{CFO} - \text{preferred dividends}}{\text{weighted average number of common shares}}$$

Coverage Ratios:

$$\text{debt coverage} = \frac{\text{CFO}}{\text{total debt}}$$

$$\text{interest coverage} = \frac{\text{CFO} + \text{interest paid} + \text{taxes paid}}{\text{interest paid}}$$

$$\text{reinvestment} = \frac{\text{CFO}}{\text{cash paid for long-term assets}}$$

$$\text{debt payment} = \frac{\text{CFO}}{\text{cash long-term debt repayment}}$$

$$\text{dividend payment} = \frac{\text{CFO}}{\text{dividends paid}}$$

$$\text{investing and financing} = \frac{\text{CFO}}{\text{cash outflows from investing and financing activities}}$$

INDEX

©2012 Kaplan, Inc.

©2012 Kaplan, Inc.

Notes

Notes

Notes

Notes

Notes

Notes

Notes

Notes

Notes

Notes

Notes

Notes

Notes

Notes

Notes

Notes